Also by Jay P. Dolan

Author

The American Catholic Experience: A History from Colonial Times to the Present

The Immigrant Church: New York's Irish and German Catholics, 1815–1865

Catholic Revivalism: The American Experience 1830–1900

Transforming Parish Ministry: The Changing Roles of Catholic Clergy, Laity, and Women Religious in the United States, 1930–1980

 (with R. Scott Appleby, Patricia Byrne, and Debra Campbell)

Editor

The Heritage of '76

The American Catholic Parish: A History from 1850 to the Present

New Dimensions in American Religious History (with James Wind)

Mexican Americans and the Catholic Church, 1900–1965 (with Gilberto Hinojosa)

Puerto Rican and Cuban Catholics in the United States (with Jaime Vidal)

Hispanic Catholic Culture in the United States: Issues and Concerns

 (with Allan Figueroa Deck, S.J.)

꙼ In Search of an American Catholicism

A History of Religion and Culture in Tension ꙼

Jay P. Dolan

OXFORD
UNIVERSITY PRESS

2002

OXFORD
UNIVERSITY PRESS

Oxford New York

Auckland   Bangkok   Buenos Aires   Cape Town   Chennai
Dar es Salaam   Delhi   Hong Kong   Istanbul   Karachi   Kolkata
Kuala Lumpur   Madrid   Melbourne   Mexico City   Mumbai   Nairobi
São Paulo   Shanghai   Singapore   Taipei   Tokyo   Toronto

and an associated company in

Berlin

Published by Oxford University Press, Inc.,
198 Madison Avenue, New York, New York 10016

www.oup.com

Oxford is a registered trademark of Oxford University Press

Library of Congress Cataloging-in-Publication Data
Dolan, Jay P., 1936–
In search of an American Catholicism : a history of
religion and culture in tension / Jay P. Dolan
p.   cm. Includes bibliographical references and index.
ISBN 0-19-506926-9
1. Catholic Church—United States—History.
2. United States—Church history.
I. Title.
BX406.3 .D65   2002   282'.73—dc21   2001058811

9 8 7 6 5 4 3 2 1

Printed in the United States of America
on acid-free paper

For Martin E. Marty

For Martin E. Marty

ACKNOWLEDGMENTS

∽ IN THE SEVERAL YEARS that it took to complete this project I had assistance from many people. Several graduate students at Notre Dame—John Quinn, Anita Specht, Kathleen Sprows Cummings, and Jane Hannon—provided valuable research assistance at various stages of this project. Fred Hofheinz and Sister Jeanne Knoerle, S.P., of the Lilly Endowment believed in the significance of the book and provided the financial assistance that enabled me to take time off from teaching to work on this project. Without the assistance of the Endowment I would not have been able to complete this book. Sections of chapter 1 were presented at a conference at Brown University. I am grateful to Sumner B. Twiss and Walter H. Conser, Jr., organizers of the conference, for their comments on this chapter. Portions of chapter 2 were presented at a seminar sponsored by Brandeis University and the College of the Holy Cross. Jonathan Sarna and David O'Brien, organizers of the seminar, were friendly critics of my work, providing solid suggestions for revision. I am especially grateful to Chester Gillis, Jeffrey Burns, and John McGreevy, who read the entire manuscript, contributing valuable comments and suggestions. My wife, Patricia McNeal, not only had to listen to me talk about this project for too many years, but has also been a valuable critic throughout the course of my work. For many years the University of Notre Dame has provided a wonderful environment in which to work. Its library staff has always been most helpful, most especially Charlotte Ames, who has been a loyal supporter of my efforts to promote the study of American Catholicism. She has been a wonderful friend and colleague for many years. Sheldon Meyer of Oxford University Press initially endorsed this project. After his retirement his successor, Peter Ginna, guided this project to its completion, providing very valuable editorial comments.

I first met Martin E. Marty in the fall of 1966 when I was a student at The Divinity School of the University of Chicago. He guided me through graduate school and over the years became not only an admirable mentor, but also a friend and colleague. The dedication of this book to him is an expression of my gratitude for his support and friendship for so many years.

October 2001   JAY P. DOLAN

CONTENTS

INTRODUCTION

∾ THE RELATIONSHIP BETWEEN RELIGION and cul-
ture has fascinated me for many years. One of my first serious en-
counters with this issue took place when I read H. Richard Niebuhr's
book *Christ and Culture*. Niebuhr's book heightened my interest, and
in subsequent years I continued to think about the historical relationship between religion and American culture. In 1981 I wrote an
essay for *The Wilson Quarterly* entitled "A Catholic Romance With
Modernity," which forced me to explore more precisely the relationship between Roman Catholicism and American culture. My focus in
this essay was to examine how Catholicism changed over time as it
interacted with American culture during the course of 200 years. I
argued that in the 1790s and the 1890s American Catholics fell in
love with modernity and in both instances they came away repentant.
Then I asserted that in the post–Vatican II era Catholics were once
again flirting with the modern world by adopting a more positive
stance toward contemporary culture.[1] In many respects this book
represents a more fully developed argument of that 1981 essay. It is
an interpretive exploration into the history and meaning of Catholicism in the United States.

I believe American and Catholic represent two souls, two strivings, to use an idea articulated by W.E.B. Du Bois. As an African
American, Du Bois experienced a "twoness—an American, a Negro;
two souls, two thoughts, two unreconciled strivings."[2] He believed

that he could be both American and Negro. Being a Catholic and an American, I have experienced a different type of twoness. It is a twoness grounded in religion rather than race. These two fundamental strivings, to be both Catholic and American, have animated me throughout my life, and they are not unreconcilable. Indeed, there exists a mutually enriching relationship between the two. For some time I have wanted to explore the historical relationship between these two very diverse traditions. One represents the tradition of Thomas Aquinas and Ignatius of Loyola. The other stands for the tradition of Jefferson and Lincoln. This book examines the interaction of these two very different traditions. More specifically, I want to explore how American culture has shaped Catholicism. I fully realize that religion can influence culture, but my primary interest in this study is how culture has shaped religion.

It was clear to me that as Catholics became more at home in the United States in the twentieth century, a public style of Catholicism began to emerge. An integral part of the ethos of this public Catholicism was to influence the shape and direction of American culture. This has been a major development in the history of American Catholicism, and I discuss this subject in chapters 4 and 5. Nonetheless, the primary focus of the book is how culture has shaped religion.

History is the study of change. This is what excites the lover of history and makes it so fascinating—to examine the human experience as it changes over time. Religion cannot escape history. Rooted in the human as well as in the transcendent, religion is subject to the ebb and flow of historical forces that influence the course of human history. The historical conditioning of religion means that religion can and indeed does change. For Catholics this was one of the great revelations of the Second Vatican Council. Garry Wills expressed it poignantly when he wrote that the Council "let out the dirty little secret. It forced upon Catholics, in the most startling symbolic way, the fact that the church changes." Prior to the council most Catholics viewed their religion in a very ahistorical manner. According to this perspective Catholicism was unchanging, always the same, and that was surely one of its attractive attributes. It was an anchor of stability in a changing world. Developments within Catholicism, however, were slowly but steadily replacing this ahistorical perspective with a more historically conditioned manner of thinking in which change became normative. According to this point of view not only did the institutional church undergo change over the course of centuries, but the doctrinal teachings of Catholicism also changed over time. John Noonan, who has written most powerfully on this issue of change, or what theologians describe as the development of doctrine, expressed this idea in the following manner: "Christianity is not a relic laid in a museum; it is not a book entombed in an archive. Christianity is alive. It lives in the living people of God. The law of life, as each of us knows from our own lives, is change."[3] Such a perspective represents a new attitude among Catholics, one that was not so widespread prior to the 1960s. Since then, an historical consciousness has taken hold among Catholics. With this development, people are more willing to accept change within the church. In this book I look at doctrine, as well as other selected aspects of Catholicism, where I believe American culture has influenced, indeed changed, the way Catholics thought about these issues.

Change often creates tension among those reluctant to give up the old and embrace the new. This was especially true in the case of Catholicism in the United States. When Catholicism was imported to North America in the sixteenth and seventeenth centuries, it was deeply rooted in European history and culture. This was the culture that shaped the soul of Catholicism for so many centuries. In North America the European tradition of Catholicism, both its doctrines and practices, interacted with different traditions and cultures. Such

interaction often occasioned the desire for change. But change threatened the status quo, and for many people this was unacceptable.
Change created tension and conflict in the community that has persisted to the present day.

The first major conflict took place in the late eighteenth and early
nineteenth centuries when an American republican model of
Catholicism clashed with the traditional European monarchical
model brought to this country by immigrant clergy and laity. Such
tension helped to shape the immigrant church of the nineteenth century and has persisted to the present day. This conflict is rooted in
the ongoing dialectic between an American model of Catholicism
and a Roman model. Another area of tension was the interaction of
immigrant religious traditions with the American model of Catholicism. In the nineteenth century the major example of such controversy involved German immigrant Catholics and an Irish Catholic
hierarchy. A similar debate arose in the twentieth century with Mexican immigrants. The attempts to reconcile such different religious
traditions make up an important part of the relationship between
Catholicism and American culture that I present in this book.

Another way of telling this story is to ask, Can a Catholic be an
American? This question has troubled Americans outside the
Catholic community since colonial times. Many believed that because of their loyalty to their religious leader, the pope in Rome,
Catholics could not be loyal to the republic. This issue haunted Al
Smith in 1928 when he ran for president. In the 1960 presidential
campaign the question surfaced once again when, in order to win the
nomination of his party, John F. Kennedy had to convince the voting
public that his religious beliefs and political responsibilities were
compatible. His success in achieving this both in the campaign and
while in office put to rest, for most Americans, the question of
whether or not a Catholic can be a loyal American.

Despite the persistent questioning of their loyalty, Catholics always believed that they could be loyal to their church as well as their nation. However, another aspect about the relationship between Catholicism and American culture has troubled Catholics for decades. Is the religion of Catholicism compatible with American culture? Are these two cultures, two traditions, at odds with each other or can they complement each other? Some say that indeed they are incompatible. Surely American society's emphasis on consumerism, secularism, and individualism appears to be at odds with the Catholic gospel. Sunday sermons never fail to include warnings against such isms. But this is a simplistic view of life, a jeremiad against worldliness that fails to look at the complexity of the human condition in order to offer a more balanced view of society. A positive perspective would focus on the complementary relationship between the two cultures. Unfortunately this relationship is too often overlooked, both in the pulpit and in the academy. I firmly believe that a person can be at home within both cultures. Just as it is possible for a Jew or a Muslim to be an American, so a person can be both Catholic and American. Like Catholicism, Judaism and Islam are religions rooted in traditions very different from those of American culture. As Islam and Judaism have interacted with American culture, they have taken on new shapes and forms. This has not happened without tension and conflict. Such a transformation became most explicit within Judaism when an entirely new denomination, Conservative Judaism, was established in the United States as a reaction against the modernization of Judaism. Similar developments have also taken place within Protestantism as it has interacted with American culture. Such interaction has resulted in new shapes and forms. New denominations have even emerged. Such developments did not occur without conflict. Indeed, conflict has been an enduring trademark of American religious history. A major reason for this conflict has been the interaction between American cultural values and the values and traditions of religions imported to the United States from abroad, as was surely the case with Catholicism.

Throughout this book I use the term culture, a word that has many meanings. It can refer to art, politics, or a way of life. I use the term to mean those values and beliefs that a group or society uses to identify itself. Since culture is bounded by time and place, it has a history. From this history emerges a cultural tradition. As this is an historical study, the concept of tradition is also used to identify the culture of Catholicism. In using the term culture I do not suggest that there is one common culture that defines Americans or Catholics. Both cultures are very diverse ethnically, politically, and theologically. Catholicism, like the nation, is ethnically very diverse. Throughout the nineteenth century more than twenty-eight different ethnic groups in the United States called themselves Catholic. Such diversity has intensified in the late twentieth century with more than fifty different language groups that are Catholic. In addition to ethnic differences there are political differences such as Irish Democrats and Italian Republicans. Generational differences also divide Catholics into such classifications as pre–Vatican II Catholics and post–Vatican II Catholics. Nonetheless, Catholicism manifests certain core values and defining beliefs. The same is true with American culture. Diverse as it is, certain values are readily acknowledged as American. It is in this sense that I use the word culture—the values and beliefs of a group or society. Given the historical nature of culture, it will change over time. Such change makes the study of religion and culture over a long period, in this case more than two hundred years, challenging as well as exciting.

In speaking about American cultural values, I do not claim that such values are uniquely American. In some respects, American is indeed synonymous with modern. The dialogue between Catholic and

American cultures has been and continues to be a dialogue between Catholicism and modernity. The American context, however, has shaped values and traits associated with modernity in a very specific manner. Democracy and religious freedom—subjects examined in this book—are good examples. Both are worldwide developments, but they also have a history that is distinctly American. It is important to note that this book is not a study of Catholicism and modernity. It is a more modest study of how certain values associated with American culture have shaped Catholicism over the course of the past two hundred years. By focusing on the American representation of modern culture, I have limited the scope of this study, thereby giving it a measure of specificity desirable for the historian.

Chapter 1 examines Catholicism in an age of democracy, the period from 1780 to 1820. The American Revolution ushered in a new age. Henceforth, democracy became a defining element of American culture. How this concept influenced Catholicism makes up a major portion of this chapter. This period was also a time when certain ideals of the Enlightenment took hold among Catholics. Such ideals shaped the way Catholics thought about their religion in this age of reason. I have argued elsewhere that a distinctive American version of Catholicism took shape in these years;[4] this chapter illustrates it in fuller detail.

Chapter 2 focuses on the turning away from a Catholicism grounded in the American democratic tradition. This was a key transition period in American Catholic history. What took place was a thorough Romanization of Catholicism in the middle decades of the nineteenth century. During these years such aspects of American culture as the rise of the public school and anti-Catholic nativism had an impact on Catholicism by reinforcing its sectarian quality.

Chapter 3 examines the period 1880–1920, when Catholicism's relationship with American culture intensified. In this chapter I expand on the study of the interaction between Catholicism and American culture. I continue to focus on democracy and how this core American value influenced the Catholic community. I also examine the European devotional style of Catholicism that flourished at that time and how it shaped Catholicism. In addition to these themes, I also study the issue of national identity—how American should immigrant Catholics become? Would becoming American mean giving up Catholicism? This question became a major topic of debate in the 1880s and 1890s. Another issue that surfaces for the first time is the Americanization of Catholic doctrine. The American cultural traditions of democracy and religious freedom persuaded some Catholics to reexamine Catholic teaching on church and state and religious freedom. As a result of such thinking, American Catholicism began to take on a distinctiveness that would set it apart from its counterparts in such countries as Italy and France. The final theme that I examine in this chapter is gender. With the emergence of the new woman in American society an awakening clearly began to take place among Catholics, which sought to modify the traditional understanding of the role of women in society. The American ideal of gender equality emerging at this time clearly influenced the shape of Catholic culture.

The five themes presented in chapter 3 become the issues examined in chapters 4 and 5. They constitute the core values of American culture that I have chosen to study. In seeking to show how American culture has shaped Catholicism, I have focused on these five areas of intersection during the course of the twentieth century. However, it also became apparent that during these years Catholics were beginning to think in a less parochial manner. Such a reorientation gave rise to the emergence of a public Catholicism that sought to influence the shape and values of American society. I discuss this development in chapters 4 and 5.

Chapter 5 also touches on some issues that have generated considerable controversy among Catholics in recent years—the ethical issues of abortion and birth control, the desire for more democracy in the management of parish life, the role of women in the church, the increased ethnic diversity of Catholicism, and the new rituals of prayer and worship that have emerged in the past forty years.

American culture has influenced Catholicism in many ways. I have selected only five areas of intersection. Clearly there are many other areas in which American culture has influenced the development of Catholicism. For example, American values and institutions have clearly shaped the Catholic educational enterprise. The evolution of bureaucracy and the nation's commitment to capitalism are other areas where American values have influenced the thinking of Catholics and the shape of Catholicism's institutions. Nonetheless, the five themes that I have selected are important issues which Catholics have been trying to come to terms with for many years. By studying these points of convergence between Catholicism and American culture, I offer an interpretation of American Catholic history that places the history of Catholicism within the larger context of American history. I hope to show that Catholicism and American culture can indeed complement and enrich each other. For two hundred years and more, Catholics have been in search of an American Catholicism. This search will never end, but it is clear that at the dawn of the twenty-first century, Catholicism is no longer a stranger in the land. It has found a home in the United States.

CHAPTER ONE

Catholicism in an Age of Democracy

∞ THE AMERICAN REVOLUTION USHERED in a new beginning for all Americans. It was the culmination of an ideological revolution that had turned American society on its head. The spirit of democracy unleashed by the Revolution inspired people to become involved in electioneering and constitution making. A new emphasis on equality repudiated a colonial society rooted in privilege and patronage. A spirit of independence, of rugged individualism, became idealized as genuinely American. Emerging from this revolution that took place in the minds and hearts of the American people was a radical restructuring of American religion. This was especially true for Catholics in the new nation.

Because of their religious beliefs, Catholics had lived as second-class citizens for much of the eighteenth century, discriminated against politically, professionally, and socially. The Revolution changed all this. New laws and new constitutions gave them religious and political freedom. Enjoying the prerogatives of full-fledged citizenship, they became involved in politics at the county, state, and national levels. Catholics embraced the idea of democracy as enthusiastically as anyone else. Enlightenment ideals of religious toleration and the reasonableness of religion also took hold among many Catholics. Such ideals shaped the way Catholics thought about their religion in this age of reason. In examining the interaction between Catholicism and American culture during this era, it is clear that these enlightenment ideals together with the democratic ethos had a most profound impact on shaping the religious world of Catholics. These two themes highlight my basic premise that American culture has had a significant influence in shaping the Catholic religion over the course of the past two centuries.

In the 1780s very few Catholics lived in the colonies, most of them of English or Irish descent. Though no one knows for certain, they probably numbered no more than 25,000, with the bulk of them concentrated in Maryland and a few thousand living in and around Philadelphia. In the years following the War for Independence, the number of Catholics began to increase and spread beyond Maryland and Pennsylvania. Large numbers of Catholics settled in Kentucky; others chose New York, and still others headed south to Virginia and the Carolinas. As the population spread out and multiplied, the institutional church began to take shape with the appointment of John Carroll as Bishop of Baltimore in 1789. Carroll was elected by the clergy, and the pope went along with their decision. At this time there were probably twenty-two priests in the entire country. Carroll remained the only bishop in the United States until 1808, when Rome appointed bishops to newly established dioceses in New York, Philadelphia, Boston, and Bardstown, Kentucky. By this time the only other major institutional developments had been the establishment of a men's college, Georgetown, in Washington, D.C., in 1789 and a seminary in Baltimore, St. Mary's, in 1791.

By 1820, at the end of this republican era, the Catholic population numbered around 160,000, and half of them lived in the Baltimore diocese. The only other denominations with more members were the Methodists and Baptists. Catholics could boast of three seminaries for young men who wanted to become priests, four men's colleges, and ten academies for women. In addition, five communities of women religious had been founded, and 208 sisters were working in the United States. The number of dioceses had grown to nine, and the clergy numbered 122, the majority of them, 88, diocesan priests; the rest belonged to such religious orders as the Jesuits, Dominicans, Vincentians, and Augustinians, all of whom had come from Europe as missionaries to the United States. Clearly the Catholic Church had expanded substantially during the republican era. In 1780 it was a small, poorly organized denomination. By 1820 it was fairly well organized, with promising educational institutions and an adequate number of priests and women religious, and was rivalling the Methodists and Baptists in size, if not in prestige.[1]

The Irish made up a large part of the Catholic community at this time. They had been coming to North America since the seventeenth century, and by 1800 a significant number of Irish had achieved social and political prominence in the new nation. Numbered among this group was Mathew Carey, who had arrived in Philadelphia in November 1784. Twenty-four years old and virtually penniless, he would eventually rise to the highest ranks of Philadelphia society. Indeed, his fame and influence would reach beyond Philadelphia as he became the foremost publisher in the nation. When he died in 1839, Carey's funeral was one of the largest that the people of Philadelphia had ever witnessed.[2]

Mathew Carey was representative of the educated Irish Catholic immigrant in the late eighteenth century. Born and raised in an upper-class home in Dublin, he was educated at a Jesuit school. His parents were involved in the intellectual and cultural life of Dublin and encouraged Mathew's education. In such an environment Carey acquired a love for books, which he nourished for the rest of his life. He also gained a taste for politics. In the late 1770s and '80s Dublin was a political beehive. Enlivened by the American Revolution and by Enlightenment political thought, Irish politicians dreamed of an Ireland free from British control. The young Carey shared these dreams.

A radical republican and an ardent patriot, he was highly critical of the English government, so critical in fact that his father was forced to ship him off to Paris so that young Mathew could avoid arrest. A year in Paris did not dampen his radicalism. He returned to Dublin as republican as ever, continuing to champion a total reform of Ireland's parliamentary system. It was not long before his politics got him in trouble once again. He was put in jail for a brief period in spring 1784. But jail did not cool his republican ardor, and by September the authorities were ready to jail him again. Such a prospect persuaded Carey that it was time to leave Ireland.

It did not take long for Carey to make his mark in Philadelphia. Within three months he published a newspaper; then he launched a magazine, *The American Museum*, that reached out to a national audience. In 1790 he published the first Catholic Bible in the United States, and ten years later he published a family edition of the King James Bible. A bookseller as well as a publisher, he developed his bookstore into one of the largest in the country. He also became one of the leading citizens of Philadelphia and worked on behalf of many charitable causes. In addition to all these activities, Carey was heavily involved in the local Catholic community and became one of the most prominent Catholics in the United States. He was a trustee of his parish, a recognized leader of Philadelphia Catholicism, and a publisher and promoter of the Catholic Bible as well as an apologist for Catholicism. As was true for many of his contemporaries, Enlightenment thought and the American thirst for democracy shaped Carey's religious world.

One of the most striking aspects of Carey's thought was his commitment to a Catholicism shaped by Enlightenment ideas. This was evident in his diary, which he began to keep shortly after his arrival in Philadelphia. His first entry, January 1, 1787, read as follows: "Began the new year with a solemn invocation of the divine being and a supplication to shield me from the manifold misfortunes that have hitherto pursued me." In referring to God as "the divine being" Mathew Carey used the language of eighteenth-century Enlightenment. When he wrote his autobiography, he prefaced it with a famous quotation from the classical writer Terence: "*Homo sum. Et humani a me nil alienum puto.*" (I am a man. And nothing human is alien from me.) This was Carey's motto, and he proudly wrote that it "animated me through life." Such attachment to the classical period, its writers, and their humanism was characteristic of the Enlightenment. In other places in his autobiography he quoted from such classical authors as Virgil and Horace, acknowledging that their wisdom inspired him throughout his life. While growing up in Dublin, he had read widely in the literature of the French Enlightenment. His personal library included the works of Locke, Voltaire, Rousseau, and Montaigne, as well as the humanists Fenelon and Erasmus.[3]

Another trait of the Enlightenment was enthusiasm for learning, and Carey, as publisher, sought to promote learning in various ways. In his magazine, *The American Museum*, he published the writings of American authors and disseminated these throughout Europe. In Philadelphia he was one of the founders of a Sunday School where poor children could receive instruction in reading, writing, and ethics.

Carey was a strong advocate of the "spirit of toleration," which, he wrote, "distinguishes this enlightened age." When he was involved in founding free Sunday Schools, he urged that they avoid "Party, Religious Bigotry, intolerance and superstition."[4] Another characteristic of the age that shaped Carey's outlook was a concern for moral values. Several times in his diary he reflected on his life, past and future. In these meditative pauses he confessed that he always wanted "to do good." This desire was an "overwhelming passion" in his life, which "I cannot resist." He wrote, "I have never seen distress without commiseration," and he always sought to provide "relief, as far as my circumstances permit." Known throughout the city for his generosity, he eventually ran out of money due to his kindness to the needy. As a result, his son had to provide him with additional income. When Carey died, a newspaper described him as an "esteemed philanthropist" and noted that "the cry of the poor, the widow, and the orphan, was never in vain at his door."[5]

This passion to do good inspired Carey to become involved in many benevolent causes. In addition to being one of the founders of the Sunday School, he also was a founder of the Philadelphia Society for Alleviating the Miseries in Public Prisons; he was the driving force behind the organization of the Hibernian Society for the Relief of Emigrants from Ireland. An inveterate pamphlet writer, he wrote essays defending the poor and the need for public charity; another one of his special concerns was poor working women.

In many respects Carey was no different from Benjamin Franklin or Benjamin Rush, two distinguished citizens of Philadelphia with whom he worked on various civic causes. Like Franklin, Rush, and many other individuals influenced by Enlightenment thought, Carey believed in the perfectibility of humankind, the moral need to reform society, and the value of voluntary organizations to attain this goal. But Enlightenment thought was not the only influence on Carey; Catholicism also shaped his thought and actions.

In addition to quoting the classics, Carey also quoted the Bible in his pamphlets. Though he had a very republican view of authority, he upheld the rights of clergy in the spiritual sphere. As a trustee of St. Mary's parish, he was intensely involved in a controversy that erupted when the local bishop arbitrarily removed a popular priest from the parish. In a pamphlet written during this controversy he described the basic beliefs of Roman Catholicism. His understanding centered on the sacraments of the church, especially Penance and the Eucharist. He believed that if any Catholics did not make a confession and receive the Eucharist within a year, they should be "debarred of divine service."[6]

As an apologist for Catholicism, Carey formed a society, the "Vindicators of the Catholic Religion from Calumny and Abuse." Included in his plan to flood the United States with books was the publication of religious books for Catholics who "because of lack of books . . . are ignorant of their religion and some even embrace other religious persuasions whose books they read."[7] After one reads his pamphlets often signed "A Catholic Layman," it becomes clear that he was well read in church history. His diary frequently mentions attendance at Sunday Mass and occasionally comments on the sermons. A strong advocate of education, he served as vice president of the Roman Catholic Sunday School Society in 1816 and 1817.

Mathew Carey remains an exemplar of the Enlightenment Catholic of the late eighteenth and early nineteenth centuries. His was a personal, interior style of religion with a strong dose of moralism. A humanist, he found inspiration in classical writers, in what he called their "genuine Roman or Grecian spirit."[8] However, the ritual and sacraments of Catholicism also nurtured his faith. Like so many people of his time who sought "to adapt their belief in God to modern ideas," Carey combined the doctrine of Catholicism with the demands of reason that was so central to Enlightenment thinking.[9] He was able to blend moralism and spirituality, faith and reason, nature and the supernatural. In this manner he integrated his religion with the culture of the age so that his Catholicism blended with Enlightenment culture then prevalent in the United States. He was Catholic to the core, but a child of the Enlightenment as well.

Carey never suggested that there was any incompatibility between his Catholicism and his devotion to Enlightenment principles. He could praise the humanism and moralism of the classical writers, and then turn to a description of how he and his wife rode to church in their carriage. For him the two realms were not contradictory. Carey's religious world was similar to that of his contemporary Benjamin Rush, who was "a fervent evangelical Christian" of the Calvinist school as well as an enthusiastic republican who supported Enlightenment causes.[10] In the 1780s and '90s many people, like Rush and Carey, reconciled apparently incompatible doctrines such as faith and reason, nature and the supernatural, and felt comfortable doing so.

Carey's religious world was not unique. Catholicism had taken many forms over the centuries, and in the late eighteenth century an Enlightenment style of Catholicism was fairly widespread. It attracted followers in England and Ireland as well as in Europe. In the United States it also had its representatives in people like Mathew Carey.

How representative of American Catholics was the religious world of Mathew Carey is a difficult question. He was clearly representative of the educated, Catholic upper class. In such cities as Philadelphia this was a sizable group. Dale Light's study of Philadelphia suggests this conclusion, as does recent work in the history of the New York Irish. The spirit of the Enlightenment permeated Philadelphia in the 1790s, when it was the leading city in the nation. Henry May, who has written the most detailed study of the Enlightenment in America, concluded that the city's elite were "Enlightened in a thoroughly eighteenth-century manner." Carey certainly fit this description and most likely so did many of the Catholic upper class.[11]

Charles Carroll of Carrollton provides another example of how the culture of the Enlightenment shaped the religious world of Catholics. Carroll was the most distinguished and indeed the wealthiest Catholic in Maryland. Active in politics, he was a delegate from Maryland to the Continental Congress as well as a signer of the Declaration of Independence. Like many children of the Maryland Catholic gentry, Carroll was sent to Europe at a young age to acquire

an education. Living in Europe for sixteen years, he received an excellent education with the Jesuits in France and later studied law in London, where he read Locke, Newton, and Montesquieu. When he finally returned to his Maryland home in 1765, he was a product of an eighteenth-century Catholic Enlightenment education. Until his death in 1832, Carroll remained a devoted Catholic and an enlightened aristocrat.[12]

The correspondence between Charles and his father, Charles Carroll of Annapolis, reveals a family shaped by eighteenth-century Enlightenment rationalism. In urging his son not to omit his daily prayers, the father wrote, "Prayer does not Consist in a set form of Words; it is the Heart the Will the Attention & intention that accompanies them that carries them like a pure sacrifice to the Throne of the Almighty." In reply to his father's advice, Charley, the name his father gave him, revealed something of his own religious inclinations. "A good conscience & a virtuous life," he wrote, "are certainly the greatest blessings we can enjoy on earth. I dont aim nor never did at cannonization; I detest scrued up devotion, distorted faces, & grimace. I equally abhor those, who laugh at all devotion, look upon our religion as a fiction, & its holy misteries as the greatest absurdities." For Charley's father, faith and reason were the foundation blocks of his religion, and he saw no contradiction between Catholicism and the rationalism of the Enlightenment. As he noted in a letter to his son, "Whatever a man may grant, whatever Rules he may lay down, whatever Doctrines he may profess, if they be inconsistent with reason and Contrary to Morality, Justice, & Religion they are in themselves void & can have no ill Effect." In addition to endorsing the reasonableness of religion, Charley also put a high value on toleration. Describing himself as a "warm friend to Toleration," he disapproved of what he called "the intollerating spirit of the Church of Rome, and of other Churches. . . . " Reflecting on his signing the Declaration of

Independence, he "had in view not only our independence of England but the toleration of all sects professing the Christian religion and communicating to them all equal rights." There is no question that he, like the rest of his family, had "an unwavering, though sorely tested, commitment to freedom of conscience." This was an integral part of the colonial Catholic tradition and certainly fit in with the spirit of toleration endorsed by the Enlightenment.[13]

Throughout his life Charles Carroll of Carrollton stressed the personal experience of religion, the reasonableness of religion, and the spirit of toleration. Such virtues represented the cornerstone of Enlightenment Christianity, and Carroll did not find such qualities incompatible with his Catholicism. Like Mathew Carey, he was able to reconcile faith and reason, nature and the supernatural, moralism and the spiritual.

The first bishop of Baltimore, John Carroll, provides another example of Enlightenment Catholicism. Like his cousin, Charles Carroll, John Carroll was sent to Europe for his education. After studying with the Jesuits at St. Omer in Flanders, he decided to enter the Jesuit order. After several years of study he was ordained a priest in 1769. When the pope suppressed the Jesuit order in 1773, Carroll returned to Maryland to work as a missionary priest. Then in 1789 he was named bishop of Baltimore. From the 1780s until his death in 1815 Carroll was the leading Catholic churchman in the United States.

John Carroll was an eighteenth-century bishop. Educated during the age of the Enlightenment, he was especially influenced by the French humanist tradition and the English Catholic Enlightenment. His extensive correspondence as a bishop has been preserved along with numerous sermons and pastoral letters, and they reveal an individual who came of age during the Enlightenment.

John Carroll was a strong believer in religious toleration. He supported the American Revolution, believing that religion had "undergone a revolution, if possible, more extraordinary, than our political one." This religious revolution introduced a new spirit of toleration in the states where "publick protection & encouragement," he wrote, "are extended alike to all denominations & R.C. are members of Congress, assemblies, & hold civil & military posts as well as others." Carroll viewed this new situation as "a blessing and advantage." In accepting the principle of religious toleration, Carroll endorsed the new American way of separation between church and state. A key corollary was the primacy of reason and persuasion over coercion. Henceforth, a person could not be forced to adhere to a particular religion. As Carroll said in one of his sermons, "in matters of faith everything must be free & voluntary."[14]

Carroll spoke of an "enlightened faith." For him reason was an important element in the shaping of a person's religion. But it was not enough. Although Carroll emphasized the importance of reason and the value of persuasion, he also wanted to add "revelation," that is grace or the supernatural. Like many people of the era who had a positive view of human nature, he saw the need to integrate it with the supernatural. He also spoke about the "rights of conscience," "the common rights of nature," "the common rights of mankind." By using such Enlightenment language about religious toleration, clearly for Carroll toleration was a natural right, not a political concession.[15]

As a citizen of the Enlightenment John Carroll was involved in civic causes, working with ministers and people of other religious traditions to promote the commonweal of Baltimore. Though he could not match Mathew Carey's reputation for philanthropy, Carroll was involved in benevolent enterprises. He had "a leading role in the founding of the Library Company of Baltimore in 1795, the Baltimore Female Humane Association, the first charity school of the city in 1798, the Maryland Society for Promoting Useful Knowledge in 1800, the Humane Impartial Society for the relief of indigent women and the

Baltimore General Dispensary in 1802, and others." He also served as a trustee of Baltimore College and St. John's College in Annapolis.[16]

Carey and the Carrolls were not alone in their thinking. The writings of apologists of the English Catholic Enlightenment were well known in the United States, and the ideas of the French Enlightenment also circulated throughout the states. Moreover, John Carroll was a popular bishop, elected to the office by the clergy and widely revered by the people. It is hard to imagine that his views were completely out of step with the rest of the Catholic community.[17] Nonetheless, an equally revealing indicator of the religious worldview of Catholics at this time was the type of religion they practiced.

Joseph Chinnici argues persuasively that Enlightenment Catholic piety prevailed during this era. The eighteenth century was a time when baroque devotionalism was riding high. As Chinnici notes, this style of piety, by encouraging "a penitential system which stressed the sinfulness of the human condition," emphasized "relics, indulgences, pious practices and saints' lives."[18] The excesses of baroque devotionalism led to its demise as the century progressed, and as the demise occurred, a different, more personal style of piety developed, one rooted in the Christian humanist tradition. A very telling indication of this shift was the design of the new Catholic cathedral in Baltimore, planned as the premier church in the nation, the showcase of Catholicism.

When Bishop Carroll and the cathedral trustees sought an architect for the new edifice, they did not turn to Europe and the baroque tradition of the eighteenth century. They looked to the nation's capital, but a few miles away, and chose the architect of the capitol building, Benjamin Latrobe, as the person to design the cathedral. Wanting a cathedral that would fit in with the times, they selected the nation's premier architect to design and build the church. Latrobe and the trustees settled on a design in the classical Roman tradition, a style "compatible with the ideals of the Enlightenment: order, harmony, discipline, reason, quiet dignity." As Chinnici rightly observes, the cathedral still stands in downtown Baltimore "as a fitting symbol of the spiritual life characteristic of the Catholic community during Carroll's era."[19]

Chinnici examines prayer books, sermons, catechisms, and popular apologetical treatises. These sources present a positive view of human nature in contrast to the baroque view of a sinful, weakened human nature. Catechisms as well as theological manuals described religion as a personal experience, with an emphasis on the interiority of religion as opposed to external acts of piety. An English Catholic writer, John Fletcher, in his book *Reflections on the Spirit of Religious Controversy*, which was widely circulated throughout the United States, defined religion in the following manner: "Religion is a system of piety and humility; and it is in holy communication with God, by prayer and meditation, that he speaks most plainly, to the heart, and unfolds the truth and beauty of his law." A widely circulated catechism touched on the same interior, personal dimension of religion. It stated, "Men owe to God an inward worship, because this is the only worship which is suited to the nature of God, who being a spirit, desires to be worshipped in spirit and truth.... Exterior, without inward, worship would be a mere farce and mockery." Such a view of religion did not focus on the differences between Catholics and Protestants. It was an irenic understanding of religion that blended in well with the environment of religious toleration prevalent in those years. In his sermons John Carroll emphasized this commonality of Christianity by referring to Catholics as "Christians," or "Catholic Christians," and by referring to the church as the "Christian Catholic church." Such a view of religion did not do away with devotional practices that were so much a part of the Catholic tradition. Indeed, such practices were encouraged, but the emphasis was always on the personal relation with Jesus and the interior disposition of the individual.[20]

This type of piety was not new to American Catholicism. It was very much in harmony with the tradition of colonial Catholicism that manifested the same qualities of a personal, interior style of religion. Moreover, this type of religion blended well with the social situation of Catholics during the republican era. This was a time when priests were scarce and churches were few and far between. To a large extent it was an age of do-it-yourself religion. Moreover, continual interaction with the dominant Protestant society often included worshiping with Protestants, marrying their sons and daughters, and being buried in their cemeteries. The irenic nature of Enlightenment Catholicism was well suited for such interaction between Catholics and Protestants.

Many people wrongly view the Enlightenment as anti-Christian or anti-Catholic. Indeed, some Enlightenment figures could fit this description, but the Enlightenment with its emphasis on reason, nature, and the human was not the enemy of Christianity, nor was Catholicism always an adversary of the Enlightenment. The Enlightenment was, as the historian Owen Chadwick has written, "new learning, and as such affected Catholic colleges, professors, and bishops."[21] It was also a *new way of believing* in which people sought to adapt their religion to the modern world. It touched Catholics as well as Protestants and Jews by altering how people thought about their God and the human community in which they lived. In the United States Enlightenment Catholicism was very evident. It represented a blending of religion and culture that was distinctive of the republican era. This conclusion is not well recognized. Catholicism in the republican era was not the same as Catholicism in the 1840s or the 1990s. As the culture of the Enlightenment reshaped the Catholicism of the baroque era, it fashioned what some contemporaries called an "enlightened piety."[22] The Catholic response to modernity in the republican era was one way in which Catholics adapted their religion to the American environment.

A second major cultural influence on Catholicism at this time was the spirit of democracy that emerged from the changes that swept through Europe in the late eighteenth century. The Enlightenment was linked to this political revolution through its emphasis on "the rights of man" and human progress. In terms of religion the Enlightenment influenced the way people thought about God and moral values, while the passion for democracy was most evident in the way people refashioned the understanding of religious authority. Intimately bound together, these two forces, the Enlightenment and the rise of democracy, produced a cultural revolution that ushered in a new age, an age referred to as the modern era. Historians date this transitional period between 1770 and 1830. In 1770 the dictates of reason and nature were becoming more recognized, and pleas for equality in the political sphere were beginning to be heard. In time reason and nature emerged as cultural goddesses while political democracy became a popular slogan. By 1830 the Enlightenment had passed into history, and "enlightened" religion had been found wanting. Political democracy had more staying power, however, becoming a permanent feature of the Western world by 1830.

In America the key event in this transition was the Revolution. On one side of 1776 was an age of privilege and deference. The aristocratic values of English society with its kings and lords were visible throughout the colonies, but most especially in the South. In Virginia the greater ruled over the lesser. The well-to-do planter lived in the great house, a home distinguished not only by its size, but also by its elaborate ornaments and orderly design. The aristocratic dress of the privileged also set them apart. Even the churches reflected the values of old England. Built of brick they were imposing structures, appropriate for the established Church of England, which enjoyed the financial and legal support of the local government. The design of the church mirrored this ordered society. People sat according to their rank in society, and the pulpit, the clergyman's perch, towered above all. A formal liturgy "read in the midst of a community ranged in order of precedence, continuously evoked postures of deference and submission. Liturgy and church plan thus readily combined to offer a powerful representation of a structured, hierarchical community."[23]

Then came the Revolution. It was a revolution of mind as well as a war for independence. The world was turned upside down, and a new nation appeared. Privilege and deference were cast aside. Freedom, independence, and equality became cherished values of the new republic. Shunning the formal, tailored dress worn by English soldiers, patriots donned hunting shirts and took up arms to fight against the king. The will of the people became supreme, and the people's choice occupied the seats of power. Rank in society counted for little in the new evangelical churches that appeared during this period, as plain tables set in the midst of the congregation replaced ornamented and elevated pulpits. People sensed that a "new order of the ages" had arrived and this Latin phrase (*novus ordo saeclorum*) became part of the nation's seal. A new type of person had stepped onto the world stage, a republican, one who had inherited "a revolutionary legacy in a world" once ruled by aristocrats and kings.[24]

This transitional age transformed American Christianity in the same manner that it changed American political life. In religion as in politics the people's choice became determinative. People sought to gain control over their own destiny, spiritual as well as political. Thus, they cast aside any monopoly that sought to control their eternal life. In Virginia this meant an end to the favored legal status of the Anglican Church. Henceforth, by law all Christian churches were equal. This marked the beginning of religious freedom for all people.

Heaven was democratized, and salvation now became a possibility for all of God's children, not just the Calvinist elect. In such an atmosphere people "wanted their leaders unpretentious, their doctrines self-evident and down-to-earth, their music lively and singable, their churches in local hands. It was this upsurge of democratic hope," wrote historian Nathan Hatch, "that characterised so many religious cultures in the early republic and brought Baptists, Methodists, Disciples and a host of other insurgent groups to the fore. The rise of evangelical Christianity in the early republic is, in some measure, a story of the success of common people in shaping the culture after their own priorities rather than those outlined by gentlemen such as the Founding Fathers."[25] This democratic spirit altered the landscape of American religion. It created a spirit of populism as the people's choice, not the preacher's prerogative, became determinative.

This new populist spirit in religion affected all denominations. It was the driving force behind the growth and expansion of Methodism; it gave birth to the Disciples of Christ and was a major reason for the popularity of Joseph Smith and the founding of the Mormon Church. It shaped the organization of Jewish synagogues as Jews sought to declare their rights and privileges. This passion for democracy also permeated the Catholic community. This was especially true of the Irish. Politically they were ardent supporters of republicanism, and this republican spirit carried over to the religious sphere. Where this was most visible was in the government of the local parish.

The vital element in the development of American Catholicism was the parish. Between 1780 and 1820 many parish communities were organized across Catholic America. Perhaps as many as 124 Catholic churches dotted the landscape in 1820, and each one represented a community of Catholics.[26] In the vast majority of these communities laymen were very involved in the government of the parish as members of a board of trustees. The principal reason for such a trustee system was the new spirit of democracy that was rising across the land. In France and Ireland as well as in the United States people were redefining the meaning of authority, coming up with a much more democratic understanding of how authority should be exercised in society. This awakening touched people everywhere, in Paris, France, as well as in Bardstown, Kentucky, changing the lives of kings as well as farmers. In Catholic communities it meant that laypeople wanted to have more control over their parish churches.

In emphasizing the influence of the democratic spirit on the Catholic parish it is well to remember that tradition played a very important role in this development. When they sought to fashion a democratic design for parish government, American Catholics were attempting to blend the old with the new, the past with the present. The establishment of a trustee system was not a break with the past, as they understood it, but a continuation of past practices adapted to a new environment. Lay participation in church government was an accepted practice in France and Germany; English and Irish lay Catholics were also becoming more involved in parish government. Thus, when they were forced to defend their actions against opponents of the lay trustee system, Catholic trustees appealed to tradition and long-standing precedents for such involvement. By blending the old with the new the trustees were able to adapt an ancient tradition to the circumstances of an emerging, new society.

The American legal system that supported the separation of church and state encouraged the development of the trustee system by classifying churches as voluntary associations or corporations. Such corporations could have their own constitutions and be incorporated in the name of lay trustees who would be responsible for the corporation's legal and financial affairs. By their very nature some American Protestant denominations endorsed the participation of the laity in congregational government; the democratic surge that took place in the republican era served to enhance this tendency. The model John Carroll chose was the Episcopal parish, with its elected vestry responsible for temporal affairs. Thus, when it came time for Catholics to think about organizing their own congregations, the Protestant example and the American legal system clearly suggested a model in which laypeople would have a prominent role.

The first step in establishing a lay trustee type of parish government was to select the trustees. This took place in a very American manner, by election. Elections would take place each year to select the board of trustees. Only those individuals who rented pews in the church were eligible to vote; this meant that white males over the age of twenty-one and of some financial means were the only people that voted. Though the trustee system could vary from parish to parish, two types were popular prior to 1820. In one type laymen were in control and the clergy looked upon as hired servants of the parish. The clergy worked for the board and were subject to the trustees' wishes. The trustees hired them, and they could also fire them. This system in which lay trustees had exclusive control over parish affairs was established in such cities as New Orleans, Philadelphia, Buffalo, New York, and Norfolk, Virginia. The other model explicitly provided for the participation of the clergy on the board of trustees and made them *ex officio* members of the board. This type of arrangement was organized in parishes in Philadelphia, Baltimore, and Boston.

The responsibilities of these trustees were rather mundane. They were engaged in what they described as "temporal concerns." In other words, they were the parish business managers and their major concern was financial: collection of pew rents, purchasing an organ, selling gravesites in the parish cemetery, determining the salary of the priest, and paying off debts. They also supervised the work of those employed by the parish, such as the organist and the priest. When the priest and the trustees did not agree on some issue, be it salary or the quality of preaching, then conflict did occur, and it was often bitter and prolonged. But as Patrick Carey, the recognized authority on lay trusteeism, notes, such conflict took place in relatively few Catholic parishes. In the vast majority of the one hundred or more parishes in the country at this time the trustee system worked well.[27]

While it is true that there were European precedents for lay involvement in parish government and American law favored a trustee system of parish government, a key influence in the adoption of the trustee system was the democratic spirit that was surging through the nation at this time.

Roman Catholicism was a religion of the Old World. Many Catholic immigrants as well as those born and raised in the land that was to become the United States recognized the contrast between the European tradition of Catholicism and the American style of independence and freedom. Moreover, they realized the need for the Roman Catholic church to adapt itself to the American situation. They were not raising questions about Catholic dogma or religious beliefs, but about the way the church operated through its bishops and clergy.

Mathew Carey recognized the need of the Irish clergy to adapt to American culture. In Ireland he wrote, "too frequently the relations between the pastor and his flock partake of the nature of extravagantly high-toned authority on the one side and servile submission on the other." In the United States people would not accept this. As he states, "This people never will submit to the regime in civil or ecclesiastical affairs that prevails in Europe." In his opinion "a different order ... prevails in this country. ... The extreme freedom of our civil institutions has produced a corresponding independent spirit respecting church affairs, to which sound sense will never fail to pay attention, and which it would be a manifest impropriety to despise or attempt to control by harsh or violent measures. The opinions and wishes of the people require to be consulted to a degree unknown in Europe." As regards bishops, he observed that "an overweening idea of the extent of episcopal authority is not suited to this meridian."[28] In Europe the monarchical tradition had left an indelible imprint on both church and state. In Carey's opinion this feudal tradition was not compatible with the American political and cultural environment. Catholics in New Orleans made the same point when they petitioned the state legislature to enact a law that would force the bishop "to govern the Catholic church here in accordance with the spirit of our national customs and political institutions."[29] This need for adaptation was paramount in the minds of many Catholics across the country.

In desiring to have the church adapt to American culture, Catholics wanted Roman Catholicism to be more in step with the times by breathing in some of the democratic spirit that was blowing across the landscape. In doing so they believed that they would be establishing "a National American Church with liberties consonant to the spirit of government under which they live." This could happen if the church adopted what they called "republican" principles in the government of the local church.[30]

In his study of trusteeism Patrick Carey has documented the link between trusteeism and republican ideology. The trustees, who often described themselves as "American Republicans," endorsed four major principles of the American democratic experience—the sovereignty of the people, popular elections, religious freedom, and a written constitution.[31]

In the old country the will of the monarch was sovereign; in the New World the will of the people was supreme. One of the more popular slogans of the day was "the voice of the people is the voice of God." Catholic trustees appropriated this maxim and applied it to the church. "Is it wise," asked a Philadelphia Catholic, "is it prudent, that those whose voice is law in everything else, should be made to feel, that in that very thing, in which they are most deeply interested they have no voice at all?"[32] The way that the voice of the people would be heard came through elections. Popular elections were considered a natural right and a natural consequence of popular sovereignty. In advocating elections in the church, trustees included not just election of trustees, but also the election of pastors and bishops. Mathew Carey felt so strongly about this that he wanted to call "a convention of the Roman Catholics throughout the Union" to consider the subject of the election of bishops and eventually send an agent to Rome to negotiate this issue.[33]

Freedom or what was often described as "the spirit of independence" was another principle advocated by Catholics. As Mathew Carey noted, the freedom exercised in the civil realm "has produced a corresponding independent spirit respecting our church affairs."[34] What he meant was that the European style of absolutism and the arbitrary exercise of authority were not suited to the American scene. Independent as Americans, they wanted to be independent as Catholics. This did not mean casting off "the spiritual supremacy of the Apostolic See," but keeping it as a bond of union, "not as the yoke of a servile dependency."[35]

The final republican principle was the need for a written constitution. Constitution writing had a long heritage in the Anglo-Saxon tradition and was very much in vogue in the republican era. From the federal level to the local level people engaged in the process of writing a constitution. In Scott County, Kentucky, a group of Catholics organized themselves into a religious society in 1806. One of the first steps they then took was to draw up a constitution. Described as a "Republican Constitution," it had a preamble and a set of articles by which they sought to regulate and define the government of the local church in Scott County.[36] Such a constitution was to serve as a protection against the arbitrary use of authority by incorporating certain checks and balances into the government of the local church. By establishing a balance of power, the likelihood of conflict would diminish. Moreover, the constitution spelled out the areas of responsibility for both clergy and laity.

These four principles—the sovereignty of the people, popular elections, religious freedom, and a written constitution—provided the rationale for the trustee system in the American Catholic community. Very American and clearly republican, they showed how much democratic thought had permeated the Catholic community. Numerous examples of such republican Catholicism exist from Scott County, Kentucky, to Philadelphia, Pennsylvania, but the most ambitious and comprehensive example took place in the southern regions of Georgia and the Carolinas. Led by their Irish-born bishop, John England, Catholics in this region fashioned an elaborate system of church government that was inspired by the spirit of republicanism.

John England was appointed the bishop of Charleston, South Carolina, in 1820. While in Ireland he was involved in the political and religious reform movements of the early nineteenth century, and this experience turned him into a liberal Catholic sympathetic to the democratic spirit of the age. When he came to Charleston, he entered a Catholic community that was bitterly riddled with dissension over the issue of authority in the local congregation. England brought peace to the community by fashioning a republican style of church government in which clergy and laity worked together. As he stated, he wanted to fashion a church in which "the laity are empowered to cooperate but not to dominate." The centerpiece of this arrangement was a written constitution that England presented to the clergy and laity in September 1823. Accepted by the assembly, the constitution endorsed the election of parish lay trustees, annual conventions of clergy and laity to discuss the needs of the church as well as lay representatives chosen to participate in these meetings. These conventions met annually from 1823 until England's death in 1842.

The constitution reflected England's belief in republicanism and the need to instill some of its qualities in the church so that the people would be more involved in the decision-making process. For England the constitution was a conscious effort to adapt Catholicism to the American republican environment. He sought to create something new in the Catholic world. However, most of the other bishops, derisively labeling him a "republican," did not approve of what they called his "republican notions."[37] In fact, no other bishop adopted England's vision of church government, and when he died in 1842, republican Catholicism lost its most powerful advocate.

Looking back at this era from the twenty-first century, an obvious question is what was the Vatican's reaction to this democratization of Catholicism in the United States? It is important to remember that the Vatican did not always enjoy the power and control over national churches that it possesses in the twenty-first century. The centralization of such control only began to develop in the second half of the nineteenth century. In the late eighteenth century the influence of Rome on the American church was minimal. The church in Europe had reached "a nadir of its prestige and influence."[38] Then along came the French Revolution, and, as Owen Chadwick states, "The Revolution did to the Roman Catholic Church what the Reformation failed to do. It appeared to have destroyed its structure if not its being."[39] For a time the church in France ceased to function, as monasteries were closed, buildings destroyed, priests executed, and the institution's very existence called into question. Napoleon's troops kidnapped the pope, Pius VI, and he died a prisoner in exile. Then Napoleon kidnapped Pius's successor, Pius VII, and kept him a prisoner for nearly six years. What was occurring in the United States at this time mattered little in the larger picture of Vatican affairs. Survival of the papacy was what mattered most in those years, not whether or not some clergy or laity were trying to democratize church government.

The spirit of democracy stamped Catholicism in this era with a distinctive mark by radically altering the manner in which authority operated in the church. Both clergy and laity had sought to reshape the traditional monarchical model of Catholicism by having the government of the local church mirror the democratic culture of the new nation. The blending of the hierarchical tradition of Catholicism with the new democratic imperative was an important development in the search for an American Catholicism, a Catholicism in harmony with the culture of the new nation.

Why did this style of Catholicism, what I call republican Catholicism, with its democratic tendencies and its Enlightenment impulses, never endure through the nineteenth century? There are several reasons for this failure, but the key one is that another understanding of Catholicism was prevalent in the United States during the age of John Carroll. A more traditional model of the church, this view emphasized the weakness of human nature, the prevalence of sin, and the need for the church and its clergy to help people overcome this worldly environment. It stressed the authority of the hierarchy and the subordinate role of the laity. The medieval monarchy, not the modern republic, was its model of government. Historians have labeled this model of Catholicism Tridentine Catholicism, after the Council of Trent, because this sixteenth-century church council promoted the reformation of Catholicism by endorsing this style of religion. Prevalent in Europe for much of the eighteenth century, it underwent a brief period of adaptation to modern thought and culture during the age of the democratic revolution that swept through the Western world. The Tridentine model was revived and restored to prominence by the middle of the nineteenth century. An exemplar of this school of thought was John England's contemporary, Ambrose Marechal.

Born in France, Marechal joined the Sulpicians, a society of diocesan priests, and was ordained in 1792 in Paris. Because of the turmoil of the French Revolution, he fled Paris, not even taking time to celebrate his first Mass as a priest. He headed for the United States, where he worked mostly as a missionary in Pennsylvania and Maryland; he also taught some courses at St. Mary's Seminary in Baltimore. After the French Revolution cooled down, he returned to France. After a few years he came back to Baltimore to teach at St. Mary's, a seminary operated by the Sulpicians. In 1817 he was appointed the archbishop of Baltimore.

As the archbishop of Baltimore Marechal strongly opposed John England's desire to promote a republican model of Catholicism beyond the borders of the Carolinas. He disparaged the innovations that England promoted in Charleston and pejoratively labeled his diocesan constitution a "democratic constitution."[40] Marechal endorsed the idea of religious liberty, but he wanted no part of democracy in the church. As far as he was concerned the spirit of democracy was the root cause for many of the church's problems in the new nation. Americans loved "the civil liberty which they enjoy," he wrote. As he stated, "The principle of civil liberty is paramount with them," and even the lowest magistrate is elected by the vote of the people. Such principles governed Protestant churches and in his opinion Catholics were "exposed to the danger of admitting the same principles of ecclesiastical government." Strongly opposing this tendency, he sought to establish the supreme authority of the clergy and weaken the power of the lay trustee system.[41] Marechal's model of the church was French and monarchical. Moreover, it was the model of church that was gaining ascendancy in France after the downfall of Napoleon in 1814.

Like Marechal, many other French clergy fled to the United States

during the revolution. Most of them subscribed to a very traditional understanding of Catholicism. Their presence was especially noticeable in Kentucky. The Kentucky Catholic community was founded in the 1780s by transplanted Marylanders who had abandoned the Chesapeake region for the economically more promising territory west of the Alleghenies. Though the majority of Kentucky Catholics were native-born Americans, there was only one American-born priest in Kentucky in 1815. The rest were Europeans, with Frenchmen being the most numerous.

The pioneer priest of Kentucky was Stephen Badin. Born in Orleans, France, he came to the United States in 1792 to escape the turmoil of the French Revolution. Ordained a priest a year later by Bishop John Carroll, he set off for the Kentucky frontier, where he worked for many years. A contemporary of Badin was Charles Nerinckx, who had emigrated from Belgium in 1805. Both Nerinckx and Badin would have a decisive influence on the development of Kentucky Catholicism. The first bishop of Kentucky was another emigré priest, Benedict Flaget. Two other bishops appointed to assist Flaget in Kentucky, John B. David and Guy I. Chabrat, were also French. In fact, of the twenty-three bishops appointed to work in the West during the first half of the nineteenth century, eleven were French.

French influence was very evident concerning piety. Enlightenment Catholicism encouraged a personal, plain style of religion that stressed the positive side of human nature, toleration, and the reasonableness of religion. Badin and Nerinckx, together with many other French clergy in the United States, promoted a stern code of morality that discouraged dancing and theatergoing. The foundation of their strict moralism was a negative view of human nature and the need to curb its evil tendencies. Their severity in the confessional was well known, and people complained continually about both. Nerinckx told people to rise at four A.M. and forbade them to dance. Badin imposed such penances as holding a hot coal while reciting the

Our Father and the Hail Mary or digging a shallow grave and lying in it a brief time each day for a week. Though they were eccentric in their understanding of the spiritual life, Badin and Nerinckx shared a fundamentally pessimistic view of human nature characteristic of European Catholicism at this time. Many Kentucky Catholics did not approve of this style of piety. Such resistance suggests that they were attuned to a more moderate and positive type of spirituality.[42]

Bishop Flaget was more balanced in his spirituality, but he too emphasized the enormity of sin and found personal strength in a spirituality centered in the crucifixion of Jesus.[43] As was traditional with priests of the Sulpician society, Flaget put great emphasis on the sacrament of Penance and viewed the administration of this sacrament as the most important work of the priest. Such an understanding of the priesthood underscored the pervasive nature of sin, the weakness of human nature, and the need for the priest to provide "divine kindness" to the people through the sacrament of Penance. Parish missions, the Catholic counterpart to Protestant revivals, were common along the Kentucky frontier, and they too promoted this understanding of Catholicism in which sin and fear were the foundation on which religion rested. These French missionaries clearly were bringing their own style of Catholicism to the new nation. They had no intention of adapting the traditional French style of Catholicism to the United States.

Kentucky was also the setting for clashes between the monarchical and republican models of Catholicism. Known as ardent Jeffersonians, Kentucky Catholics supported a republican view of government in both the civic and religious spheres. Since the absence of clergy along the rural frontier encouraged lay leadership in the church, most congregations organized themselves into a religious society and then wrote republican constitutions that supported the idea of lay trustees. Badin resisted what he called such "extravagant pretensions of Republicanism" and continually opposed any manifestation of lay independence. Flaget also had to deal with such independence and acknowledged that the people were indeed "good republicans."[44] The contrast between the two opposing views of the church was captured very clearly in a letter written by the French-born bishop of New Orleans to a Vatican official:

> It is scarcely possible to realize how contagious even to the clergy and to men otherwise well disposed, are the principles of freedom and independence imbibed by all the pores in these United States. Hence I have always been convinced that practically all the good to be hoped for must come from the Congregations or religious Orders among which flourish strict discipline. . . .[45]

In a hierarchical church discipline was essential, while independence and freedom were counterproductive to the goals of an organization based on authority and the chain of command.

The democratization of Catholicism in the aftermath of the Revolution marked the first major challenge that the culture of the new nation presented to Catholicism. The influence of the Enlightenment was most noticeable in the practice of religion among middle- and upper-class Catholics, clearly influencing the way Catholics talked about their religion as well as the way they practiced it. Nonetheless, it did not present the same type of challenge that the democratic impulse did. The encounter between Catholicism and democracy was a clash over authority in the church, not the personal piety of individuals. By challenging the traditional model of authority, it posed a threat to the hierarchy's control over church affairs. Moreover, the encounter between Catholicism and democracy took place in the public forum, where it sparked prolonged and bitter debates. What took place in Philadelphia in the 1820s illustrates how contentious the debate over democracy in the church could become.

St. Mary's parish was the showcase of Philadelphia Catholicism.

Founded in 1765, it could boast of a distinguished history by the early nineteenth century. Its parishioners belonged to the most respectable and affluent segment of society; several of its members had distinguished themselves during the Revolutionary War. Nonetheless, for much of the 1820s the parish was in a state of turmoil. At issue was the question of authority. The trustees claimed the right to appoint and dismiss the clergy, and the bishop denied such claims. The dispute divided the parish between those loyal to the bishop and his traditional, monarchical view of the church, and those who wanted a more participatory, democratic style of church government. Large public meetings took place to rally support for the more liberal, democratic faction. In 1822 a trustee election riot took place in which parishioners, armed with clubs and bricks, fought one another in front of the church; then the bishop excommunicated the pastor of the parish; the democratic party of parishioners petitioned church authorities in Rome to intervene on their behalf; they also asked the local courts and even the state legislature to intervene and rule in their favor. Authorities in Rome finally did intervene. To restore peace in the church, they disciplined both the bishop and the priests involved in this most recent controversy over authority; because of his incompetence the aging Bishop Conwell was stripped of his authority as the bishop of Philadelphia; the two contentious clergymen who had been challenging the bishop's authority were reassigned to another diocese. Rome then appointed a new bishop, Francis Kenrick, who would set out to restore order and authority to the church in Philadelphia. With the appointment of Kenrick the experiment in democracy in St. Mary's parish came to an end.

In October 1829 the bishops of the United States met in Baltimore for their first provincial council. Convened by the new archbishop of Baltimore, James Whitfield, the council sought to bring some order and discipline to the church. Given the recent turmoil in

Philadelphia, the bishops were anxious to address the issue of trustees and the involvement of laymen in the government of the church. They wanted to abolish, or at least drastically weaken, the system of electing lay trustees. In addition, they wanted all new churches to be deeded to the bishop, thus weakening the power of boards of trustees who often held the deed to the church property. "It would be of great good to religion," they noted, "if this simple plan were universally adopted and the system of church trustees entirely abolished."[46] In expressing their dissatisfaction with the trustee system the bishops were rejecting the "republican" model of church government that John England was promoting in South Carolina. Rather than try to blend the democratic model of church at the local level with the Catholic tradition of episcopal authority, they endorsed an exclusively monarchical model in which the bishop ruled supreme in all church affairs. This was an important decision that clearly marked "the beginning of the growth of exclusive episcopal power in the government and management of the church."[47] More than a mere administrative decision, it was a reaction against the long-standing attempt of many Catholics, both clerical and lay, to adapt Catholicism to American culture through the democratization of church government. In effect, what the bishops were saying was that the traditional style of Catholicism with its emphasis on episcopal absolutism was to be the manner in which Catholicism would adapt to the culture of the new nation.

After the downfall of Napoleon in 1814, the fortunes of the church in Europe began to change. Within the next generation European Catholicism underwent a remarkable revival. By 1829 Catholicism in the United States was becoming more Roman than ever before.

The central feature in this restoration was the strengthening of the papacy and the increasing centralization of the church in Rome. More and more Catholics believed that a strong papacy was the key to the church's salvation in the nineteenth century. This mentality became known as ultramontanism, a belief that Catholicism must be Rome-centered with all authority resting in the papacy. As the pope's authority increased, the likelihood of the continuation of an American style of Catholicism politically independent of the Vatican diminished. A hierarchical model of the church with power and authority concentrated in the office of the papacy was antithetical to the republican model that encouraged democracy in the local church.

More was at work in these years than just the restoration of papal authority. The traditional religion of Catholicism, Tridentine Catholicism, was also revived. This style of piety conflicted with the "enlightened religion" that was so much a part of the Catholic ethos in the republican era. Tridentine Catholicism emphasized the primacy of revelation over reason; it nurtured a spirit of intolerance toward other religions rather than tolerance; and it endorsed a pastoral strategy based on sin and fear. Moreover, it was very similar to the ethos of evangelical Protestantism that was on the rise in the United States. This emphasis on sin and conversion became a dominant feature of both Catholicism and Protestantism in the nineteenth century.

The restoration and Romanization of Catholicism signaled the end of the American experiment with democracy in the church. The decline of the Enlightenment undermined the "reasonable piety" of the Carroll era. An additional change challenged any attempt to Americanize Catholicism in the republican era, the massive immigration from Ireland and Germany that began in the 1820s. Immigration brought a new class of Catholics to the United States in very large numbers. Unlike the educated, middle-class Catholics of the republican period, these newcomers were unskilled workers who provided the muscle and brawn needed to fuel the Industrial Revolution. They brought with them an understanding of Catholicism developed in the sectarian environment of their homeland, where Catholics viewed

Protestants as oppressors of their religious liberties. In particular, Irish nationalism at this time took on an increasingly sectarian, Catholic tone quite different from the more tolerant mood of the republican era. Moreover, the religion of republican Catholicism was a religion of the elite that emphasized an "enlightened piety," whereas the traditional religion of Tridentine Catholicism with its emphasis on such emotion-laden themes as sin and fear was more suited to an evangelization program targeted at the lower classes. This is precisely what occurred with the revival of the parish mission and evangelical Catholicism in both Europe and the United States. In addition, the immigrants came at a time when the traditional model of Catholicism was undergoing a revival in Europe. Thus, the religion that nurtured them in their youth and the religion they carried with them to the United States was antithetical to the religion of the Carroll era.

Because of its decisive impact on the shape of the church, the immigrant period in American Catholic history (1820–1920) has overshadowed the republican era. Yet, one of the more ambitious attempts to fashion a Catholicism in harmony with American culture took place in these years. It represented the first major effort of Catholics to blend the religion of Catholicism with American culture. By the 1820s the time to achieve some type of harmony between the two had passed. Tradition had won out over modernity. This did not happen without conflict and dissension—conflict that ripped apart a number of parish communities in cities like Philadelphia. The majority of church leaders rejected the democratic impulse and enlightenment piety. They chose to stand against the culture, championing a vision of the church that was more medieval than modern. This view would become more evident in the middle decades of the nineteenth century.

CHAPTER TWO

The Romanization of Catholicism

ᨠ Dᴜʀɪɴɢ ᴛʜᴇ ᴛʀᴜsᴛᴇᴇ ᴄᴏɴᴛʀᴏᴠᴇʀsʏ at St. Mary's parish in Philadelphia a group of parishioners published a pamphlet, a common practice in those days, that expressed their dissatisfaction with the clerical leadership. They bemoaned the "sundry abuses" that afflicted the church in Philadelphia, which they attributed to "the arbitrary and unjustifiable conduct of certain foreigners, sent among us by the Junta or Commission, directing the Fide Propaganda of Rome." These foreign clergymen, the letter went on to state, had "uniformly shown themselves hostile to our institutions, and completely ignorant of our country." Moreover, they had exercised their power "in too many instances, in a despotic and arbitrary manner." In a telling section of the letter the parishioners marked the moment of change with "the decease of our ever to be lamented father and friend, Archbishop Carroll. During his lifetime," they wrote, "his moderation and private virtues kept peace in the church . . . ; but . . . these states unfortunately have not been blessed with a second Carroll, who was a native of our country, and who, consequently, was well acquainted with our institutions, and respected them, as well as our individual rights. . . . " This reference to Carroll highlighted the contrast between the republican era when Catholicism had adopted certain features of American culture and the subsequent, antebellum period when Catholicism took on the features of a European model of Catholicism.[1]

A significant feature of this model was its emphasis on church authority, and the obedience this demanded stood in stark opposition to the American liberal tradition of intellectual independence. Nonetheless, it became a trademark of Catholicism in the antebellum era. In particular, it enhanced the authority of the bishop, encouraging an episcopal style quite different from that of John Carroll. Francis Kenrick personified this new breed of bishop.

Born in Ireland and educated in Rome, Kenrick came to Philadelphia in 1830 as bishop, determined to restore order and discipline in the church. His Roman seminary education appeared to be decisive in shaping his understanding of the church in the modern world. He had lived in Rome at a time when the papacy was beginning to regain its prestige. This was a time when the Catholic Church adopted a militant posture against the forces of liberalism emerging in Europe. The noted church historian Roger Aubert described this shift as a turning "away from the modern ideas of progress and back toward a tradition rooted in the Catholic Middle Ages."[2] Kenrick endorsed this vision of Catholicism, the heart of which was loyalty to the papacy.

One of his first tasks was to establish his authority over the laity. Since St. Mary's parish still remained a center of conflict, Kenrick moved decisively against the republican-spirited laity. He showed up uninvited at one of the public meetings of the pewholders in order to address the people. "He told them," wrote Fr. John Hughes, "that they must not dare to control him in the exercise of his episcopal authority." He would wish no other trustees in the parish as long as "these gentlemen would confine themselves within their proper limits, and not presume to meddle, directly or indirectly, with his authority." The trustees continued to resist Kenrick. The bishop then put the parish under interdict. This effectively closed St. Mary's since no religious services could take place while the parish was under

interdict. After suffering under this rule for one month, the trustees finally gave in and accepted Kenrick's authority. Then in 1832 the first diocesan synod passed a law that stated that title to every new church built in the diocese would be in Kenrick's name rather than in the name of a board of lay trustees. By abolishing the tradition of lay trustees, Kenrick sought to remove any taint of democracy in the government of the local church. Democracy was clearly incompatible with his vision of the church, a vision that was more monarchical than democratic, more European than American.[3]

John Hughes was another new breed bishop of this era. Irish-born but educated in a seminary in Maryland, he personified the church militant. Ordained a priest for the diocese of Philadelphia in 1826, he experienced firsthand the troubles in St. Mary's parish. Siding with the bishop, Hughes applauded the manner in which Kenrick asserted his authority. Ordained a bishop in 1838, he went to New York to assist the aging prelate, John Dubois, whom he eventually succeeded upon Dubois's death in 1842. A combative type, Hughes did not hesitate to enter the fray, be it a debate with a Protestant minister or a contest with a republican-spirited board of trustees. In New York he met both.

Shortly after his arrival in the city, Hughes crossed swords with the trustees of the Old St. Patrick's church. In a pastoral letter he challenged their authority to hire and fire parish personnel, including the clergy. "From that time," he wrote, "I made war on the whole system. I wrote upon it, gave a series of lectures which lasted for six months on the scandals it had produced and the evils it had entailed on the Catholic religion throughout the United States." He believed that it was "expedient to adopt a new mode of government ... I had to stand up among them as their bishop and chief ... To knead them up into one dough, to be leavened by the spirit of Catholic faith and of Catholic union."[4] Hughes eventually prevailed over the trustees. Under his direction the diocesan synod of 1842, following the

example of Kenrick in Philadelphia, approved several directives that effectively weakened the power of lay boards of trustees. The bishop clearly wanted to dismantle what he called "this uncatholic system." As far as Hughes was concerned, he was the boss in the church, not the lay trustees. As he stated, "Episcopal authority came from above and not from below and Catholics did their duty when they obeyed their bishop." Hughes treated the clergy in much the same manner. His will was law, and when some clergy complained about this and discussed the necessity of priests' rights, Hughes told them "that he would teach them [County] Monaghan canon law; he would send them back to the bogs whence they came."[5]

Hughes's militant and autocratic style of leadership was suited to the rapidly expanding Catholic community of New York. Overwhelmed by immigration from Ireland and Germany, the church needed someone like Hughes to bring a measure of unity and solidarity to a very diverse and rapidly growing population. When he failed to get government approval of public funds for Catholic schools, he led the crusade for parochial schools. In the pulpit he stood up to nativist bigots, staunchly defending the religion of the immigrants. After riots in Philadelphia in the summer of 1844 had led to the burning of Catholic churches, Hughes urged the Catholics of New York to defend their churches lest they too be torched. Because of his militant stance against possible attacks on the city's Catholic churches, no churches burned in New York during the summer of 1844.

Democracy in church government was clearly incompatible with Hughes's view of the church. Like Kenrick he looked to Rome, not the United States, for his understanding of how authority was to be exercised in the church. The desire to democratize Catholicism in the United States faded as men such as Kenrick and Hughes took over the leadership of the church. Though this democratic impulse would

never entirely disappear, the church was moving toward a more monarchical, less democratic style of church government. The Vatican Council of 1870 decisively pushed the church in this direction when, by proclaiming the infallibility of the pope, it encouraged the centralization of the church in Rome. Such centralization of authority filtered down throughout the church, enhancing the authority of both bishop and pastor.

The plain style of religion so prevalent in the republican era of Catholicism persisted into the 1820s and '30s. This was most visible in the simplicity of church architecture and decoration. One European Jesuit, John Grassi, described the churches in the United States as "unpretending structures, without ornament." Notably absent were the statues and pictures commonly found in Roman Catholic churches in Europe. For missionaries from Europe, this was something of a culture shock. Ambrose Marechal, the French-born archbishop of Baltimore, "grieved" very much that the Baltimore cathedral was "almost completely lacking in decoration." He wanted "to buy two statues, namely one of Our Lord and Saviour and one of the Blessed Virgin" for the cathedral, but "none whatsoever could be found in these regions."[6] Devotional works also emphasized a plain style of religion by stressing an interior, personal piety that deemphasized the mediating role of priests and sacraments. This type of spirituality blended in well with the social situation of the Catholic community in which there was a scarcity of both clergy and churches. But change was under way. Another style of religion, devotional Catholicism, imported by European clergy and laity, was pushing aside the "enlightened piety" that distinguished the republican period of Catholicism. The emergence of devotional Catholicism was one of the most important developments associated with the rise of ultramontanism.

The heart of devotional Catholicism was the exercise of piety or what was called a devotion. Popular devotions distinct from the Mass have arisen throughout the history of Roman Catholicism. Unlike the Mass, which was celebrated in Latin, the language of popular devotions was the vernacular. Each devotion has a specific focus—e.g., the passion of Jesus—and for this reason the spiritual life of an individual became centered on a particular person—e.g., Jesus, Mary, or one of the saints—and the devotion connected with that person. Though they could be performed privately and most often were, devotions were also celebrated in church at public ceremonies presided over by a priest. Devotional Catholicism enjoyed a renaissance in the nineteenth century. Most of these devotions had originated centuries earlier, and after a period of neglect in the late eighteenth century, they were revived with new vigor during the papacy of Pius IX. Promoted by the papacy, this style of piety became a trademark of the ultramontane era. Some of the more popular devotions at this time were those dedicated to the Sacred Heart of Jesus, to Jesus in the Eucharist through public exposition of the Blessed Sacrament, to the passion of Jesus, and to the Immaculate Conception of Mary, as well as the recitation of the rosary, and, of course, devotion to such saints as St. Patrick, St. Joseph, and St. Anthony. The emphasis on these devotions fostered a culture of devotionalism that became "the heart and soul of immigrant religion."[7]

The rise of devotional Catholicism began with the large influx of immigrants in the post–1820 period. Already a noticeable trend by the 1840s, it gained popularity in the 1850s. By the 1860s it had become a distinctive feature of American Catholicism. The most convincing piece of evidence for this shift was the proliferation of prayer books and devotional guides. From 1800 to 1880 eighty prayer books were published in English in the United States; fifty-eight were published after 1840, with twenty-six appearing in the 1850s. The multiplication of devotional guides—books devoted to a few specific devotions such as those to the Sacred Heart, the Way of the Cross, and the rosary—followed the same trend. One hundred thirty such guides were published between 1830 and 1880, with 98 percent being published after 1840; once again the decade of the 1850s surpassed other decades in terms of the largest number of publications, with fifty-one, or 39 percent of the total number of devotional guides published in that decade.[8] Not only were many more prayer books in English now available to people, but the style of religion promoted by these books was decidedly different from the plain style of religion associated with early nineteenth-century Catholicism.

Historian Ann Taves in her analysis of these prayer books has convincingly documented this shift. Prior to 1840, prayers books included only a few devotions—the rosary and benediction of the Blessed Sacrament being the most popular. After 1840 the number of devotions increased dramatically, featuring such rituals as devotion to the Sacred Heart of Jesus, the passion of Jesus, the Way of the Cross, and devotions in honor of St. Joseph, as well as numerous others. Devotional guides reflected the same trend with devotions to Mary, the Blessed Sacrament, the Sacred Heart of Jesus, and the passion and death of Jesus being the most popular.[9]

The significance of the 1840s and '50s was again underscored in the development of the Catholic revival, or, as it was more commonly known, the parish mission. European missionaries imported the parish mission to the United States. In many ways it was similar to the Protestant revival meeting that was enjoying a renaissance in the antebellum period. Catholic revival meetings increased significantly during the 1840s, with three times the number of missions being held in this decade as in the previous one. The trend continued in the 1850s with a large increase, and the numbers continued to climb throughout the following decades. Through its sermons and rituals, the parish mission fostered devotional Catholicism. Moreover, the mission was also a primary occasion for the sale of large number of prayer books and devotional guides as well as rosaries, pictures, and other religious articles.

The emergence of devotional Catholicism in the antebellum period resulted in a definite change of attitude among Catholics in the United States. In the republican era belief in tolerance was a notable feature of Catholicism, and this disdain for religious bigotry in turn fostered tolerance of other Christian churches. Throughout the nation Catholics and Protestants learned to live together. They attended services in each other's churches, sometimes out of necessity, more often out of genuine interest and curiosity. Protestants gave money and land for the construction of Catholic churches and sent their children to Catholic schools. Catholics and Protestants were partners in politics, and religiously mixed marriages were common. In the era of the immigrant church, however, a siege mentality emerged, fostering a militant sectarian attitude that was no friend to tolerance. A major reason for this was the emergence of a nativist crusade in the antebellum era. Targeting both Catholics and the foreign-born, this crusade subjected Catholics to intense discrimination. Catholics came to believe that they were under attack. Reinforcing this mentality was a devotional ethos that nurtured the persecuted complex.

The link between devotionalism and this new siege mentality was most clearly visible in the devotion to the Sacred Heart of Jesus. Since their founding in the sixteenth century, the priests of the Society of Jesus, the Jesuits, had promoted this devotion. An Italian-born Jesuit, Benedict Sestini, who was on the faculty of Georgetown College, founded a devotional magazine, *The Messenger of the Sacred Heart*, in 1866 to promote devotion of the Sacred Heart "in response to the forces of darkness that Sestini saw threatening Christian civilization." The magazine promoted the Apostleship of Prayer, a voluntary association to spread devotion to the Sacred Heart. In stark contrast to John Carroll, Sestini viewed the spiritual life as a "deadly struggle" with the forces of evil. For him Jesus was "fighting with us, in us and for us" as "the ever-recurring assaults of the world" filled the spiritual life with struggle and strife. This devotion also encouraged loyalty to the papacy, which Sestini viewed as under siege by the forces of rebellion. "All attacks of human or satanic malice and power" against the papacy would not prevail, wrote Sestini. For him the pope "shall always emerge victorious from the onslaught" because of the intervention and power of the Sacred Heart. Sestini continually used the language of battle and war, struggle and strife, to describe the situation of Catholics. The only remedy to overcome the attacks of evil, be they human passions, rationalism, or the troops of Garibaldi who were occupying Rome, was devotion to the Sacred Heart.[10]

Coupled with the prevalent siege mentality was a sectarianism that had been developing since the early nineteenth century. One reason for this was the new type of Irish Catholic who was immigrating to the United States in these decades. In the republican era many Irish immigrants, Mathew Carey included, brought with them "fiercely antisectarian ideals" that were developing in Ireland in the 1780s and '90s as political leaders sought to establish an independent Ireland founded on the republican principles of equality and toleration. By 1800 this movement had collapsed. Sectarian ideals once again were to prevail in Ireland. As the decades passed, Irish society became progressively more sectarian, resembling in many respects the Jim Crow South in the United States in the latter part of the nineteenth century. In the South the dividing line was race. In Ireland it was religion. The Catholic Emancipation movement of the 1820s, led by Daniel O'Connell, solidified this sectarian spirit.[11]

An early manifestation of such sectarianism took place on July 12, 1824, in New York City. This was Orange Day, the anniversary of a key event in Irish history when at the Battle of the Boyne in 1690 the Protestant armies of King William defeated the Catholic forces of

King James II. This signaled the final triumph of England over Ireland, of Protestantism over Catholicism. Ever since, Irish Protestants have marched on July 12 to celebrate their victory over Catholics. In 1824 the march took place in Greenwich Village, a settlement on the outskirts of the city, populated mostly by Irish Catholic weavers. The local Orangemen paraded through the streets accompanied by fife and drum. Fortified by frequent visits to the local grog shops, the Orangemen continued their celebration into the early evening hours. A group of Irish Catholic men challenged some of the Orangemen as they left one of the taverns, demanding that they put away their Orange flags, which Irish Catholics found very offensive. They refused and a brawl ensued. When it was over, the police arrested thirty-three Irish Catholics and not one Orangeman. A similar riot took place in Philadelphia in 1831. This time American nativists joined the Irish Protestants in their celebration of Orange Day. The sectarianism that surfaced on Orange Day had found a powerful ally in nativism.[12]

Anti-foreign and anti-Catholic, nativism was a powerful social movement that developed in the pre–Civil War period in response to the large influx of Catholic immigrants. Unprecedented and indeed unwelcome, such massive immigration changed the social profile of the nation. In the decade after 1845 three million immigrants arrived in the United States; large numbers of them were Irish and Catholic. In the 1830s the city of Buffalo, for example, was overwhelmingly American with as much as 85 percent of its population being American born; by 1855 the city had changed radically. In that year about 74 percent of the population was foreign born.[13] Similar transformations took place in other cities. This dramatic rise in the foreign-born population was a major reason for the rise of nativism.

The burning of a Catholic convent in Charlestown, Massachusetts, in 1834 launched the nativist crusade that would color American life for the next quarter century. Church burnings and Bible riots, as well as anti-Catholic lectures and books, kept feelings and attitudes at a high level of intensity. College students at some of the nation's most prestigious institutions debated such questions as the compatibility of Catholicism with American government. At Yale one debating society declared that "the Roman Catholic religion [is] inconsistent with free government." Students at the University of Pennsylvania believed that nativists were justified in burning the homes of their Catholic neighbors during the Bible riots of 1844; at the University of Georgia one group of students supported the proposition that Catholicism "should not be tolerated in the United States." Indeed, in the 1850s, wrote a noted historian, "the average Protestant American had been trained from birth to hate Catholicism." Such an attitude favored a sectarian culture in which religious bigotry built seemingly impenetrable walls of division between Catholics and Protestants. The founding of the Know Nothing party in 1850 thrust the issue onto the national political stage. Rooted in nativist bigotry, the party's motto was "Americans must rule America." Its members even had to take an oath that they would not vote for any foreigners, Roman Catholics in particular.[14]

By 1854, four years after its founding, the Know Nothing party had over one million members. It had elected eight governors, more than one hundred congressmen, and the mayors of Boston, Chicago, and Philadelphia, as well as thousands of lesser officials throughout the United States. The rise of the Know Nothing party astounded many Americans and led Abraham Lincoln to observe that "our progress in degeneracy appears to me to be pretty rapid. As a nation, we began by declaring that all men are created equal. We now practically read it all men are created equal except Negroes. When the Know Nothings get control, it will read all men are created equal, except Negroes, and foreigners and Catholics."[15]

Americans' fear of Catholicism was perhaps understandable. A small, insignificant denomination in 1800, by 1860 it had become the largest denomination in the country. In a brief thirty-year period, 1830–60, its population had increased by almost 900 percent, numbering 3.1 million by 1860. It also had become a church of immigrants as Irish and German immigrants stamped Catholicism with a very foreign identity. Such a heavy foreign membership set the church apart from the rest of society at this time. The convert, Isaac Hecker, spoke for many Americans when he observed that the Roman Catholic "Church is not national with us, hence it does not meet our wants nor does it fully understand and sympathize with the experience and dispositions of our people. It is principally made up of adopted and foreign individuals."[16] Such an attitude did not bode well for Catholics in an age of rising nativism.

The anti-foreign, anti-Catholic climate of the antebellum era clearly put Catholics on the defensive. Protestantism still remained the heart and soul of American culture, defining and shaping its major institutions. Since the vast majority of Catholics were now foreign born, this made them very suspect in an age when only Americans were thought to be fit for public office. Pushed to the margins of society by the forces of nativism and anti-Catholicism, Catholics began to build their own enclaves in the immigrant neighborhoods. Religion became their badge of identity, and the local parish became the hub around which much of their lives revolved. Socially and religiously they had become separated from American society.

In addition, the Catholic intellectual tradition that was taking shape at this time on both sides of the Atlantic stood in opposition to the American liberal tradition. Democracy, together with an emphasis on the rights of the individual and intellectual freedom, were the main elements of this tradition. The Catholic deviation from democracy in church government and the intense commitment to the authority of the pope and his clerical representatives at the local level was not in harmony with the liberal intellectual tradition. Thus, intellectually as well as socially and religiously, Catholics stood on the margins of American society.

Devotional Catholicism blended in with this historical situation, helping to shape and sharpen the ethos of this emerging Catholic culture. Ann Taves has argued this point convincingly in her study of Roman Catholic devotionalism. Though acknowledging the importance of nativism in the formation of a Catholic subculture, she writes that "mid-nineteenth-century Catholic theology and practice itself fostered the creation of an enclosed Catholic subculture and indeed was able to use nativist hostility to reinforce American Catholics' view of themselves as a beleaguered minority banding together to protect itself from the attacks of its enemies."[17] Rather than being passive agents, victims of nativist forces who were forced into isolated communities, Catholics self-consciously built up a strong community that was centered on the immigrant parish. This was their strategy of survival in a nation that was not very welcoming.

By the 1850s the ultramontane revival had clearly left its mark on the emerging immigrant church. As one bishop proudly proclaimed, the American church was "Roman to the heart."[18] Nonetheless, as Roman as Catholicism was becoming at this time, American cultural influences, in particular nativism and anti-Catholicism, were transforming the culture of Catholicism. Another important influence was the emergence of the common school, or what is now known as the public school.

Schools funded by tax money was an idea that had gained wide support in the pre–Civil War period. At this time many reform movements were sweeping across the nation. Support for publicly funded schools was part of this wave of reform, which began to peak in the 1830s and 1840s, with the result that by 1860 every state had some public education. Rooted in the Protestant culture of the United States, the public school movement encouraged an American Protestant imperialism. Its supporters promoted it with a crusader's zeal, and before long the schoolhouse became the established church of the American republic.

As spectacular as this movement was, it had a fundamental flaw. It was rooted in a white, Anglo-Saxon, Protestant ideology that was not very tolerant of those outside this culture. For Catholics the culture of the public school was alien and its benefits questionable. It was this basic conflict between the ideology of the common school and Roman Catholicism that led to the development of the Catholic school system. By the end of the nineteenth century the parochial school had become a distinctive trademark of American Catholicism. It was the cornerstone of an extensive independent, Catholic educational system eventually comprising high schools, colleges, and universities that was unparalleled in the United States.

Another feature of the immigrant church was the national parish, a parish organized by nationality rather than by territory. Congregations organized by nationality were not a uniquely Catholic idea. Protestant denominations, Methodists in particular, also developed such parishes in response to the influx of immigrants. Catholics, however, clearly had the largest number of national parishes. In the republican period the national parish was the exception; the norm was the territorial parish in which all people living in a designated geographical area belonged to the same parish. Such territorial parishes generally disregarded any distinction of people based on nationality. But the arrival of large numbers of immigrants posed a problem. Even though they might have lived in the same area of the city, German and Irish Catholics were not willing to worship in the same church. Each group wanted to worship and pray in its own language, following the tradition and customs of the Old World. The national parish was a pragmatic response to this problem. By the middle of the nineteenth century it had become the principal institution that the immigrants established in their attempt to preserve the religious life of the old country.

The emergence of the "new city" in the nineteenth century reinforced the development of the national parish. As cities were expanding their boundaries in the course of the nineteenth century, they gradually became more segregated according to class, race, and ethnicity. The immigrant neighborhood was especially distinctive. As one observer noted, the immigrants "create for themselves distinct communities, almost as impervious to American sentiments and influences as are the inhabitants of Dublin or Hamburg."[19] Distinctive landmarks of urban America, they possessed an innate magnetism that attracted the immigrants. Once the newcomers settled in, these neighborhoods became their reference point within the larger, more impersonal city. A key institution in these neighborhoods was the national parish. During the century of immigration it would remain the most enduring cultural institution in the neighborhood, nurturing and sustaining the religion of the immigrants.

As foreign and alien as Catholicism was to most Americans, a sizable number of American Protestants did become Catholic. It is estimated that 57,400 Protestants became Catholic between 1831 and 1860. Two of the most famous converts were Orestes Brownson and Isaac Hecker.[20] American-born writers and intellectuals, they both wanted to make Catholicism more American. At this time they were clearly rowing upstream, but their hope of a more American version of Roman Catholicism was rooted in a timeless search to link Catholicism more closely with American culture.

Born in 1803, Brownson spent much of his adult life searching for the true religion. At first a Presbyterian, he later became a Universalist preacher; then he joined the Unitarian church and even went so far as to found his own Church of the Future in Boston; in 1844 he converted to Catholicism. By this time he was a well-known writer, and his conversion raised more than a few eyebrows. To become a Catholic at this time was a bold decision. For an American-born Protestant like Brownson it meant entering into an alien world. He described the significance of such a decision in the following manner:

> To pass from one Protestant sect to another is a small affair, and is little more than going from one apartment to another in the same house. We remain still in the same world. In the same general order of thought, and in the midst of the same friends and associates. We do not go from the known to the unknown; we are still within soundings, and may either return, if we choose, to the sect we have left, or press on to another, without serious loss of reputation, or any gross disturbance of our domestic and social relations. But to pass from Protestantism to Catholicity is a very different thing. We break with the whole world in which we have hitherto lived; we enter into what is to us a new and untried region, and we fear the discoveries we may make there, when it is too late to draw back. To the Protestant mind this old Catholic Church is veiled in mystery, and leaves ample room to the imagination to people it with all manner of monsters.... We enter it, and leave no bridge over which we may return. It is a committal for life, for eternity. To enter it seemed to me, like taking a leap in the dark; and it is not strange that I recoiled, and set my wits to work to find out, if possible, some compromise, some middle ground on which I could be faithful to my Catholic tendencies without uniting myself with the present Roman Catholic Church.[21]

Until his death in 1876 Brownson was a spokesman for the Catholic religion. One of his first forays into the public arena was his ill-fated campaign to make the Irish more American. At this time the tendency was to equate Catholicism with being Irish and Protestantism with being American. Brownson fought against this characterization. He published his views in a series of articles in his *Brownson's Quarterly Review*, arguing that the Irish and all other immigrants "must ultimately lose their own nationality and become assimilated in general character to the Anglo-American race." The Irish resented this, accusing Brownson of being anti-Irish and soft on anti-Catholic nativists.[22] Brownson had clearly endorsed the Americanization strategy, that is, the need for Catholics to adapt to the American culture. He reiterated this theme two years later at a July commencement address at St. John's College, the essence of which was published in fall 1856. Brownson celebrated the American nation, "a people," he wrote, "with a great destiny, and a destiny glorious to ourselves and beneficent to the world."[23] The essay, "Mission of America," was very much in the spirit of "Manifest Destiny," an expression and belief in vogue at this time that celebrated the providential role that the United States possessed. He rejected the idea that Catholics should " ... separate themselves from the great current of American nationality, and ... assume the position in political and social life of an inferior, a distinct, or an alien people, or of a foreign colony planted in the midst of a people with whom they have no sympathies.... " Rather he wanted them to "take their position as free and equal American citizens, with American interests and sympathies, American sentiments and affections, and throw themselves fearlessly into the great current of American national life.... " For Brownson being American meant possessing "self-reliance, energy, perseverance," what he called "the chief elements of success." Most important, Brownson believed that the future of America rested in the hands of Catholics. As he stated, "It is only through Catholicity that the country can fulfill its mission.... The salvation of the country and its future glory depend on Catholics." He concluded his paean to

America and Catholicism with the warning that it was "the duty of all Catholic citizens . . . to be, or to make themselves, thorough-going Americans." Those who would not he considered "'outside barbarians' and not within the pale of the American order."[24]

It would be hard to find a more explicit endorsement of Americanization. However, it was not unchallenged. At the end of the commencement ceremony Archbishop John Hughes arose and addressed the students. As one person noted, Hughes "harangued the graduates with completely opposing views, denying the existence of the advantages the laws of the country are said to offer Catholics, which Brownson had taken pains to emphasize; asserting further that liberty for Catholics existed only on paper, and not in fact, and exhorting them to prepare for days of oppression and persecution in the future."[25] Hughes also wanted Brownson to avoid any "allusion to the nationality of our Catholic brethren" and did not want him to "write or say anything calculated to represent the Catholic religion as especially adapted to the genius of the American people as such."[26]

Hughes was trying to walk the line that separated the proponents of a Catholicism that would be strongly Irish and one that would be very American. He wanted to avoid controversy in this sensitive area of religion and nationality. He certainly was not anti-American. Like John Carroll, the Irish-born Hughes could celebrate the genius of the American republic. He did not hesitate to applaud the United States, "a country," he wrote, "which, in its civil and social relations, has exhibited so fair an opportunity for developing the practical harmonies of Catholic faith, and of Catholic charity. . . ."[27]

However, he would not go so far as to support the idea that "the doctrines of the Catholic Church may be, so to speak, Americanized."[28] In a letter to Brownson he denied the convert's contention that "if the Catholic religion had been or could now be presented to the American people through mediums and under auspices more congenial with the national feelings and habits, the progress of the Church and the conversion of Protestants would have been far greater."[29]

What Hughes was saying was that Catholicism cannot and should not adapt itself to the American culture. In his essay Brownson hinted at such an adaptation in a very inchoate manner, but he never explained how it would happen. The most he could say was that "grace does not destroy nature, nor change the national type of character. It purifies and elevates nature, and brings out whatever is good, noble, and strong in the national type." If Catholicism could be "adapted to the wants of the simple, the rude, the barbarian, and the savage," he said, surely it could adapt itself to the "active, energetic, self-reliant American character."[30]

The controversy between Brownson and Hughes was about more than just the issue of nationality. Brownson clearly wanted Catholics to become more American, while Hughes saw this emphasis on nationality as divisive. He wanted to emphasize the Catholic dimension of American Catholicism. He was intent on preserving the Catholicism of the Old World in the United States and establishing an immigrant church strong enough to withstand the attacks of a nativist American society. But Brownson wanted the religion of Catholicism—"Catholicity" was the word he used—to adapt itself to the American culture. He never explained how this would take place, and within a year he repudiated this idea, most likely because of Hughes's strong objection. The repudiation took place in a review he wrote of Isaac Hecker's book *Aspirations of Nature*. In a most explicit manner Brownson denied any "design to Americanize Catholicity," thus distancing himself from any group, or "new school" to use Hughes's phrase, that sought to achieve this. As he stated, "We are also opposed to every thing which looks like accommodating Catholic teaching to the tastes and temper of the age or country." He went on to say, "Americanism does very well in the political order . . . but it cannot be transferred to the church without heresy and schism."[31] Brownson's strong repudiation of his earlier position and Hughes's equally strong condemnation of any attempt to "Americanize Catholicity" clearly indicate that they were speaking about the relationship between religion and American culture.

The "new school" that Hughes referred to was a small group of clergy and laymen in New York City who met in the mid-1850s to discuss issues of mutual interest. Their chief concern was to show the compatibility between American culture and Catholicism. As Hughes stated, they wanted to "show that the Catholic religion and the American Constitution would really fit each other as a key fits a lock; that without any change in regard to faith or morals, the doctrines of the Catholic church may be, so to speak, Americanized— that is represented in such a manner as to attract the attention and win the admiration of the American people."[32] Conversations about the need for Catholicism to become more American were commonplace among this group of Catholics. Such discussion became more structured in the 1860s when some New York priests established a theological society, the Accademia, so that they could discuss the situation of Catholicism in the United States. They wanted the church to be "radically different from what it had been in the Old World. It had to be open to the uniqueness of its new milieu and reflect that milieu."[33] For these clergymen this definitely meant more democracy in a church whose bishops had become increasingly authoritarian. Other issues they discussed were the infallibility of the pope, the use of English in the Mass, mandatory celibacy for the clergy, and their right to have beards and not wear the clerical collar. Such discussion groups were very suspect in a church that was becoming a mirror image of European Catholicism.

Brownson's fellow traveler on the road to Rome, Isaac Hecker, spent the best years of his life promoting the idea of an American

Catholicism. Born in New York City in 1819, Hecker began to search for a spiritual home. Like Brownson he was initially attracted to transcendentalism, even living for a brief period in the transcendentalist community at Brook Farm. Then in 1844 he converted to Catholicism. After his conversion he joined the Redemptorist religious order and was ordained a priest in 1849. He eventually left the Redemptorists and in 1858 founded a new religious order, the Paulists, officially known as the Missionary Society of St. Paul the Apostle.

Hecker's most creative work was done in the 1850s and '60s. In two books, *Questions of the Soul* and *Aspirations of Nature*, along with several essays, he sought to articulate the genius of Catholicism and its relation to the United States. Like Ralph Waldo Emerson and many other transcendentalists, Hecker focused on the individual's search for the transcendent. According to Hecker this search would only be complete when it was united with the Catholic Church, the external authority that the individual needed to succeed in this search for the divine. Like Joseph Smith, founder of the Mormons, who also lived in this antebellum age, Hecker believed in the special providential destiny of the United States. The doctrine of providence was the core of his theology, so much so that his "religious imagination was dominated by the vision of the future triumph of the Church, the coming of God's kingdom on earth."[34] This was a special land chosen by God, where the final chapter of sacred history would be written. For Smith the Mormons were the chosen people who would write that last chapter of sacred history—the coming of God's kingdom on earth. For Hecker it was the American Catholic church. In his opinion the providential destiny of America would be realized only when America became Catholic.

Hecker believed that the destinies of the United States and American Catholicism were so bound together that Catholics alone would be able to guide the nation toward "its highest destinies." To achieve this goal it would be necessary for Catholics "to put aside

European ways and adapt to American conditions."[35] In a letter to his colleagues in the Redemptorist order he wrote, "So far as it is compatible with faith and piety, I am for accepting the true American civilization, its usages and customs; leaving aside other reasons it is the only way in which Catholicity can become the religion of our people." In a letter to a Catholic laywoman he reiterated this point, writing that "our faith must take root in our national characteristics...."[36] He went on to tell her that "every age has its own characteristics" and therefore the type of spirituality suitable for American Catholics must be reflective of the age in which they lived.

What this spirituality consisted of exhibited some of Brownson's ideas, concepts that were certainly in the air at this time among many American intellectuals. These included such ideas as personal initiative, self-reliance, freedom of action, and a positive attitude toward the world. Hecker's positive regard for the world or what he called "the age" was rooted in his belief that the divine Spirit becomes more manifest as history unfolds; that is, with each passing age God becomes more present in the world through the medium of the church. Such a positive view of the world clashed with the negative view promoted by most Catholic preachers at that time. Like the Jesuit Sestini, they viewed the world as corrupted by sin, something to be endured, not redeemed; Catholics would find their salvation within the church in such a manner that their isolation from society would be increased. Hecker's vision was just the opposite. For him Catholics should go out into society to transform it and bring about the final triumph of the church and the coming of God's kingdom.

Hecker's vision of religion was so dynamic that he envisioned Catholicism transforming American society. But this could not take place until Catholicism became more American. One of his most explicit statements in this regard came shortly before his death in a comment regarding the recent establishment of Catholic University in Washington, D.C. "The work of the new University," he wrote, "planted in the political center of this free and intelligent people, will tend to shape the expression of doctrines in such wise as to assimilate them to American intelligence—not to minimize but to assimilate. To develop the mind there is never need to minimize the truth; but there is great need of knowing how to assimilate the truth to different minds."[37] This was the challenge Hecker posed for his generation—how to adapt Catholicism to American culture within the limits presented by the Catholic faith. This would always remain the challenge for anyone seeking to adapt Catholicism to American culture. The other side of the challenge was to avoid capitulation to the culture with the result that Catholicism would lose its identity as well as its integrity.

Throughout his life as a Catholic Hecker strived to shape his religion to the American environment. He founded a new religious order that sought to unite Catholicism and American life; he wrote books and essays that articulated a new apologetic with the hope that his reasoning would penetrate the hearts and minds of Protestant Americans; he encouraged a new type of spirituality that emphasized sanctity in the world and not apart from it; he founded a press to distribute religious pamphlets and books; he established a periodical that would address the issues of the day; and he lectured throughout the nation, hoping to gain converts to Catholicism. Like many visionaries, however, he was not a systematic thinker. He presented a vision, a theology of history, with the United States and Catholicism as the central features of this theology, but he did not explain how his vision would be reconciled with the Catholic faith tradition. Such vagueness would leave his writings open to misinterpretation by others who did not share his unique vision.

The American-born converts Hecker and Brownson were clearly the most prominent Catholics of the antebellum period who endorsed the idea of Catholicism becoming more American. However, they were not very representative of the majority of

Catholics. Nor was this a good time to push the idea of making Catholicism more American. Mass immigration had greatly changed the social profile of the church; the large numbers of foreign-born Catholics, mostly Irish and Germans, wanted to preserve the culture and religion of the old country—they wanted the church to be Irish or German, not American. The restoration of Catholicism and the increasing importance of Rome and the papacy as the vital center of Catholic life was a development that was at odds with any attempts at Americanization. The episcopal leaders of the church in these decades, Hughes and Kenrick being two prominent examples, were clearly dead set against any efforts to make Catholicism more American; they were Roman to the core. Much like German Lutherans in the Missouri Synod, Catholic Church leaders chose to stand apart from American society, strongly resisting any attempts to Americanize Catholicism. Their focus was on the immigrant newcomers whose needs they sought to meet by building up an institution that included churches for worship, schools for education, hospitals for healing, and numerous other institutions and organizations. This was a positive and creative response to the challenges posed by a society that was religiously very sectarian but still open to the peoples of the world who were migrating to the United States in search of a better life.

In the middle decades of the nineteenth century Catholicism clearly evidenced both European and American cultural influences. It was neither a totally foreign institution as some of its critics argued, nor was it a very American church as some of its members had wished. It was a blending of both European and American cultures. This mingling of cultural influences would continue in the post–Civil War period as Catholics sought to come to terms with the emergence of modern America. The search for an American Catholicism still remained an elusive quest.

CHAPTER THREE

In Search of an American Catholicism

ᖷ IN NOVEMBER OF 1889 thousands of Catholics gath-
ered in Baltimore to celebrate the one hundredth anniversary of the
establishment of the Catholic hierarchy in the United States. One explicit purpose of the three-day celebration was to honor the memory
of John Carroll, the first American Catholic bishop. However, other
themes captured the imagination of the speakers in the course of this
centennial event. One refrain heard time and again was "the progress
of the church" during the preceding one hundred years. This was a
time of Catholic boosterism. Speaker after speaker proudly noted the
growth of the church since the time of John Carroll. Once a small denomination, it had now become the largest church in the nation with
some nine million members. "But while we rejoice in the numerical
strength of the Catholic religion," noted James Gibbons, the cardinal
archbishop of Baltimore, "we rejoice still more that ... the church ex-
hibits an organic vitality, an exuberant spirit, a vigorous activity and a
sturdy growth which afford a well-founded hope of unlimited expansion in the future."[1]

Archbishop John Ireland of St. Paul, Minnesota, spoke Sunday evening at vesper services held in the cathedral. By 1889 Ireland had
emerged as a leading figure in the American Catholic community.
Surely one of the most gifted preachers in the country, his sermon that
evening echoed the sentiments of Gibbons. Ireland's favorite theme
was that Catholics must "make America Catholic." Once converted to

"the supremacy of the supernatural," America's "singular mission" was to bring forth in the world "a new social and political order, based more than any other that has heretofore existed upon the common brotherhood of man, and more than any other securing to the multitude of the people social happiness and equality of rights. In our own are bound up the hopes of the billions of the earth." Then, in a flourish of optimism he summed up his dream—"The Church triumphant in America, Catholic truth will travel on the wings of American influence, and with it encircle the universe." The church and the nation would be united under the banner of Catholicism, and together they would shape the future of the world. Such optimistic nationalism fueled by religious imperialism is difficult to understand in the post-Vietnam, post–Vatican II era, but in the 1880s and '90s energetic nationalism was commonplace. Ireland and many other Americans believed that they were living in "the greatest epoch of human history" and were "assisting at the birth of a new age." A nation of destiny, the United States would be the midwife of a new world order.[2]

Catholics had come of age by the closing decade of the century. Members of the largest denomination in the country, they were much more confident about their place in American society in the 1890s than they were in the 1840s. They were proud to be Catholic and were not hesitant to display this pride publicly. John Ireland expressed this confidence and pride as well as anyone. One major reason for such confidence was the presence of a sizable Catholic middle class. Part of the celebration of the centenary in Baltimore was a two-day congress in which some 1,200 laymen from across the country gathered together to honor the memory of John Carroll, as well as to discuss such issues as education, literature, temperance, youth, and the relationship between labor and capital. These delegates, selected by the bishops of their respective dioceses, represented the cream of the Catholic middle class, with merchants, lawyers, and physicians

making up the largest groups of delegates. The city of Baltimore mirrored this social profile.

Though still heavily concentrated in blue-collar, semi-skilled or
unskilled occupations, some 30 percent of Baltimore's Irish
Catholics were employed in skilled work or low white-collar occupations in 1880. In the next twenty years they would progress even further up the occupational ladder. What was true in Baltimore was also
true for other cities. Second-generation Irish Catholics, those born in
the United States of immigrant parents, were experiencing significant upward mobility by the 1880s.[3] It was among this group that
the feeling of confidence and optimism about the future of the
United States was most visible. This was the class that sent delegates
to the Baltimore congress. They were the ones who had pianos in
their parlors, lace curtains on their windows, and steam heat in the
winter. The bulk of the Catholic population was still working class
and largely foreign born, mainly recent arrivals from towns in southern Italy or Eastern Europe. These Catholics defined the immigrant
church of the 1890s. But they did not speak the language of John Ireland. The Italians, Polish, and other recently arrived immigrants focused their energies on maintaining their ethnic culture rather than
celebrating the superiority of American society and culture.

In celebrating the union of Catholicism and American culture or
what he called the church and the age, John Ireland highlighted the
issue of the relation between religion and culture. It is fair to say that
in the 1890s one of the most discussed issues within middle-class
Catholic America was the relationship between Catholicism and
American culture. Like the republican era this was a time of major
transition in American Catholic history, when Catholicism's relationship with American culture came under intense scrutiny. During the
1880s and '90s a very public debate took place in the pulpit, in newspapers, and in journals. The clergy were the ones most involved in this

debate, with bishops leading the charge on either side of the issue. Some like Ireland and Gibbons wanted to see Catholicism become more in tune with the age. "We should speak to our age," said Ireland, "of things it feels and in language it understands. We should be in it, and of it, if we would have its ear.... The Church of America must be, of course, as Catholic as ever in Jerusalem or Rome; but so far as her garments assume color from the local atmosphere she must be American"; or as another preacher stated, the Catholic church must "become American without ceasing for an instant to be Catholic."[4]

Not everyone agreed with such an enthusiastic endorsement of the age. Bishop Bernard McQuaid of Rochester was one of the more prominent personalities who disagreed strongly with Ireland's exceedingly positive assessment. McQuaid was ardently American and supported such American ideals as the separation of church and state as well as democracy. However, he saw the age as one dominated by "infidelity" or "unbelief," terms he used to describe his times; for him it was an ungodly world, and the main enemies of the day were liberalism and socialism. McQuaid was very representative of those Catholics who believed that their religion was under seige in this rapidly developing modern society. When Ireland surveyed the landscape, he saw democracy, a thirst for knowledge, progress, and a new world order with Catholicism leading the way into the future. But McQuaid saw agnosticism and unbelief, the enemies of organized religion.[5] These different perspectives revealed a fundamental divide within American Catholicism in the 1890s, a division that would last well into the twentieth century. A Baptist preacher described this division in the following manner:

> There are two distinct and hostile parties in the Roman Catholic Church in America. One is led by Archbishop Ireland. It stands for Americanism and a larger independence. It is sympathetic with modern

thought. It believes the Roman Catholic Church should take its place in all the great moral reforms. It is small, but progressive, vigorous, and brave.

The other party is led by the overwhelming majority of the hierarchy. It is conservative, out of touch with American or modern ideas. It is the old medieval European Church, transplanted into the Nineteenth Century and this country of freedom, interesting as an antiquity and curiosity, but fast losing its power and consequently, growing in bitterness.[6]

What was taking place within Catholicism at this time was also happening in other denominations. In the nineteenth century, American Judaism underwent significant change. For more than two centuries orthodox Judaism was the chosen religion of American Jews. By the mid-nineteenth century a reform movement began to take hold within the community. Imported from Europe, Reform Judaism sought to bridge the divide between tradition and the modern world. In the United States this resulted in the use of English in worship services, the singing of hymns, men and women sitting together at prayer services, and the use of the organ as well as less strict dietary laws. Led by Rabbi Isaac Mayer Wise, the Reform movement was too liberal for more traditional Jews, too American and Protestant for their tastes. Tensions increased and reached the breaking point in the mid-1880s, when a group of more moderate Jews founded a new denomination within American Judaism. Known as Conservative Judaism, it was a response to the challenges presented by modernity, specifically modern American culture. It was a halfway station between the traditional Orthodox expression of Judaism and the more recent Reform movement. Much like Catholicism, Judaism in the United States has continually grappled with the encounter between tradition and modern culture. For Jews the result has been a fundamental split that resulted in three distinct denominations, namely Orthodox, Conservative, and Reform Judaism.

American Protestants also experienced division as they sought to adapt to the emerging modern culture of the late nineteenth century. This was an age of unbelief. Prior to the middle of the nineteenth century "atheism or agnosticism seemed almost palpably absurd." However, by the end of the century unbelief had become a definite option for Americans. This shift underscored the difficulties that modern culture presented for traditional religion. As the historian James Turner wrote, "In trying to adapt their religious beliefs to socioeconomic change, to new moral challenges, to novel problems of knowledge, to the tightening standards of science, the defenders of God slowly strangled Him." At one time science reinforced belief in God, but by the late nineteenth century "science had little use for God."[7] The major force in this development was Darwin's theory of natural selection. His work challenged the fundamental Christian dogma of God's creation of the world and its human inhabitants. As this culture of unbelief was developing, the modern university focused its attention on the scientific method of inquiry. This enthusiasm for science weakened the influence that traditional theology had enjoyed in the academy. New views about the Bible raised questions about the historical validity of the sacred stories recorded in the scriptures. Protestants debated these issues, politely at first and then more contentiously. What resulted was a major split within American Protestantism.

Historian Martin Marty has described this division as the emergence of the two-party system within Protestantism. This split cut across denominational lines so that some Congregationalists had more in common with some Methodists than with other Congregationalists. Marty labeled one group "Private Protestantism" and the other "Public Protestantism." Private Protestants emphasized the salvation of the individual through a conversion experience, the religion of revivalism, and a negative view of the world, which they depicted as the kingdom of the ungodly. More focused on the social order, Public Protestantism sought to transform the world into the kingdom of God. For public Protestants an individual's salvation took place in the world, not apart from it. The modernist-fundamentalist debate of the early twentieth century widened this divide. The modernists who stood with public Protestants wanted to adjust the Christian faith to the standards of modern culture, whereas the fundamentalists who came out of the camp of private Protestantism were militantly anti-modernist. Emphasizing the experience of personal conversion and the inerrancy of the Bible, their religious tradition has helped to shape Protestant evangelicalism in contemporary America. This split that began to emerge in the closing decades of the nineteenth century has permanently divided American Protestantism. For Protestants a major issue still remains the fundamental question of how religion should relate to modern culture.[8]

The modernist conflict that split apart Jews and Protestants at the turn of the last century did not have such severe consequences among American Catholics. The fault line that separated tradition from modernity, which first appeared in the republican era, widened considerably in this period. Some minor schisms did take place, and some individuals abandoned the church because of its staunch opposition to the findings of the new theology of the era. But no fundamental rupture occurred within the church. A major reason for this was the Catholic tradition of recognizing the church's teaching as definitive, indeed infallible. If church authorities declared that the findings of the new theology were erroneous, then it must be so. As an old saying stated, when Rome spoke, the issue was settled (*Roma locuta est, causa finita est*). Such central control of Catholic teaching did not allow for widespread dissent in 1900.

Throughout this period, the 1880s until World War I, Catholicism and American culture intersected in a number of areas. One very visible issue was the persistent desire for democracy in the local church. This would not go away despite the episcopal campaign to abolish trusteeism in the middle decades of the nineteenth century. Another issue was the devotional life of the people. The immigration of so many European Catholics strengthened the devotional style of Catholicism that had taken shape in the antebellum period, and few people saw any reason to change. Nationalism or loyalty to an old world homeland and culture while living in America was another point of intersection between religion and culture. Though a topic of debate in the republican era, it took on much greater importance during this period. Another area where Catholicism and American culture were at odds was over the issue of theology or doctrine. The same intellectual and scientific forces that sowed dissension among Protestants threatened to divide Catholics.

Finally, a fifth issue that began to surface at this time among some segments of the Catholic community was a discussion about the role of women in society. These five issues offer excellent examples of the interaction between Catholicism and American culture.

Democracy

THE FIRST AND MOST persistent issue that sparked debate was the question of democracy in the government of the local church. It had first emerged at the time of the democratic revolution, and even though the hierarchy sought to abolish the trustee form of parish church government, the thirst for democracy never entirely disappeared. Where it was most visible in this period was in the parish communities of the new immigrants from Eastern Europe who sought to adapt their old-world style of parish life to the demo-

and belonging in the New World. More than an insurance institution, the mutual benefit society became a source of initiative in the broader community, and among the Polish "the great work of the society...is the formation of a parish."[11]

Wherever the Polish settled, they organized a mutual benefit society. Feeling a deep need for their own national parish where they could hear sermons in Polish and practice their own religious customs, the society would collect money to purchase land for a church; then they would petition the local bishop to send them a Polish-speaking priest. Once a priest arrived, the church was built and the parish began to take shape. Even though every parish community was not organized in the same way, a definite pattern of lay initiative existed in each instance. Sometimes people acted on their own, sometimes they acted with the aid of a priest, but with few exceptions the source of the initiative was the people's mutual benefit society.

A key issue in the establishment of Polish parishes was the ownership of property. Most often, the parish was incorporated in the name of the mutual benefit society, whose officers became the trustees of the parish. This arrangement conflicted with the prevailing custom in the late nineteenth century of bishop and clergy owning all church property. Thus, the stage was set for conflict, and conflict there was. In virtually every city where they settled, Polish Catholics went to battle over the issue of the ownership of church property. From their point of view, the tradition of the old country allowed for lay involvement in parish affairs, and they sought to continue this arrangement in the United States. As one Polish editor stated, "In the old country the founders and benefactors [of a parish] had a voice not only in the running of church affairs, but in the selection of the pastor. Here in America, the founders and benefactors of the Polish churches, that is the Polish people, should certainly have the same rights and privileges."[12]

cratic culture of the United States. Like the Irish and Germans before them, these immigrant Catholics wanted to have a voice in the organization and government of the local church. This was an entirely different issue from John Ireland's crusade to make America Catholic. This debate took place at the local parish level and engaged laymen as well as clergy. It was not about making America Catholic, but about democratizing local church government. The Polish provide the best example of how the thirst for democracy still permeated the immigrant church in the closing decades of the century.[9]

In the old country the parish was the center of village life for Polish Catholics. "The most important events of individual, familial, and communal life" took place there, by gathering people together and giving them a sense of identity as both Polish and Catholic. When they immigrated to the New World, the parish became the primary form of association among Polish Catholics. It was "simply the old primary community, reorganized and concentrated" in the United States.[10]

The organization of the parish in the Polish community followed a pattern similar to that of other immigrant groups. When people first arrived, they generally attended services in a local Catholic church. For many Poles, this often meant a German church since those from Prussia and Austria could understand German. But this was not a satisfactory arrangement. Like all immigrants, they wanted to pray in their native language and sing Polish hymns, not German ones. To achieve this end, Polish immigrants organized themselves into a mutual benefit society, whose express purpose was to found a Polish parish church.

The mutual benefit society was a common organization in immigrant communities. Most often transplanted from the Old World, such societies provided insurance benefits for their members in times of sickness and death, giving the newcomers a sense of identity

The editor had made an important point. In the Old World, Polish nobles enjoyed the right of patronage and could not only appoint parish priests, but also exercise control over parish affairs. In the New World the people wanted to transform "the old world individual patron into a more democratic form of collective patronage."[13] In other words, following the American love of democracy, the newcomers wanted to democratize an old-world custom so that the people had a voice in parish affairs. But the bishops and clergy, many Polish priests included, did not agree. For them, the clergy, not the people, should run parish affairs and hold title to all church property. The laypeople did not give in on this issue. They resisted strongly and even endured excommunication, rather than go along with the tradition of clerical control in parish affairs. Such resistance was a fact of life in Polish parishes across the country, and parish battles, complete with street riots, church demonstrations, and appeals to Rome were commonplace. In fact, conflict over the issue of ownership of church property and lay involvement in the government of the local church was the cause for the first major schism in American Catholic history.

Schism in the American Catholic church had occurred throughout the nineteenth century. Generally, it involved dissident parish congregations who chose to separate from the Roman Catholic Church because of a difference of opinion with their bishop over the issue of ownership of parish property. Most often, time healed the wound, and the people rejoined the church. Things did not go so smoothly among the Polish, however. During the 1890s schismatic independent churches began to emerge in Chicago, Buffalo, Scranton, and other cities in the Northeast. Then, in 1904, Rev. Francis Hodur, leader of the Scranton independents, called a meeting of several independent parishes. This gathering was the formal beginning of the Polish National Catholic Church. A key issue in the dissidents' platform focused on democracy in the government of the local church. Hodur became the bishop-elect of the new denomination and remained its leader until his death in 1953. Though it never reached more than 5 percent of the entire Polish population, the existence of the Polish National Catholic Church served as a continual reminder of the struggle for democracy that took place in the immigrant church.

Immigrant Catholics from other parts of Eastern Europe followed a pattern similar to the Polish in the organization of their churches. Like the Polish, they too sought to democratize an old-world tradition, namely the right of patronage of a local noble in order to gain control over parish affairs. This would mean ownership of church property, an elected board of trustees, and even removal of uncooperative pastors. In their mind the rationale for this was simple and clear: "The people have built the churches," wrote a Lithuanian immigrant, "therefore the people are the owners of the churches; and not the will of the bishop or of the Pope, but that of the people must be the rule in the parishes."[14] As with the Polish, conflict broke out in these communities, and parish battles were frequent. Some Slovak and Lithuanian parishes went into schism and formed independent churches, rather than give in on this question of ownership of church property. Among the Ukrainians, Eastern-rite Catholics who followed a tradition of worship different from Latin-rite Catholics, the issue of democracy in the local church was a major reason why many Eastern-rite Catholic clergy and laity left the Roman church in the early twentieth century.

That thousands of Eastern-rite Catholics along with thousands of Poles, Lithuanians, and Slovaks would leave the church over the issue of lay involvement in parish government illustrates how critical the issue was. The insistence of these Catholics on preserving their authoritative role in managing local church affairs was such that they would endure excommunication, rather than give in on this point. At the same time the Catholic hierarchy, along with the majority of the clergy, were so adamant they were willing to allow thousands of laypeople to leave the Roman Catholic church, rather than give in to their demands on this issue. An irresistible force had met an immovable object, and the encounter produced bitter and prolonged conflict. Nationality differences certainly intensified the conflict, but more than just cultural differences were involved. Fundamentally, it was a conflict between two radically differing views of the church and its relation to culture. One view advocated a model of church that emphasized a democratic functioning of authority with an emphasis on local autonomy, a church that could adapt itself to the American culture of democracy. According to this model, laypeople and clergy would work together sharing responsiblity for the organization and government of the parish. The other view supported a monarchical model of the church that was unchanging and fixed regardless of its local environment. Championed by the hierarchy, this view emphasized the authority of the clergy over the laypeople, with the bishop exercising supreme authority over everyone, priests and people alike.

Despite the efforts of Eastern European immigrant Catholics to democratize the church, Roman Catholicism steadily marched toward a more monarchical, less democratic style of church government. A directive issued by the archdiocese of Milwaukee in 1907 clearly articulated this way of thinking: "The Church is not a republic or democracy, but a monarchy;... all her authority is from above and rests in her Hierarchy;... while the faithful of the laity have divinely given rights to receive all the blessed ministrations of the Church, they have absolutely no right whatever to rule and govern."[15] By this time the clergy were in control of the church, and the desire for a more democratic church became an unfilled wish.

Democracy has been a central feature of American culture ever since the republican era. The noted French traveler Alexis de Tocqueville noted this in his commentary on American society in the 1830s. He also observed that Catholics took to democracy like ducks to water; in his opinion they constituted "the most republican and most democratic class in the United States." He also noted that they were "the most submissive believers."[16] De Tocqueville had highlighted a paradox that has remained consistent throughout American Catholic history. As Americans, Catholics embraced democracy; as Catholics, they remained submissive to church authority. To live in a culture fiercely proud of its democratic heritage and to belong to a church in which democracy has no place has presented a dilemma for Catholics. Successive waves of European immigrants sensed this and wanted to make Catholicism more democratic. But the hierarchy insisted that this was not the Catholic way of governing the local church. Nonetheless, the desire for democracy in the church has never disappeared. In the United States such a desire will always remain a cultural imperative that will challenge the manner in which decisions are made in the Catholic community.

Devotional Life

ANOTHER ISSUE LEFT OVER from the republican era was the shape of Catholic devotional life—the manner in which Catholics prayed and worshiped. The decline of the Enlightenment and the emergence of devotional Catholicism in the mid-nineteenth century had transformed the piety of Catholics. The immigration of large numbers of eastern and southern European Catholics in the closing decades of the nineteenth century reinforced this turn toward a more elaborate, devotional style of religion.

The new immigrants carried with them an attachment to devotional Catholicism. The elaborate tradition of baroque piety, revived in the nineteenth century, had shaped the religious world of most of

these people. The churches they built in their new country strongly reflected this. The interiors of these temples were busy places, with numerous statues of saints, each associated with particular devotions, throughout the church. Statues of the Sacred Heart of Jesus, of Mary, of Joseph, and of St. Anthony were quite popular. In addition, each ethnic group often had a small shrine in their churches honoring their own special patron, such as Our Lady of Mt. Carmel among the Italians. Some of these shrines were replicas of old-country shrines where the immigrants once prayed. Stained glass windows, imported from Europe, also added an old-world flavor to these churches. The celebration of religious festivals was another trait of devotional Catholicism that emerged at this time. In the antebellum period Catholics were not inclined to parade through their neighborhoods, publicly proclaiming their faith. By the late nineteenth century they were no longer so cautious. The best example would be found among the Italians.

In East Harlem, New York City, Italians devoted an entire week in July to honor Our Lady of Mt. Carmel, a devotion imported from Italy. Even the statue of the Madonna of Mt. Carmel that had a place of honor in the church was brought from the old country. The highlight of the festival was the procession through the neighborhood. Thousands of marchers took part in the parade, and several bands accompanied the marchers. Incense and the sounds of Italian religious hymns filled the air as the procession made its way up and down every block of Italian Harlem, where the devout lined the streets as the Madonna made her way through their neighborhood. In Chicago, St. Louis, San Francisco, and in other cities Italian communities celebrated similar festivals in honor of the saints of the old country.[17]

The growth of devotional confraternities increased dramatically in this period. There were separate confraternities for men and women, each based in a parish. They had an explicitly religious purpose—to encourage devotion to a particular saint through a ritual of prayers and acts of piety such as attendance at Mass. Among women, confraternities honoring Mary were most popular; one of the more popular confraternities for men was the Society of St. Vincent de Paul, which honored its namesake through acts of charity on behalf of the poor. These confraternities also had a social function, because they provided Catholics with an opportunity to bond together. By coming together as Catholics, they were able to strengthen their sense of identity. This social function blended in well with the confraternity's explicitly religious purpose and helped to nourish the culture of devotional Catholicism.

The improvement and expansion of the print culture in the late nineteenth century also aided the popular appeal of devotional Catholicism. Magazines and newspapers promoted devotion to popular saints by highlighting their heroic lives and the miracles attributed to their heavenly intercession. The print media publicized parish missions that were on the increase in these years by printing stirring accounts of these revivals and the dramatic impact they had on people's lives.

This was also a time when Catholic parochial schools were becoming a major force in the shaping of the Catholic culture. In these schools religious instruction formed an important part of the curriculum. In addition to learning the religion of the catechism, the young students were introduced into the celestial community of the saints and the elaborate network of devotions that brought these heavenly relatives into their lives. Statues and paintings of various saints decorated every room in these schools; prizes for academic excellence were most often statues, holy pictures, medals, or books of a religious nature. Devotions to Mary during the month of May were especially popular. At a Jesuit men's college in New York, St. Francis Xavier, " ... Elaborate processions of the entire student body arranged according to rank—first classes, then sodalities, and finally clergy—

marched from the school to the church, bearing a statue of Mary for the opening and closing of the month. Special altars decked with flowers in honor of the Virgin were erected in classrooms or study halls."[18]

During these years devotion to Our Lady of Lourdes and the use of water collected from the Marian shrine at Lourdes, France, became very popular. In 1858 a young peasant girl reported seeing visions of Mary at a grotto near the town of Lourdes in southern France. A spring appeared at the site, and the water was acclaimed for its healing power. Devotion to Our Lady of Lourdes became very widespread in France, and soon it was imported to the United States. Priests at the University of Notre Dame promoted this devotion through their devotional magazine *Ave Maria*. They had water from the shrine at Lourdes shipped to Notre Dame. Then they mailed it to people who requested the water. Those who used Lourdes water believed very strongly in its healing power; their letters, describing the cures they experienced, were published regularly in *Ave Maria*. As historian Colleen McDannell writes, "Through using Lourdes water, Catholics could experience the power of the French shrine at a distance."[19] Devotion to Our Lady of Lourdes and the use of water collected at the shrine clearly underscored the European dimension to devotional Catholicism at this time. Like the Italian devotion to Our Lady of Mt. Carmel and numerous other devotions, devotion to Our Lady of Lourdes was rooted in the European tradition of Catholicism. It clearly marked Catholicism in the United States with a foreign stamp. Although Latin was the language of the Mass, the principal worship service for Catholics, the vernacular, the mother tongue of the people, was the language used in the devotional services that honored a saint or a particular aspect or event in the life of Jesus. By providing people with the opportunity to pray in their mother tongue as well as sing the hymns and practice the devotions that their ancestors had taught them in the old country, the rituals of devotional Catholicism helped to strengthen the faithful's ethnic identity. In this manner devotional Catholicism fostered a European religious and cultural tradition among immigrant Catholics.

However, as strongly European as devotional Catholicism was, American culture did leave its mark on the religious life of Catholics. This was most noticeable among the Irish middle class, who were striving for an American middle-class identity in the midst of an Irish Catholic culture. One way in which this endeavor took place was through the appropriation of a middle-class domestic ideology. This ideology took on a religious quality among both Protestants and Catholics in the course of the nineteenth century. The centerpiece of this value system was the family. For both Catholics and Protestants the appropriation of this domestic value system was one way to adapt to the emerging modern society. The family became the bulwark against the vices of modernity. "Without a strong family," exclaimed Catholic writers, "economic and political structure would crumble.... Social, spiritual, and personal ills could be averted if the family coped with hardship and maintained its integrity." Established by God, the family was to foster certain domestic virtues such as order, purity, cleanliness, stability, and refinement. Novels, advice books, and newspapers promoted these virtues so that Catholic men and women would become more acceptable not only to God but to society as well. One emigrant's guidebook encouraged "each man 'to endeavor to raise himself in the social scale which would require scrupulous neatness and cleanliness ... both in person, dress, and house management.'" Middle class families had an array of religious artifacts that they could purchase in order to create a religious atmosphere in the home. Crucifixes, religious engravings and lithographs, blessed candles, and statues were commonplace in many Catholic homes. Among Catholics the appropriation of Victorian domestic virtues came with a European twist. The model for middle-class refinement and gentility was the Catholic aristocracy of France. For upwardly mobile Catholics France became "their center of culture." Convent schools administered by religious orders of women from France became popular; English translations of French advice books were common; and use of the French language became associated with the culture of the upper class.[20]

This turning back to Europe underscores an important point about the encounter between Catholicism and American culture. It never was a simple either/or choice between American or Catholic, or in this instance American and European. Rather, what was most common was a mingling of the two cultures. The world of devotional Catholicism was very European, but it also evidenced a measure of American influence. This was a time when Catholics in the United States were seeking to find a religious expression that was most suitable for them. Most found it in the European devotional tradition that they carried with them when they immigrated to the United States. Those who had been born in the United States, chiefly the Irish middle class, incorporated an American domestic ideology into their religious culture. Neither completely European nor totally American, they blended the two religious cultures into an expression of religion that suited their conception of themselves. In many respects a similar mingling of cultural traditions was taking place among Jews in the United States at this time. This was most visible among Reform Jews who sought to make their worship more American and less tied to the traditions of the Old World. This Americanization of Jewish ritual eventually became too much for many Jews and led to the founding of Conservative Judaism.

The blending of cultures in the prayer life of Catholics took place with every successive generation as American-born Catholics sought to fashion a spiritual life that was meaningful and applicable to the

American environment. Devotional Catholicism emerged at a specific time in the history of American Catholicism, and it suited the needs of an immigrant church very well. As time passed, Catholics distanced themselves from their European immigrant heritage. They would then seek to discover a style of prayer and worship more in tune with the American environment. This would take place in a most dramatic manner in the post–World War II era. The resulting controversy would rival the experience of Judaism in the late nineteenth century, when schism rent the Jewish community.

National Identity

THE SAME ISSUE THAT Orestes Brownson and John Hughes had debated in the 1850s once again became a topic of discussion in the 1880s and '90s. Unlike in the 1850s, however, this debate was widely contested throughout the country. The point at issue was how American immigrant Catholics should become.

In the decades after the Civil War immigration changed the nation and its churches. Between 1865 and 1915 as many as 25 million immigrants arrived in the United States—four times the number who had arrived in the preceding fifty years. The vast majority of them settled in the nation's cities. In places such as Chicago, New York, Milwaukee, and Detroit immigrants made up more than 80 percent of the population. One striking feature of this wave of immigration was its diversity. The majority of these immigrants came from many different countries in eastern and southern Europe. Some cities housed as many as twelve or fifteen different ethnic groups; each group put its own stamp on the city's neighborhoods, transforming them into immigrant enclaves. Little Italys and Little Polands sprang up in such cities as New York and Chicago, stamping those cities with a cosmopolitan quality that was not so evident in the 1850s. The Catholic

Church had become an immigrant institution in the antebellum era, but just two groups, the Irish and Germans, comprised the bulk of the foreign-born population. By 1915 as many as twenty-eight different nationalities or language groups called themselves Catholic. The largest of these were the Irish, Germans, Italians, Polish, French Canadians, and Mexicans; together they accounted for at least 75 percent of the Catholic population.

Such ethnic diversity split the Catholic Church into many different national churches. Each immigrant group was inclined to organize its own parishes. These were community institutions that Catholics established to preserve the religious life of the old country. They were also social institutions that strengthened the social fabric of the community by nurturing families as well as faith and by promoting education as well as Sunday Mass. By organizing their national parishes, immigrant Catholics hoped to hear sermons in their mother tongue, practice the devotions and customs of the old country, and raise their children in the faith of their fathers and mothers. Each group established schools and organized charitable and social organizations as well as devotional confraternities. Immigrant Catholics also formed their own ethnic "leagues," federations loosely organized according to nationality. This enabled clergy and people to join together to finance and establish such institutions as high schools, hospitals, orphanages, and cemeteries that served their particular ethnic group. The clergy of each group often met to establish policy for their own ethnic community. They also stayed within their own league or ethnic group. Rarely, if at all, was a Polish priest assigned to an Irish parish or vice versa. Each ethnic community generally had one priest whose prestige was such that people considered him to be the clerical leader of the group; even the bishop would consult this unofficial leader on issues related to the priest's particular ethnic group. In many respects these ethnic leagues were similar to the synods or conferences that divided Protestant denominations along the lines of ethnicity. In reality, they constituted a church within a church.

The closing decades of the nineteenth century were a time of increasing nationalism in the United States. One expression of this trend was jingoism, an extreme form of nationalism that judged America to be, as John Ireland stated, "God's chosen nation to guide the destinies of mankind."[21] Such intense nationalism resulted in a spirit of expansionism that propelled the nation into war with Spain in 1898. When the war was over, the United States was left with an overseas empire. Nativism was another expression of nationalism. The rise in immigration and the unusual diversity of peoples who settled in the nation fueled the flames of nativism. Economic distress in the 1890s intensified these antiforeign, anti-immigrant feelings. As historian John Higham wrote, "The period resounded with organized campaigns to arouse a vigorous 'Americanism.' Flag exercises, replete with special salutes and pledges, spread throughout the public schools along with agitation for inculcating patriotism."[22] Once again the Catholic Church was singled out for attack because of its large foreign-born population. Another development was the rise of Anglo-Saxon nationalism. This fostered a climate of racism that enkindled intense feelings of prejudice against Italian, Polish, and Slavic Catholics. In addition, Protestant nationalists viewed Catholic loyalty to a Roman papacy as a threat to national security. Some even feared an armed takeover of the nation by papal soldiers. This was the context in which the debate over the Americanization of immigrant Catholics took place. Once again Catholicism and American culture intersected at the crossroads of nativism and national loyalty. The issue at stake was not democracy in the church or the style of piety or prayer. It was rather a debate over the relationship between religion and nationality. Indeed, it was a question of national identity. Would

Catholicism in the United States be a church of foreigners or would it become an American church?

The issue of the relationship between religion and nationality affected all Catholic immigrant groups. But the one group that sparked a national, indeed international, debate over this issue was the Germans. Next to the Irish, the Germans were the most numerous and most powerful group in Catholic America. Between 1860 and 1890 more than 2.9 million Germans immigrated to the United States. This was the high point of German immigration, and about 35 percent of these immigrants, approximately one million, were Catholic. Catholic Germans carried with them the bitter memory of the *Kulturkampf*, a power struggle between a largely Protestant German government and German Catholics in the 1870s and '80s that took the form of religious persecution against Catholics. This experience resulted in *Kulturkampftrauma*, "a deeply engrained distrust toward anyone outside the 'Ghetto Church.'"[23] This distrust surfaced in the United States when Catholics, chiefly of Irish descent, promoted the Americanization of their German co-religionists. Another element that entered the debate was the minority status of German Catholics in the church. In terms of numbers the Irish had gained control of the American Catholic hierarchy. The Irish were the chief power brokers, and the Germans resented their second-class status. They desperately wanted to strengthen their position in the church and did so by doggedly working to maintain their distinctive religious culture.

German Catholics believed that the key to their survival as Catholics was the maintenance of the German language. "Religion and nationality go hand in hand," wrote one German priest. "Religion sustains nationality, and nationality is an aid to religion," he said, and the key to keeping "true to the faith" was encouraging language and nationality.[24] A prominent German layman, Henry J. Spaunhorst, in a talk to an assembly of German Catholics spoke for many when he said, "We love our mother tongue; we regard the customs and practices, which we inherited from the old fatherland or from our parents, with honor. What could be more natural? How can we acknowledge our heritage any better than through exhalting our language which our parents bequeathed to us."[25] At a similar gathering a few years later, Dr. Ernst Lieber, a prominent political figure in Germany, emphasized to his immigrant audience the importance of maintaining the German language. "The German language ... is your mother tongue," he said. "The language which comes from the heart and goes into the heart. It is said: if one calls 'mother,' it does not come right from the heart. If, however, one calls '*mutter*,' yes that comes from the heart." He then linked language to a love of mother and father. Indeed, for Lieber language was what connected the child with the entire parental household. He went on to link the mother tongue to prayer, what he called the "queen of the heart." He concluded his talk in the following manner: "Make your dollars in English but converse with our Lord God in our good old German language!"[26] For German Catholics the bond between language and faith was so strong that their rallying cry throughout these years of debate became "Language saves Faith." Under this slogan they steadfastly resisted any attempts to weaken their attachment to German language and culture.

The sequence of events that sparked a national debate over nationality and religion is well known. It began in St. Louis, a German Catholic stronghold, in the early 1880s when a group of priests petitioned the Vatican, asking that German parishes and pastors be granted the same status as English-speaking (i.e., Irish) pastors and parishes. They believed that German Catholics, priests and laity alike, were second-class citizens in a city where the Irish clergy were in control. Then, in 1886, a German priest from Milwaukee, Peter Abbelen, traveled to Rome to present a similar petition to church authorities on behalf of the clergy in the German triangle region of Cincinnati, St. Louis, and Milwaukee. The clergy wanted more independence for German Catholics; in effect, they wanted to establish their own national church. In his letter Abbelen emphasized the importance of maintaining the German language and the traditions of the fatherland. He also raised an issue that would be repeated time and again—the rapid and forced Americanization of German Catholics, which, in his opinion, would inevitably lead to a "deplorable falling away of them from the Church." "Let the 'Americanization' of the Germans be a slow and natural process," he wrote; "let it not be hastened to the prejudice of the religion of the Germans. They will kick against the goad."[27]

Abbelen's petition infuriated John Ireland and other bishops. Ireland and John J. Keane, the bishop of Richmond, wrote a lengthy letter to church authorities in Rome arguing against Abbelen's petition. A key argument in the bishops' letter was the widespread feeling in the United States that "the Catholic Church is composed of foreigners; that it exists in America as a foreign institution, and that it is consequently, a menace to the existence of the nation."[28] To grant the wishes of the German clergy would verify the suspicions that Protestant Americans had about Catholics. Other bishops also wrote to Rome defending their treatment of German Catholics and arguing against any special privileges for them. The letter-writing campaign of the bishops carried the day. The response of Roman authorities to the Abbelen petition recognized the legitimacy of separate parishes for diverse language groups—a practice already widespread—but refused to grant the Germans any further privileges.

The *Kulturkampf* was the crucible in which German Catholics formed their intense love of language, faith, and fatherland. Religious persecution had hardened their commitment to their religion and their culture, and they did not want to lose either one. For English-

speaking Catholics, mostly of American birth and Irish descent, the
nationalist climate in the United States fanned the flames of their patriotism. In the 1880s and '90s these two fiercely national loyalties
clashed. John Ireland expressed this American nationalism better
than anyone. Born in Ireland, educated in the United States as well as
in France, he served as a priest and later a bishop in St. Paul, Minnesota. In a talk he gave on American citizenship Ireland delivered a
paean to what he labeled the "providential nation." He believed that
"a divine mission has been assigned to the Republic of the United
States. That mission is to prepare the world, by example and moral
influence, for the universal reign of human liberty and human rights.
America does not live for herself alone; the destinies of humanity are
in her keeping." It is hard to imagine any of Ireland's contemporaries
surpassing him in his messianic patriotism. He proudly followed in
the tradition of John Winthrop, who had inaugurated the sacred history of the nation in 1630 when he christened it with the biblical
phrase "city on a hill." Toward the end of his talk Ireland touched on
the topic of immigration. He said, "A well-directed immigration will
not be detrimental to American spirit or to American loyalty." Then,
hitting a theme he would strike again and again, he spoke out against
encouraging any "social and political organizations or methods
which perpetuate in this country foreign ideas and customs." He further stated, "Efforts to concentrate immigrants in social groups and
to retard their Americanization should be steadily frowned down.
There are in America self-constituted leaders of foreign-born citizens
who speak of Americanization as a term of reproach; with these men
public opinion should deal severely."[29] America was his love, and he
was proud to be an American citizen, but he was also proud of his
faith. In one of his more memorable lines, he proclaimed his dual loyalties: "Catholic I shall be in faith, and American in nationality."[30] In
Ireland the Germans had met their match. There was no question

where he stood on this issue of nationality, and he would not budge. Neither would the Germans.

In 1891 the feud over national loyalties erupted once again. The catalyst this time was a German Catholic layman, Peter Paul Cahensly. Chiefly through his efforts, an emigrant aid society, the St. Raphaelsverein, was founded to assist German Catholic emigrants. In 1890 the leaders of the various national branches of the society met in Lucerne, Switzerland, and drafted a letter to the pope outlining ways and means to protect the faith of immigrants after they arrived in the United States. Cahensly delivered the document to the pope in April 1891. Citing losses to the church in the United States of "more than ten million souls," the Lucerne Memorial made several recommendations for the care of immigrants in the United States. They echoed some of the same issues of the Abbelen petition. These included separate parishes for each nationality, administered by priests of "the same nationality to which the faithful belonged," catechetical instruction in the mother tongue, separate parochial schools for each nationality, equal rights for the clergy, and representation within the hierarchy of each nationality.[31]

Once the Lucerne Memorial became public, the nationality debate exploded. Some Catholics saw it as a foreign plot to gain power in the American church and Germanize it. Ireland labeled it "Cahenslyism" and the name stuck, thus unjustly singling out Peter Cahensly as the chief culprit of an imagined political conspiracy. For more than a year a public debate took place in newspapers and journals; charges and countercharges faced off in the battle. On one side was Ireland and those who wanted immigrant Catholics to become American; on the other side were the Germans, who wanted more recognition of their needs and rights in the church. The common enemy of the Germans was the Irish, whom they feared "would Americanize everything." In due time, Pope Leo XIII responded to the Lucerne Memorial, saying that its proposals were "neither opportune nor necessary." Once again German Catholics lost the fight to gain more status and power in the American church.[32]

For German Catholics life went on in their parishes as before, but they remained quite defensive about their place in the American church. As time passed, they became more American, and the slogan of "Language Saves Faith" was seldom heard among the Germans. But the nationality debate never really ended. The French from Quebec likewise fought to preserve *la langue et la foi*; the Polish, Italians, Slovaks, and numerous other groups waged similar battles.

The leaders of the church, its bishops, two-thirds of whom were of Irish descent in 1900, wanted the immigrants to become American and leave behind their foreign traits. But the immigrants' cultures were so entwined with their religion that to give up their cultures, symbolized most concretely in their languages, meant losing part of their religion. This was a major challenge that Catholicism faced in the United States. Protestants faced the same challenge with the Lutheran experience offering perhaps the closest parallel to that of the Catholic encounter with American culture. Both religious traditions followed similar patterns in seeking to resolve the issue. Each ethnic group set up its own federation or league, unofficially in the case of Catholics, and formally in the case of Lutherans. By allowing these separate national churches to exist, church officials recognized the people's need to express their religion according to a specific cultural tradition. They also believed that Americanization would take place over time. When they sought to speed up the process, forcing immigrants to become more American than they could tolerate at that time, conflict inevitably erupted.

Since the United States has been and continues to be a nation of immigrants, the relationship between religion and nationality has remained a critical issue for the nation's many denominations. How

Americanized immigrant Catholics should become was an issue that generated heated discussion in the late nineteenth and early twentieth centuries. Decades later, immigrants from Latin America and Asia would raise the issue once again.

The Americanization of Doctrine

ENTANGLED WITH THE NATIONALITY issue was the question of just how distinctive Catholicism in the United States was and indeed should become. Was its distinctiveness merely one of nationality, or was there something more at issue? Was Catholicism somehow different in the United States from Catholicism in Italy or France? Did this difference have something to do with doctrine? Clearly some people thought so. They were of the opinion that a school of thought was developing in the United States that promoted the idea of "an American Catholicity which is in advance of past times, which differs materially from the faith once delivered to the Church and always preserved by her, which boasts of a freedom from restrictions which bind the ages of the past." Thomas Preston, the powerful chancellor of the New York archdiocese, was a leading critic of this "American Catholicity." He believed that indeed it was "falsely representing... the one true religion which we are bound to defend and profess."[33] Roman authorities also believed that such a pattern of thinking did exist, and in 1899 they persuaded the pope to issue a letter condemning what he called "Americanism."

The leading figure in the school of thought that advocated an American Catholicity was John Ireland. He was involved in all the major issues that Catholics debated in the closing decades of the nineteenth century. However, the one issue that propelled him to notoriety and eventually led to his fall from the pedestal of ecclesiastical prominence was his unrelenting crusade to unite the "Church and the age," making them in harmony with each other. What was at issue in what he called "the new, most glorious crusade" was neither democracy in local church government, nor the style of people's piety, nor nationalism.[34] What Ireland emphasized in his campaign to make America Catholic was more fundamental, indeed more doctrinal. In searching for a Catholicism that would be more American than what it had previously been, he was pushing for a change in the traditional understanding of what the church should be. Ireland, as well as some of his supporters, were advocating ideas that were fundamentally in opposition to the current Catholic teaching that viewed the church as unchangeable. His opponents, both in the United States and in Rome, interpreted Ireland's campaign to unite the "Church and the age" as a dagger aimed at the heart of Catholic doctrine.

Ireland, however, did not consider his crusade to be a threat to Catholic doctrine. He believed that he was loyal to the tradition of Catholicism. Nonetheless, he spoke the language of change in an age when changes in religion were regarded as very suspect. In adapting to American culture, Catholicism—the word he used was the *Church*—"must herself be new, adapting herself in manner of life and in method of action to the conditions of the new order, thus proving herself, while ever ancient, to be ever new, as truth from heaven is and ever must be."[35] What this meant was that Catholicism should adopt new ways to present its message to American society. This involved change, and Ireland realized the challenge that this posed. "The Church never changes," he said, "and yet she changes." This was the dilemma that confronted any Catholic who sought to change what was believed to be an unchangeable tradition. To solve the problem, Ireland distinguished between the divine and the human, the essentials and the accidents. "The divine never changes," he wrote; "it is of Christ, the same . . . forever. But even in the divine we must distinguish between the principle and the application of the principle; the application of the principle, or its adaptation to environment, changes with the circumstances. And thus, at times, there seems to be a change when there is no change." The "Church," he stated, "… while jealously guarding the essentials" should be ready "to abandon the accidentals, as circumstances of time and place demand."[36]

For Ireland, such accidentals included integrating Catholic parochial education into the public school system, abandoning an intolerant attitude toward Protestants, and supporting the separation of church and state, as well as freedom of religion. In essence, what Ireland was trying to do throughout his life was, in the words of Dennis Dease, "to justify his deep-seated conviction that the Church must initiate an over-all rapprochement with a modern culture which at some point in the past had passed her by."[37]

More than ethnic identity was at issue with John Ireland. He realized the need for the church to adapt to the age. In his mind it had done this in the past and must do it once again. However, as Dease stated, "Ireland inevitably ran up against the problem of change in the Church; he knew that the Church must at times listen to the voice of the world and read the signs of the times. Yet Ireland's basic concept of the Church was ahistorical: he regarded the Church as transcending history and as unchanging in essence."[38] For this reason Ireland never fully reconciled his intense, personal desire for change and his Catholic faith, which told him that Catholicism was immune to change.

To describe Ireland's concept of the church as ahistorical is to introduce an idea emerging in the nineteenth century, historical-mindedness, or what is called the modernist mentality. According to this perspective religion is historically conditioned and subject to cultural adaptation. A more immanent understanding of God and history and the concept of a progressive realization of the kingdom of God was also linked to the modernist mentality. As the modernist impulse permeated the Catholic intellectual community, doubts began to arise about the prevailing understanding of the church as a timeless, unchanging institution. This school of thought, known as neo-Scholasticism, was regarded as the official Catholic philosophical and theological system. According to the neo-Scholastic mind, Catholicism was the one true religion and could not and indeed did not change. The doctrines of the church were truths revealed by God, "eternal and immutable . . . they subsisted in the flux of history untouched by its vagaries and particularities."[39] Such an ahistorical perspective on Catholic doctrine ruled out any suggestion that this doctrine could or should change. However, Ireland and others spoke in such a way that a person could logically conclude that Catholicism and change were compatible. That is precisely why they met such fierce opposition both in the United States and in Rome.

Joining Ireland in this search for an American Catholicism was John Keane, the bishop of Richmond, Virginia, and later the rector of Catholic University. A major ally of Ireland, Keane was an intellectual heir of Isaac Hecker. Like Hecker, he had a progressive notion of history in which the church, in adapting itself to the age, would take on a new shape as the new century dawned. For both Keane and Hecker the basis for this development was the doctrine of divine providence, according to which God directs the progress of both church and world. Denis O'Connell, rector of the North American College in Rome, was another important figure who endorsed Ireland's vision. He lobbied key ecclesiastical figures in Rome to gain their support for Ireland's gospel of Americanism. James Cardinal Gibbons, archbishop of Baltimore, was another supporter of Ireland's progressive view, as was John Lancaster Spalding, bishop of Peoria, Illinois. Though not as involved as the others in promoting the new crusade, he too believed that the church must "fit herself to a constantly changing enivronment, to the character of every people, and to the

wants of each age."[40] Allied with this school of thought were the Paulists, a religious congregation founded by Hecker, and the Sulpicians, seminary professors who taught in some of the more important American seminaries.

Labeled by their contemporaries as liberal, or as one priest stated, people who were "in touch with the time.... Constantly lecturing, talking, writing," they promoted what they called their "movement" with energetic vigor.[41] Like Ireland they shared a positive view of the age. They believed that they were living in a new era to which the church must adapt. Their work was to "bridge the chasm separating the Church from the age, to dispel the mists of prejudice which prevent the one from seeing the other as it is, to bring the Church to the age, and the age to the Church." The church was not to stand apart from the world, but was to take its place in the midst of the world so it might "win the age." Ireland described the age as one ambitious for knowledge, an age of democracy, of social justice, and material progress. Buoyed by an unrelenting optimism, they looked to the future with confidence.[42] This was a decided change from the antebellum period, when Catholics regarded American society with a great deal of suspicion and apprehension.

Those who opposed the idea of an American Catholicity were labeled conservatives by contemporaries. The conservative position supported an institutional concept of the church, defining the church "primarily in terms of its visible structures, especially the rights and powers of its officers."[43] According to this point of view, the church is immune to change because it is a divine institution. They also were hostile toward Protestants, wary of government reform efforts, and alienated from the progressive thinking of the age. They were not at all enthusiastic about the opportunity of uniting church and age. For them, Catholicism was incompatible with modern culture. They were patriotic Americans, but being Catholic had nothing to do with being

American. Their crusade was not to unite church and age, but to strengthen the immigrant church so that it could withstand the attacks of the modern world.

William Kerby, a young Catholic priest, described the conservative temperament in the following manner:

> The Conservative ... looks back at the past and into books. He thinks of how much the world is out of plumb. He shudders at the recklessness of modern states, mourns over the heresies which develop daily; ... The Conservative has nothing new to say, he is merely stationary, if he talks or writes he does two things, no more, no less. He constantly repeats principles absolutely true and denied by no one Catholic; secondly, he insinuates that the Liberal denies those principles.[44]

The leaders of the conservative wing were Michael A. Corrigan, archbishop of New York, and his mentor and friend, Bernard J. McQuaid, bishop of Rochester; allied with them were most of the German hierarchy and clergy, together with the Jesuits. The conservative position was also the majority viewpoint among clergy and laity.

The controversy over how American Catholicism should become raged throughout the late 1880s and into the 1890s. It was a bitter and prolonged debate. An important dimension to the entire controversy was its Roman connection. At this moment in history the Jesuits were close allies of the papacy. They also were the pope's strongest defenders against any attempts to modernize church teaching. The Italian Jesuits in Rome, in particular, played a crucial role in the American controversy by continually attacking what they believed was the unorthodox, indeed heretical, platform of the liberals. Moreover, a climate of suspicion pervaded the Catholic Church in Europe. This arose from new developments in biblical studies and theology that seemed to challenge orthodox Catholic teaching. The

American controversy was caught up in this atmosphere, and it too became suspect in Rome.

The liberal American position centered on a number of issues. Education, the most important issue, set the tone for the debate and hardened the lines of division. With Ireland leading the charge some liberals were eager to seek a compromise with the public school enterprise. They wanted to find some way for Catholic children to receive both religious and secular instruction in state-supported public schools. They also yielded more authority to the state in the realm of education than the conservatives would tolerate. Conservative prelates like McQuaid attacked any effort at compromise with what he viewed as "Godless" public schools. German Catholics vigorously defended the parochial school since it was a central element of their campaign to maintain their distinctive ethnic culture. In the end, efforts to establish public schools that included religious instruction failed.

Another contentious issue was membership in secret societies. Fraternal societies with secret rituals of initiation were very popular in the late nineteenth century. Fearful that they would attract men away from the church, conservatives wanted to forbid Catholics from joining them, while liberals were more tolerant about membership in such societies. Conservatives got their way in 1894 when church authorities in Rome issued a decree condemning such secret societies as the Knights of Pythias, the Odd Fellows, and the Sons of Temperance.

A third issue was the attitude toward Protestants and Protestantism. Conservatives were generally very suspicious of Protestants, while liberals were more tolerant. For conservatives such tolerance smacked of religious indifferentism, which they regarded as one of the great heresies of the nineteenth century. When Gibbons, Ireland, and Keane took part in the international Parliament of Religions in Chicago in 1893, their participation caused a great furor. The pope soon issued a letter instructing Catholics not to attend such inter-faith gatherings.

Other major aspects of the American position touched more directly on certain church doctrines, including support for democracy as the best possible form of government, separation of church and state, and freedom of religion. Few Americans would have challenged these ideas, but the ideas were not very popular in Rome. The church in Italy was still suffering from the political and military takeover of the papal states in 1870. The pope had become a "prisoner of the Vatican," and the Italian government had promulgated laws injurious to the welfare of the church and its clergy. During the course of the nineteenth century Catholicism in Italy had taken on a character very different from its American counterpart. Liberalism and democracy were regarded as enemies of the church; religious freedom meant religious indifferentism, an idea that was anathema for Catholics. Moreover, many churchmen regarded the temporal power of the pope as a doctrine of faith; for some it was an infallible doctrine that "all Catholics must firmly hold."[45] Such thinking was based on the idea of the union of church and state, with the church being the more perfect and superior society in this unique marriage. Italian nationalists, however, had little regard for this idea when they took over the papal territories in Italy.

Clearly, the Italian experience of Catholicism was radically different from the American experience, and this greatly influenced how church authorities in Rome, the Jesuits in particular, regarded Ireland's campaign to unite church and age. In Rome it was said, that he was "well known as a liberal and revolutionary bishop." No more pejorative description could be imagined than to call a Catholic prelate "liberal and revolutionary." These words evoked memories of the bloody French Revolution as well as radical philosophical ideas that challenged the very core of Catholic faith. In *Civilta Cattolica*, an influential Jesuit journal closely linked to the papacy, one Jesuit wrote that people in the United States breathed in "the infected air" of liberalism and this "has more effect on them than the Decalogue."[46] Another Jesuit described those people who advocated what he called the "bold and deceitful maxims of . . . Americanism" in the following manner:

> These would argue that where faith and morals are not compromised, one might go out to meet Protestants at least half-way on the road which separates us. These "zelanti" proclaim that the Church must make herself American, suppressing in one sweep the use of foreign languages and especially those of ancient origin, sacrificing Catholic schools to send their children alongside their Protestant peers to the institutions of the State, tolerating secret societies, associating with Protestants . . . sliding on certain doctrines . . . such as that outside the true Church there is no salvation, lifting to heaven the complete separation of Church and State and condemning union [of Church and State] as one of the most lamentable calamities . . . [47]

For these priests what was at issue was not only the issue of Catholic schools or mingling with Protestants, but also key points of Catholic doctrine. In their opinion those who supported the Americanist position were advocating positions contrary to Catholic belief.

The effort to gain a papal condemnation of the Americanist movement gained momentum in the mid-1890s with the Jesuits leading the charge. The first indication of their success was an 1895 encyclical letter on the state of Catholicism in the United States. Though the encyclical, *Longinqua oceani,* was very laudatory about the progress of the church, a brief but telling section of the letter alluded to the American system of government. Pope Leo XIII wrote, "It would be very erroneous to draw the conclusion that in America is to be sought the type of the most desirable status of the Church, or that it would be universally lawful or expedient for State and Church, to be, as in America, dissevered and divorced."[48] This was a clear repudiation of the liberal, Americanist position that endorsed the separation of church and state. The union of church and state with the church ruling over the state had been a key Catholic doctrine since at least the Middle Ages. With the decline of monarchy and the rise of democracy such a position no longer seemed very plausible. But among church authorities in Rome, and for most other Catholics, the doctrine was never questioned. To suggest that the American model, in which the Catholic Church had no right to interfere in the affairs of the state and no right to prevent the free exercise of religion, should become the norm for nations throughout the world was to challenge the legitimacy of an ancient, and indeed seemingly immutable, Catholic doctrine. This amounted to heresy. Given the gravity of the situation, it would only be a matter of time before a more definitive condemnation of the Americanist school of thought occurred.

This took place in 1899, when Pope Leo XIII issued a letter, *Testem Benevolentiae*, which condemned a constellation of ideas he labeled "Americanism." This condemnation followed the publication in 1897 of a French translation of a biography of Isaac Hecker written by a fellow Paulist, Walter Elliott. When Elliott's biography was first published in 1891, with a glowing preface by John Ireland, it hardly created a ripple of controversy. But when some liberal French Catholics published it in France, a furor ensued throughout Europe. Felix Klein, a liberal French priest, wrote a thirty-five-page preface praising Hecker in glowing terms, comparing him favorably with such individuals as Augustine and John of the Cross, even proposing him as not only "a man of our times, but a man of the future."[49] The book was an instant best-seller, going through seven editions in a brief period. Liberal clergy in France liked Hecker and Ireland's understanding of the church and the age. They also favored the American system of democracy and separation of church and state. This position clashed with that of ecclesiastical conservatives in France who supported a monarchical form of government. A war of words ensued. Charles Maignen, a French priest, led the attack against the liberals. He believed that Americanism was "one of the greatest dangers threatening the church," and church authorities in Rome supported his position.[50]

Pope Leo XIII stated that it was a French translation of "the book entitled *The Life of Isaac Thomas Hecker*" and the ideas contained therein "concerning the manner of leading a Christian life" that prompted him to issue the letter. What the pope condemned was the fundamental principle that "the Church ought to adapt herself somewhat to our advanced civilization, and relaxing her ancient rigor, show some indulgence to modern popular theories and methods." What he was saying was that Catholicism cannot change by adapting itself to culture; what he meant by Catholicism was "the doctrines in which the deposit of faith is contained." He and his Jesuit advisers understood the Americanist movement to be concerned with issues of doctrine. Moreover, he went on to state that the idea that there can be "a church in America different from that which is in the rest of the world" is in opposition to the unity of doctrine and government that distinguishes the Catholic Church, whose center is in Rome. For Leo XIII, the idea of an American Catholicism was fundamentally flawed. Roman Catholicism was one and same throughout the world and did not allow for any cultural adaptation.[51] To suggest otherwise was heresy. As the *Civilta Cattolica* stated, whoever wavers as regards Catholic principles or "adapts himself to the times or makes compromises may call himself whatever he wishes, but before God and the Church he is a rebel and a traitor."[52]

In addition to emphasizing these basic principles, the pope also singled out certain ideas found in Hecker's biography as erroneous. These included a de-emphasis of external guidance in the spiritual life, the placing of natural virtues ahead of supernatural virtues, the suitability of active virtues for the present age, a disdain for the religious life, and the desire for new ways and methods to seek converts.

Though the pope did not explicitly condemn Hecker, Ireland, or the others, the ideas he labeled as erroneous were ideas that these men had championed. Though they never fully developed them or foresaw the implications of their thinking, the liberals were promoting a cluster of ideas alien to the prevailing neo-Scholastic school of thought. Compounding the problem was a difference of perspective or worldview. The Americanist movement not only suggested that Catholicism was able to change, but that it should change. In Rome where the neo-Scholastic school of thought was dominant, Catholicism was viewed as immune to change. When these different perspectives clashed in the controversy over Americanism, tradition prevailed over change. It was not the first time that the church in Rome and the church in America had experienced such cultural conflict, nor would it be the last.

In the United States the reaction to *Testem Benevolentiae* was predictable. Liberals like Ireland claimed that the ideas attributed to them in the papal letter were alien to them and never existed in the United States. Conservatives like McQuaid and Corrigan were pleased that the pope had condemned the liberal ideas of the Americanists. Even though the papal letter ended Ireland's "glorious crusade" to unite church and age, it hardly ended the debate over the need for Catholicism to adapt itself to modern culture.

The controversy over how American Catholicism should become was part of a larger issue concerning the relation of Catholicism to modernity. Although the papal axe effectively silenced Ireland's crusade to unite church and age, it did not quiet other voices that were seeking to reconcile religion and modern thought. They carried on the search for an American Catholicism, but expressed it in a different manner. They wanted to fashion a Catholicism that was in tune with modern thought, or as one writer put it, " ... to advance the harmony between ancient truth and modern thought, between liberty and authority, between faith and reason.... "[53] This was a more profoundly intellectual enterprise than Ireland's Americanist movement. Its proponents were seminary professors and some few academics who shared Ireland's progressive view of history as well as his optimism that church and age could be reconciled. But they took this perspective to a different level by expressing their vision in theological and philosophical language.

A clear link emerged between the Americanists and the modern theologians who followed them. The Americanists wanted Catholicism to "adapt itself to the values of the modern American republic," while the modernist theologians wanted Catholicism to adapt itself to the best that modern philosophy and science had to offer. The theologians took the desire for adaptation beyond the pragmatic, political platform of the Americanists and fashioned an ideology of theological adaptation that represented the "theological and philosophical expression of Americanism."[54] Like the Americanists, they argued that if Catholicism was to survive in the United States and in the modern world, it would have to reconcile itself with the age. But for them this meant more than political, social, or cultural adaptation; it meant reconciling the ancient beliefs of Catholicism with modern thought.

Moreover, the individuals involved in this search were more self-consciously aware of its enormous implications. They "were the first American Catholics," wrote historian Scott Appleby, "to perceive and to fully confront the range of intellectual challenges posed to religion by nineteenth-century scientific, historical, and literary-critical scholarship."[55] It is fair to say that John Ireland did not fathom how seriously his enthusiasm to unite church and age would challenge Catholic doctrine.

Historians described this new breed of Catholic intellectuals as modernists. They were not a united movement, but a group of individuals who were eager to take the best that modern scholarship had to offer and apply it to various aspects of the Catholic doctrinal tradition. Modernism was more of an orientation than a school of thought, a perspective that sought to reconcile the dogmas of religion with the intellectual discoveries of modern culture. It was quite widespread in Europe, with France being the principal center; modernist thinkers were also prominent in England and Italy. By the 1890s the modernists had clearly destroyed the tranquillity of the Catholic intellectual world. They were challenging such fundamental doctrines as "the nature of revelation, of biblical inspiration and of religious knowledge, the personality of Christ and his true role in the origins of the Church and of its sacraments, the nature and function of the living tradition in the Catholic system and the limits of dogmatic evolution, the authority of the Church's magisterium, and the real import of the concept of orthodoxy, the value of the classical apologetic." As historian Roger Aubert stated, "These were genuine problems and they called for an answer."[56] In studying these issues the modernists sought to break away from the neo-Scholastic school of thought and its ahistorical perspective by adopting a more historical, critical approach. This view would not meet with a favorable reception from church authorities in Rome. It should also be noted that the masses of Catholics both in Europe and the United States were not involved in this search for a modern Catholicism. Though the American phase of the modernist movement was insignificant in comparison to its European counterparts, it gave a very good indication of how intent some Catholic intellectuals were to fashion a Catholicism that was in step with the modern age.

The issue that received most attention in the 1890s was Darwin's theory of evolution and his concept of natural selection. The debate over evolution among Catholics was not as prolonged and divisive as it was among Protestants. Nonetheless, it was a very popular theme in the 1890s. The key person involved in this discussion was John Zahm, a Holy Cross priest on the faculty of the University of Notre Dame and an accomplished scientist and educator. In the 1880s he entered into the evolution discussion. He lectured widely and wrote numerous essays promoting the compatibility between science and religion. By the 1890s he had clearly endorsed the theory of evolution and was widely praised for his efforts. In 1896 he published his major work on the topic, *Evolution and Dogma*. With this book, the culmination of his thinking on evolution, he confirmed his reputation "as a leading Catholic apologist and educator."[57] Zahm's endorsement of theistic evolution eventually attracted the attention of Catholic theologians in Rome and elsewhere who viewed evolution as hostile to religion. By 1898 the opposition to Zahm had escalated to such an intense degree that church authorities in Rome condemned his book, an action that forced Zahm to abandon his efforts to reconcile Catholic theology and modern science.

Neither the condemnation of Zahm nor the condemnation of Americanism diminished the number of articles that appeared in Catholic journals discussing the reconciliation of Catholicism and modern thought. In the early years of the twentieth century a flurry of intellectual activity focused on the reconciliation of the modern sciences and religion. Writers favorably cited the work of French or English modernists and claimed that Catholicism was compatible with the modern age. An important center of this school of thought was St. Joseph's Seminary in New York.

Established in 1896 and directed by priests of the Society of St. Sulpice, St. Joseph's Seminary prepared young men for the priesthood. Following the lead of seminaries in Boston and Baltimore also administered by the Sulpicians, St. Joseph's Seminary sought to modernize the traditional program of formation and adapt it to American culture. This meant a modification of a stern French Sulpician tradition of seminary formation, a mentality that "often regarded as a sin against the spirit to complain of cold rooms, bad food, poor hospital treatment, long kneeling at prayers, and other violations of the rules of health and common sense."[58] Other adaptations included the encouragement of physical exercise, lectures given by distinguished visiting scholars, both Protestant and Catholic, and reading rooms where students could study some of the best secular magazines and newspapers along with the usual collection of Catholic periodicals. Seminarians also attended classes at New York University and Columbia University. But the Sulpicians wanted to do more than promote physical fitness and good reading habits. The faculty at St. Joseph's sought to teach the modern approach to such ancient disciplines as history, philosophy, and theology. This meant a rejection of the traditional neo-Scholastic methodology with its ahistorial, classicist perspective and an endorsement of an historical, critical approach in theology. In this way they hoped to achieve "a synthesis of modern science and revealed truth."[59]

The study of the Bible was undergoing much revision at this time. Propelled by the new history and its concern for data and new techniques in textual criticism, the study of the Bible was undergoing dramatic changes, a highly controversial development that would rock the foundations of American Protestantism. The threat to Catholicism was also ominous. A major issue was the authorship of the Pentateuch, the first five books of the Bible; another was the meaning of inspiration and inerrancy in the Bible. At St. Joseph's and other Sulpician seminaries the latest advances in Bible studies became part of the curriculum. The writings of European scholars who supported a more modern approach to the study of the Bible were also made available to the students.

Another important development at St. Joseph's Seminary was the 1905 founding of a journal, *New York Review*, which sought to educate the American clergy in the new theology emerging in Europe. Its goal was to reconcile an ancient faith with modern thought. As one of its editors stated, the purpose of the journal "is not to abandon the old in favor of the new, but rather to interpret with becoming care and reverence the old truths in the light of the new science." What this meant was "to provide for the American Catholic church the epistemological, theological, apologetic, and ecclesiological foundations for the new worldview" that was emerging at this moment in history.[60]

For the theologians at St. Joseph's Seminary the Catholic strategy was clear. It had to reconcile the ancient truths of Catholicism with modern thought. But they were the minority in the church. The majority opinion did not endorse the historical-critical methodology of the modernists, labeling as heretical their efforts to create a synthesis between the traditional beliefs of Catholics and modern thought. Since those who defended the traditional view of theology were also in control of the seats of power in Rome, they were able to persuade the papacy to condemn any efforts at modernization within the church.

Pope Pius X, successor to Pope Leo XIII in 1903, issued an encyclical against modernism in 1907. In one blow the pope destroyed the efforts to reconcile Catholic theology with modern thought. The encyclical, *Pascendi Dominici Gregis*, spelled out the "errors of the modernists" and prescribed concrete remedies to curtail and combat further efforts to modernize Catholic theology. In the United States the effects of the condemnation of modernism soon became apparent. *New York Review* ceased publication within a year after the encyclical appeared. Seminaries became a special target of concern. Soon their libraries began to close their doors except for a few hours a week;

suspicious books were even removed from library shelves. The pope admonished seminarians, young men who were preparing to be the future leaders of the church, to keep "their enthusiasm for learning ... under control."[61] An intensive campaign to purge all vestiges of modernist thinking from Catholic seminaries emerged. Even the slightest suspicion of modernist thinking was enough to damage a person's reputation; instructors in seminaries and other clergy had to take an oath against modernism. The fear of heresy "settled over episcopal residences, chanceries, seminaries, and Catholic institutions of higher learning. Security, safety, conservatism became national imperatives. Free intellectual inquiry in ecclesiastical circles came to a virtual standstill. The nascent intellectual movement went underground or died. Contact with Protestant and secular thinkers was broken off. It was as though someone had pulled a switch and the lights had failed all across the American Catholic landscape."[62]

The condemnation of both Americanism as well as modernism effectively stopped the attempt to reconcile Catholic thought and doctrine with the intellectual and scientific advances of the modern era. Public discussion in this area ceased, and Catholic progressives "put their energies into social programs and service activities."[63] This served to strengthen neo-Scholastic thought and its fundamental premise that canonized the immutability of Catholicism. According to this perspective religion was immune to culture; seeking to fashion an American Catholicism was unthinkable, indeed heretical. At least so it seemed at the time. As Frank Sheed, a well-known Catholic publicist in the pre–Vatican II era, stated, "The Modernist revolt ... was crushed: but it was not answered:... their questions remained— to explode sixty years after."[64]

What happened in American Catholicism at that time is similar to what took place among American Protestants. Conservative, evangelically inclined Protestants reacted very strongly against any modernist influence in religion. This opposition focused on the new theories about biblical inspiration, the question of biblical inerrancy, and most especially the theory of evolution. For all practical purposes these Protestants separated themselves from other more liberal-thinking Protestants who were seeking to reconcile religion with an emerging modern culture. Evangelical Protestants developed a distinctive theology known as dispensationalism and built up an impressive subculture of colleges, Bible schools, and congregations. Catholics also separated themselves intellectually from modern American culture and focused on strengthening the institutions of the church.

Gender

THE CLOSING DECADES OF the nineteenth century were also a time when many American Catholics began to rethink their attitude about the role of women in society and the church. A major reason for this development was the growth of the women's movement in the United States.

Traditionally the home had been the woman's domain, but this began to change over the course of the nineteenth century as women sought to become more involved in the public arena. By the 1890s the concept of the "new woman" had emerged. Representing the culmination of an era that had witnessed the "birth of a new womanhood," the new woman "integrated Victorian virtues with an activist social role."[65] Educated and middle-class, the new woman was involved in colleges, clubs, settlement houses, politics, and the professions. Her goal was to improve society by extending the values of the home into the public arena. The emergence of the new woman did not go uncontested. Some people feared that such a development would lead to the moral breakdown of society. Fearful that it might make women too independent, people argued against the value of higher education for women; others wanted women to become as educated as men. Critics claimed that by entering the professions and losing their identity as nurturing and mothering individuals, women would bring ruin to the home. But many women, searching for a new identity at this time, pursued careers in such areas as medicine, religion, law, and politics. The debate over the new woman affected much of American society by changing the way women thought about themselves and their role in society. Within the Catholic community interest in this issue was widespread.

The traditional Catholic view of women was not very different from what many other Americans believed. Grounded in a Victorian ideology of domesticity, this view championed the home as the proper sphere of women's activity. Catholic advice literature enshrined the home as "the true woman's kingdom"; this was "her domain, her garden, her paradise, her world"; and she should never think of any other sphere of activity.[66] Parish mission preachers reinforced this view of women in sermons on the duties of parents by invariably portraying the mother as the moral guardian of the family with child rearing being her primary role. For Catholic women the model mother was Mary, the mother of Jesus. Asking women to be as perfect as Mary added a special dimension to the prevailing domestic ideology. For some women it provided inspiration; for most, however, it was another burden added to the role of being a mother. Indeed, a woman's salvation depended on how well she fulfilled her responsibility as the moral guardian of the family. The only other option for Catholic women was the religious life. Thus, according to Catholic tradition the home and the convent were the only two spheres where women belonged.

The convent, or the vocation of the nun, was quite popular among Catholics at this time. In 1850 there were 1,375 nuns in the United

States; by 1900 the number had grown to almost 40,000. For Catholics the life of a nun was a divine calling that placed a woman on a pedestal below the priest but high above the single or married woman. Clearly, many young women chose this vocation because it offered them many opportunities, such as teaching or nursing, unavailable to the housewife in an immigrant community. Viewed as a positive alternative to marriage, life in the convent presented the opportunity for further education as well as leadership positions in the religious community to which they belonged. Most nuns became teachers. They comprised the labor force, a cheap one at that, needed to staff the increasing number of parochial schools being established in the Catholic community. Others were involved in a variety of social services that ministered to the sick, the orphaned, the delinquent, and the homeless.

By the 1890s Catholics began to question the traditional view of women and advocated a more public, activist role in society. The advocates of this new understanding of women were not the foreign-born immigrant mothers, but educated, middle-class American-born women. In embracing the model of the new woman, they chose the single life rather than married life or the convent. Though clearly in the minority in the community, they evidenced the influence of the women's movement on Catholics. In her study of Detroit Catholicism Leslie Tentler noticed the emergence of this new consciousness among Catholic women. As she stated, "An important minority among Catholic women now envisioned their lives in less limited terms than their mothers and grandmothers had done. Catholic women began in the 1890s to join benefit societies in large numbers, and in that same decade they were instrumental in organizing and sustaining a surprisingly large number of parish groups devoted to adult education. In different ways, these developments in women's church-related organizations reflect the growing sense of their members that women not only possessed a clear individuality apart from the family but that they might in good conscience enlarge the boundaries of 'woman's sphere.'"[67]

Advocates of the new model of woman did not challenge the vocation of the nun, which Catholics held in high esteem. Rather their focus remained on the traditional role of women and the challenges that a modern society presented. Men as well as women debated the issue of the "new woman" in newspapers and periodicals. *Donahue's Magazine*, an Irish monthly published in Boston, added a special section devoted to women's issues in 1893; not surprisingly one of its editors was a woman. *The Catholic World* featured many articles on issues related to the role of women in society. A frequent theme was the new opportunities emerging for women. According to one writer, the nineteenth century opened up "almost limitless possibilities in the various occupations and professions."[68] This was indeed true as new opportunities in education and the professions became available for single women. *Donahue's Magazine* ran a special six-month segment on career options open to women; among the possible careers were doctor, designer, bookkeeper, real estate broker, and insurance agent. Writing in the same magazine, a writer identified as a married working woman expressed amazement that many men still believed "that a woman's proper sphere is a cube, bounded by the walls and roof of her own home."[69]

A series of articles in *The Catholic World* on the public rights of women emphasized the opportunities available for the single woman. "It is time," noted a schoolteacher, "that we ceased educating girls with the idea of marriage always before them. Let us rather help them to develop into practical usefulness any natural gifts they may possess with a view to making themselves skilled workers in some special work." She went on to note that "woman is taking a new position in the world, and we should therefore begin now to fit the *fin de siècle* girl, who must be the twentieth-century woman, for the duties that are coming to her." Another writer stressed the intellectual development of women. Challenging the idea that "woman's sphere is domestic," she noted that "the truth is that in our present precarious condition there is but a small percentage of women whose duties are restricted to the home circle. For this reason every girl should be taught to develop her powers, mental and physical. She should be encouraged to lean upon herself, and to discover her peculiar talent." Another author, Mary Dowd, blended traditional ideas about domesticity with support for woman's suffrage. She believed that if women did receive the vote they would be able to reform society. She also spoke about the rights and opportunities of single women. Describing the emergence of this new woman, the single woman, "to be one of the greatest reform movements of the age," she stated that "this class, including all others obliged to support themselves, have the moral right, and should have the social and legal right to enter whatever professions or fields of labor they choose and are capable of filling."[70] The cultural reorientation that was taking place in American society regarding the issue of gender clearly had an impact on some Catholics.

This was also a time when Catholic women were entering the professions in sizable numbers. They were especially prominent in the teaching profession. In many cities they comprised more than half of the teaching faculty in the public schools. This was especially ironic since the hierarchy had made such a strong push for parochial schools. But these schools remained the domain of women religious, whereas the presence of so many Catholic women in the public schools clearly made them more attractive to Catholic parents. Laywomen joined clubs and were especially active in the Chautauqua movement and the settlement house apostolate. Laywomen also organized citywide charitable organizations and "did for the new immigrants what the Vincent de Paul Society did for the older immigrants."[71] The national

Catholic Congress held in Chicago in 1893 in conjunction with the World's Columbian Exposition included a day especially focused on women; at these sessions participants listened to talks that high-lighted the contribution of women to art, literature, and reform.

In promoting the idea of the new woman, Catholics were quick to point out that she really was not that new. One writer stated, "There is no such thing as a new woman; she is just the same one you have known all along since she first sang you to rest. It is her sphere that has become enlarged...." By appealing to their tradition, which, they boasted, had "a record of noble deeds of Catholic women in educa-tion," Catholics were able to appropriate the model of the new woman, baptizing it with historical precedent. For this reason the new woman appeared acceptable to Catholics and did not pose a threat to the traditional ideology regarding women.[72] It was their confidence as educated, middle-class Catholics and their belief in the richness of Catholic tradition that enabled them to join the American idea of the new woman with the Catholic tradition of the true woman. In this manner they created an alternative view of the new woman that allowed Catholics to enter the expanding public sphere of women's activity while remaining safely within the boundaries of Catholic tradition. One area in which this mingling of cultural tradi-tions took place was higher education.

In the mid-1890s no Catholic women's college existed. However, by the turn of the last century two women's colleges were in opera-tion, the College of Notre Dame of Maryland and Trinity College in Washington, D.C. By 1918 a total of fourteen Catholic women's col-leges had opened their doors to a continually increasing number of students. Clearly, a major reason for this dramatic increase was the emphasis American society placed on the value of higher education for women. Since American higher education was expanding at this time, Catholics became especially active in reshaping their educational system so that it could compete with the developments taking place in American society.[73]

In the 1890s and early twentieth century Catholics debated the propriety and value of higher education for women; some critics claimed that "smartness is not becoming to women" and urged them to stay in the home; for others there was "no doubt that girls are fitted to receive a college education."[74] Bishop John Lancaster Spalding was an active advocate of higher education for women. In one of his more widely quoted addresses on the topic he forcefully spoke about "woman's right to the highest education." "Woman's sphere," he said, "lies wherever she can live nobly and do useful work. The career open to ability applies to her not less than to man." In acknowledging the advances made in the United States where "women have access to all kinds of schools, and to nearly all the professions," he praised the efforts of women religious to open colleges for Catholic women.[75] He viewed them as the capstone of the Catholic educational system. Thomas Gasson, a Jesuit and president of Boston College, also spoke out on behalf of higher education for women. He strongly criticized those who would oppose the education of women, and to support his argument he appealed to the Catholic tradition that boasted of "learned women."[76]

A major reason for establishing women's colleges was the fear that the many Catholic women who were attending secular colleges would lose their faith in such an environment. As one Notre Dame professor stated, "Catholic girls in large and increasing numbers are flocking to non-Catholic colleges, to the injury or loss of faith, and they will continue to do so until we supply them with Catholic colleges."[77] The danger of losing the faith has always been a major motivating force in the drive for Catholic schools. It helped to inspire the growth of the parochial school, and it clearly was a reason for promoting higher education for women as well as for men.

The curriculum in these women's colleges helped to prepare students for professional careers. This development was most visible in the type of occupations held by graduates of these schools. A 1932 study of twenty-three Catholic women's colleges found that an overwhelming majority of their graduates were unmarried teachers; social workers, secretaries, journalists, and librarians were the next largest occupations, and most of these women were also single. Graduates had also entered such fields as law, medicine, theater, and interior decorating.[78]

The emergence of the new woman at the turn of the last century had a decisive impact in the Catholic community as more and more women moved beyond the home and sought to become involved in the public sphere. The traditional domestic ideology of woman as mother and moral guardian of the family was the prevailing thought among most Catholics and indeed among most Americans, regardless of their religious persuasion. Nonetheless, change was in the air as more women sought to redefine the role of woman in a modern age, specifically in American society. This posed a special problem for Catholic women. While they were encouraged to become educated and involved professionals, the home was also championed as the chosen place for women to find fulfillment. Such mixed signals tended to create a great deal of ambiguity about the place of women in the church and in society. This was a predictable consequence when people sought to mingle different cultural ideals.

The debate over gender is a clear example of how the shifting values of culture can affect traditional belief. Catholic tradition upheld the sanctity of the home and the mother as moral guardian of the family. However, an emerging modern society proposed a new image of woman who would have very different roles than her traditional predecessor. This posed a dilemma for most religious denominations that had sanctified the role of woman as domestic queen. In the twentieth century the emergence of the new woman, together with the challenges it presented to the traditional model, would become even more pronounced. Among Catholics the genteel discussion of the turn of the last century eventually gave way to a widespread debate about the role of women in the Catholic community.

The role of women in the Catholic Church has been a subject of much debate in recent decades, but the foregoing discussion suggests that it is not an issue that first surfaced in the late twentieth century. In the United States this has been a topic of discussion that began in earnest more than one hundred years ago and has yet to be resolved to the satisfaction of the entire community. It remains a classic example of how cultural developments can and indeed do shape religion.

This era, 1880 to 1910, was a key moment in the continuous search for an American Catholicism. As in the republican era, the encounter between Catholicism and American culture was profound, indeed more so than in the preceding 1820–1880 period. This era was a major transitional period in American Catholic history. A cultural awakening took place in these years, and Catholics, mainly of the middle class, sought to adapt the traditions of Catholicism to American culture.

John Ireland's campaign to unite the church and the age was a key indicator of how desirous Catholics were to adapt the traditions of Catholicism to American culture. Coupled with this was the desire to adapt Catholic thought to the best that modern philosophy and science had to offer. After a brief flourish, both of these efforts collapsed. More than ever, the church became centered in Rome, and the church in the United States became more closely linked to the Vatican. This transformation strengthened the conservative forces within American Catholicism and reinforced its aversion to modern thought. The Romanization of Catholic piety accompanied the Romanization of the Catholic intellect. Devotional Catholicism was the style of piety that the immigrants cherished, and it remained so throughout this era; any American influence was minimal.

Eventually, Catholicism would become more international in its perspective and more sympathetic to modern culture and the variety of its expressions. This would weaken the Roman influence within Catholicism and usher in a reevaluation of Catholic thought and piety. But this change would not occur until the 1950s and '60s.

The interaction between traditional Catholic thought on gender and the ideology of the new woman that first emerged in the period from 1880 to 1910 did not cease. The traditional view remained dominant, but the new Catholic woman, better educated and more professionally involved, continued to appear. By her very presence she would continue to challenge the hegemony of the model of domestic queen. Another area where the influence of American culture persisted is found in the debate over nationality. Americans became more and more nationalistic as time passed. This nationalism reached unprecedented levels during and after World War I as the crusade for Americanization gained widespread popularity. Then, in the 1920s, new immigration laws brought a halt to the massive influx of immigrants. All of these developments forced immigrant Catholics to temper their old-world loyalties. Such nationalistic feelings would never totally disappear, but they did grow weaker as fewer and fewer newcomers came to the United States to rekindle these flames of nationalism. Church leaders also discouraged the persistence of old-world loyalties and strongly endorsed the national crusade for Americanization. Like the other issues examined in this chapter, the debate over nationalism—more accurately over whose cultural traditions would define Catholicism in America— was unavoidable.

CHAPTER FOUR

Competing Visions

∾ ON A FRIDAY EVENING in early September 1920 the neighborhoods of Auburn Park and Englewood, located on the South Side of Chicago, came alive with the sound of music. People lined the streets to welcome what was described as a "mammoth parade...the biggest ever featured" in the area. A reporter noted that "one hundred and eighty-six decorated machines and floats passed before the reviewing stand." Leading the parade were a drill team and band. Neighborhood businesses sponsored the floats and residents built the machines; prizes were awarded for the best floats and machines. The parade was the inaugural event in the annual carnival of St. Sabina parish, and it attracted a record-breaking crowd. The carnival went on for a week, and among its many attractions were "twenty funny clowns, the liveliest of merry go rounds and a giant Ferris wheel" along with sixteen booths and concessions. When it came time to count the receipts, the grand total of $15,000 was contributed to the parish building fund. This was a hefty sum, more than the parish collected throughout the entire year at the weekly Sunday collections.[1]

Fund-raising fairs were commonplace in late nineteenth century America. In the Catholic community they were a way to raise money for a rapidly expanding institution that needed churches, hospitals, orphanages, and schools. Not only were such fairs popular, they were indeed essential in a new parish like St. Sabina that had to finance the building of a church and school. Each year from 1916 to 1928 the parish sponsored a carnival, and as one parishioner recalled, "The carnivals were outstanding. . . . People worked very hard for those. That was one of the big sources of revenue for the building fund."[2]

Parish carnivals, however, did more than raise money. They also helped to build a sense of identity and solidarity among parishioners. A key ingredient in shaping this group identity was ethnicity. The people's commitment to a distinct cultural tradition, be it Irish, Polish, or Italian, remained very prominent among Catholics in the post–World War I era. In the 1920s the immigrant church was very much alive, and Catholicism continued to be a religion rooted in diverse ethnic traditions. The national parish was the key institution in maintaining the people's loyalty to a specific ethnic heritage and strengthening their sense of identity as Catholics. This commitment to the culture of the immigrants, most especially the new immigrants from eastern and southern Europe, would force Catholics once again to address the question of national identity. What would be the relationship between Catholicism and American culture? Would Catholicism in the United States continue to remain a church of foreigners, or would it become an American church? Such a question took on a special urgency in the postwar era when a revival of nativism focused its attacks on Catholics and immigrants.

St. Sabina's parish provides a glimpse of how central the local parish church was in sustaining the ethnic heritage of the people and strengthening their identity as Catholic in a society that was staunchly American, still very Protestant, and one that looked upon Catholics as outsiders.

Sabina's was an Irish parish with as much as 60 percent of the parishioners American-born Irish. Some foreign-born Irish also lived in the parish, and they contributed a distinctly Irish flavor to the neighborhood. Even though some Germans and French belonged to the parish, it was the Irish who ran St. Sabina's. The executive committee for the 1920 carnival was 100 percent Irish and male; the pastor was Irish, and many of the sisters who taught in the parish school were also of Irish descent. The school curriculum even included a course in Irish history. The intensely Irish character of St. Sabina's not only reflected the people's commitment to their ethnic heritage, but it also set them apart from people of other nationalities.

The Irish in St. Sabina's neighborhood had moved there from the city's working-class neighborhoods such as Bridgeport, Canaryville, and Back of the Yards. Auburn Park was a blue-collar neighborhood "made up of ... small people—streetcarmen, policemen, firemen, city workers, who in those days didn't get much in the way of pay— people with big families" as one parishioner recalled.[3] Nonetheless, moving to this new neighborhood was economically a step up for these people; many parishioners traveled to work on the streetcars and trains that linked Auburn Park with downtown Chicago. The Union Stockyards, located on the city's South Side, was also a major employer for the residents of Auburn Park; in fact, one of the nights of the carnival was designated as Stockyards Night.

Thomas Egan, the founding pastor of St. Sabina's, described Auburn Park in 1916 as "a prairie, with a few families and lots of mud." The movement of the city's population in the 1920s toward the South Side transformed the farmland into a residential neighborhood. By the 1930s as many as 7,000 people belonged to St. Sabina's. Most of them had chosen to live in Auburn Park mainly because of the Catholic parish and its school. Because a large number of them owned their own homes, their commitment to the parish and the neighborhood remained steadfast.

In Chicago the parish defined the neighborhood, and as far as Catholics were concerned the neighborhood was the parish. When asked where are you from, Catholics would most often reply with a parish name. In Auburn Park a Catholic would not say, "I'm from the South Side" or "I'm from 79th Street"; he or she would say, "I'm from Sabina's," because they were proud of it. A practice common in many cities where Catholics lived, it underscored the strong relationship between the parish and the neighborhood. When real estate developers sought to sell homes in these communities, they would advertise them as a "St. Sabina Two-Flat" or a "Little Flower Bungalow." As one developer remarked, the parish "was used to identify a section of the city."[4]

As the local parish became the center of people's lives, it ordered their universe. Parishioners raised money to build the church, school, convent, and rectory. This was their church, and they were proud of their accomplishments. This was where they prayed; its school educated their children. As the social center of the neighborhood, the parish sponsored dances that became legendary among the young people. It was also the recreational center of the area with a host of athletic organizations and a community center and basketball court that seated 1,800 people. For some the attachment to the parish was so strong that they considered it, as one person said, "like . . . a part of your family."[5]

The historian John McGreevy has argued that the Catholic neighborhood was "layered with religious meanings."[6] This was certainly true in Auburn Park. By integrating religion and neighborhood, the parish defined the neighborhood, giving it a sacred character. This took place in a myriad of ways. Each day the celebration of Mass in the church brought God into the midst of the congregation; the church steeple towering over neighborhood bungalows reminded people of God's presence; the sound of church bells was another reminder of the divine. The statues or small religious shrines in the yards of Catholics was another visible sign of God's neighborhood presence. At Easter time the priest often went through the neighborhood, blessing the homes of the people, driving out the demons of past times. Perhaps the most comprehensive sign of the sacred character of the neighborhood was the religious processions that journeyed through the city streets, both defining the boundaries of the Catholic neighborhood and enveloping it with a religious aura that only such processions could provide. In this manner the parish permeated the neighborhood with a religious quality that was uniquely Catholic. Together with its many social, educational, religious, and recreational organizations it created a Catholic milieu in which the faith of the people would develop and flourish. Viewed from this perspective, the carnival was more than just a way to raise money. That was its explicit purpose, but it also brought people together, strengthening their loyalty to the parish and the neighborhood. In so doing, it reinforced the bond between religion and neighborhood, transforming Auburn Park into St. Sabina's parish.

The strong bond between neighborhood and parish in St. Sabina's was not unique. The 1920s was the golden age of the Catholic parish. This was a time that one observer described as one of "prodigious parochial activity."[7] Each parish had numerous societies that sought to meet the needs of parishioners of all ages. Some parishes sponsored as many as eleven or more such social events as dances, plays, minstrel shows, card parties, bazaars, and picnics throughout the year. Chicago's Catholic newspaper had a special section that reported on the various activities in the city's parishes; it covered a full page. In New York the local Catholic newspaper published a weekly column, "What's Going On in City Parishes," to keep its readers informed about parish activities; it filled a page and a half of notices. Clerical magazines carried many articles that instructed priests about the value of parish theater groups and other types of parochial activities. In these years the priest was described as "cult leader, confessor, teacher, counselor, social director, administrator, recreation director for young and old, and a social worker." A member of Sacred Heart parish in New York City recalled this time in her life. Echoing the observations of St. Sabina's parishioners, she said, "My recollection of Sacred Heart is a very happy one, of my own family, my friends, and neighbors. Our lives were centered around Sacred Heart church and one another."[8]

This intimate bond between church and people not only strengthened the sense of identity among Catholics, it also set them apart from their Protestant and Jewish neighbors. In doing so, it reinforced the religious and cultural ghetto that Catholics had created in the United States. This trait first developed in the pre–Civil War era when Catholics began to fashion their own subculture, an island community set apart from an unfriendly society. This separatist quality persisted into the post–World War I era. The noted convert Dorothy Day wrote in her autobiography that "Catholics were a nation apart, a people within a people, making little impression on the tremendous non-Catholic population of the country." Another writer described the Catholic subculture as a "sectarian compound" where all friendships and feuds took place. A St. Sabina parishioner recalled that Catholics "were on the defensive . . . raised in a kind of enclave, maybe you should call it a ghetto." A foreign visitor described the situation in the following manner: "The Catholic Church is . . . a thing apart in the heart of the American body politic. It collaborates in its own time and in its own way, but in the long run it remains distinct and does not fuse."[9]

A major reason behind the persistence of the Catholic subculture was the distinctive belief system that was so much at odds with the normative Protestant religion at this time. Catholics were fairly well integrated into American society when it came to work and politics, but their religion placed them in an orbit different from the rest of the nation. Anti-Catholic attitudes still remained an integral part of the Protestant ethos in the 1920s. Because of their religion Catholics were still viewed as outsiders in the land of their birth, and they keenly felt the resultant discrimination. As one observer in the 1920s noted, "Protestantism is the only national religion, and to ignore that fact is to view the country from a false angle." He went so far as to state that those who prefer Catholicism to Protestantism "are considered bad Americans and sure to be frowned on by the purists."[10] It was precisely this situation and the attitude it fostered that persuaded Catholics to stay close to their own kind.

Another major reason behind the persistence of the Catholic subculture was the ethnic and foreign complexion of the Catholic population. Even though immigration was beginning to decline in the 1920s, the nation still had a very sizable immigrant population. In Chicago first- and second-generation immigrants made up almost two-thirds of the city population in 1930; more than half of the city's Catholic population still belonged to national parishes. A recent study of Chicago's industrial workers emphasizes the persistence of ethnicity in the 1920s. Although men and women worked with people from different ethnic and racial groups, "at the end of the day they headed home to worlds segregated according to race, skill, and ethnicity." They lived in a fragmented world, divided from people of other races and nationalities. In this world ethnicity was a key fault line. Community leaders sought to maintain this fragmentation and the culture of separateness it fostered by "keeping ethnic Chicagoans tied to national communities." To achieve this they "put their greatest energy into ensuring the survival of basic ethnic institutions" such as schools, mutual benefit societies, banks, and churches.[11] Similar patterns of churches and neighborhoods defined by nationality were present in most cities. In Philadelphia Italians lived in their own neighborhoods segregated from other nationalities. The influx of Italian, Polish, and French Canadian immigrants to Boston necessitated the establishment of thirty-five national parishes between 1907 and 1930. In Connecticut valley towns such as Waterbury and Naugatuck ethnic rivalries and conflicts were very visible, widening the chasm that separated one ethnic community from another.[12]

In the 1920s the nation was undergoing a nativist revival. Anglo-Saxonism and anti-Catholicism were "the two leading nativist traditions" at work in this period. The historian John Higham labeled these years "the tribal twenties" because of the rabid nationalist and racial fervor that ignited violent attacks against immigrants and Catholics. A major consequence of these social conditions was the revival of the Ku Klux Klan "as an instrument of modern American nationalism."[13] People joined the Klan for a variety of reasons, but the order's basic message explains its extraordinary appeal. "Average white Protestants were under attack: their values and traditions were being undermined, their vision of America's national purpose and social order appeared to be threatened, and their ability to shape the course of public affairs seemed to have diminished."[14] High on their list of scapegoats were Catholics and immigrants. By attacking immigrant Catholics, the Klan and its supporters strengthened their own sense of identity as white Protestant Americans. The attacks, mostly verbal, only served to strengthen the immigrants' sense of identity as Catholic outsiders. Prohibition was another social movement in the 1920s that targeted immigrant Catholics as roadblocks to the restoration of a Protestant middle-class culture. In their desire to maintain a society free of the evils of alcohol, Prohibitionists divided society into the wets and the drys. Because of their cultural traditions the vast majority of immigrant Catholics opposed Prohibition and thus were labeled wets. This served to reinforce their outsider status.

The anti-Catholicism of the Klan was reminiscent of the anti-Catholic nativism of the 1840s and '50s. The standard accusations of a corrupt church intent on a political takeover of the nation appeared frequently in Klan publications. The alleged tyranny of the church was described as incompatible with the nation's democratic institutions. Catholics must learn, as one Klan leader said, that "our government is on the banks of the Potomac and not on the Tiber in Rome." As far as the Klan was concerned, it was impossible to be a good Catholic and a good citizen because the church was "fundamentally and irredeemably, in its leadership, in politics, in thought, and largely in membership, actually and actively alien, un-American, and usually anti-American." In his classic study of nativism John Higham concluded that within the Klan "anti-Catholicism actually grew to surpass every other nativistic attitude." This attitude persisted throughtout the 1920s and helped to defeat Irish Catholic Al Smith in his 1928 bid for the presidency.[15]

Immigrants, too, were targets of some of the Klan's more bitter rhetoric. One Klan pamphlet described them as "diseased minds and bodies and souls," and such "ignorant and unskilled, covetous and greedy" individuals should not be allowed to enter the United States.[16] Such xenophobia contributed to the climate that enabled passage of the Johnson-Reed Act in 1924 restricting immigration.

Anti-Catholicism was not limited to the Klan. Such intolerance was widespread throughout society, and the prejudice it fostered seriously affected Catholics. A prominent layman, Admiral William S. Benson, described the effects of such prejudice on Catholics:

> They meet bigots in their work, in their neighborhood life, in the organizations to which they belong. If they are teachers, they are in danger in many instances of being discharged. If they are in public life, their religion loses them votes and prevents them, perhaps, from giving their full services to their city, state or country. In some way or other we are all handicapped.[17]

That the Klan focused on Catholics and immigrants as the scapegoats for society's ills was not surprising. The number of Catholics had risen to close to eighteen million by 1920; new churches and schools were appearing across the urban landscape with frequent regularity. Members of the largest denomination in the country, Catholics publicly exhibited a confidence and pride that was not so noticeable in the late nineteenth century. Large parades of men who belonged to the Society of the Holy Name were very common at this time. One such parade in the nation's capital in 1924 included 100,000 marchers. The stated purpose of the society was to defend the holy name of Jesus, and as they marched down the avenues of the nation's capital, they exhibited a combative and proud demeanor. In Chicago an international religious congress complete with a parade down Michigan Avenue and a Mass in Soldier Field Stadium attended by an estimated 150,000 people took place in 1926. Such large, public demonstrations clearly challenged the hegemony of the Protestant ethos in the United States. The large numbers of Catholics involved in city politics was another reminder of how far they had come since the pre–Civil War era. This, too, evoked the fear of a Catholic takeover. The presence of large numbers of immigrants challenged the nativist belief articulated by none other than President Calvin Coolidge that "America must be kept American."[18] Nationally, the foreign-born represented 13 percent of the population in 1920; in some cities the percentage was much higher. Many city neighborhoods were overwhelmingly ethnic, and such dominance sparked fear in the hearts of many Anglo-Saxon Protestants. Because of its large foreign-born population the Catholic church remained a suspect institution.

National Identity

IT WAS THIS SOCIAL context that inspired a movement among church leaders to make immigrant Catholics more American and less tied to their ethnic heritage. At the heart of the issue was the relationship between Catholicism and American culture. John Hughes and Orestes Brownson had debated this issue in the 1850s. It was the lifetime concern of Isaac Hecker, and John Ireland's dream was to fashion an American Catholicism. Pope Leo XIII put an end to that idea in 1899, when he issued the encyclical letter *Testem Benevolentiae*. It is somewhat ironic, then, that less than twenty years later church leaders were trying to Americanize Catholic immigrants. At first glance it appears that, compared to the movement of the 1890s, this effort was more cultural than doctrinal. Nevertheless, church leaders were really asking people to put aside one expression of their religion, be it Polish or Mexican, to adopt a more American style of Catholicism. Moreover, the 1890s debate over how Catholicism should adapt to American culture was largely a discussion among the clergy and some middle-class laity. In the postwar period it became an issue that preoccupied the church at the local, neighborhood parish level. More than an intellectual debate, it was an issue that would affect how people worshiped and educated their children.

The public image of Catholicism was also a primary concern of church leaders. The hierarchy has always worried about how other Americans would view the Catholic Church, and this concern was felt most acutely in the nativistic climate of the 1920s. In addition, church leaders who sought to make American Catholics out of immigrants were overwhelmingly American by birth and education, and many were of Irish descent. Their understanding of what it meant to be Catholic in America resembled the practice of religion in English-speaking parishes, where people of Irish descent generally made up the majority of the population.

The more recently arrived immigrant groups became targets of the hierarchy's push to turn immigrants into Americans. In the 1880s and '90s the nationality debate involved the Germans. In the 1920s

the Polish were a prime target for Americanization. Polish nationalism was on the increase during the World War I. The hope of a
restored Polish nation inspired many Poles to travel to Europe to
fight the Germans. When the United States entered the war, thousands more enlisted in the armed struggle. Chicago alone sent more
than 10,000 Polish men overseas. Elaborate flag ceremonies attended by thousands of people took place in Polish parishes to celebrate
the heroism of the young men who had gone off to fight the Kaiser.
Parishes organized parades whenever recruits left for boot camp or
the battlefield. Bands played, boy scouts marched, and church choirs
sang as they marched from the church to the local railroad station.
Patriotic speeches celebrating the glory of Polonia were always part of
the community ritual. In this climate of heightened nationalism
there occurred one of the more famous campaigns to Americanize
Polish Catholics. Given the heightened nationalism of the Polish, it
was clearly the worst possible time to undertake such an effort.

The setting for this encounter was Chicago, and the main protagonist was George Mundelein, who became the archbishop of
Chicago in 1916. In his very first interview after being appointed to
Chicago, Mundelein confirmed his belief in Americanization when
he stated, "The people of the United States must be Americans or
something else. They cannot serve two masters."[19] Like many
Americans at the time, Mundelein opposed the idea of a "hyphenated American." But the Polish wanted to serve two masters—to be
both Polish and American. While they wanted to be politically loyal
to their adopted country, they also wished to remain culturally
Polish. As hyphenated Catholics they were not only vulnerable to
attacks from the nativists, but also from their new archbishop.
Mundelein's thinking became clear when he began to initiate policies
that were aimed at curtailing the growth of national parishes and cultures. His predecessor, Archbishop Quigley, had sought to accom-

modate the needs of the diverse immigrant groups by establishing many national parishes. Mundelein abandoned that policy in favor of establishing parishes organized by geography or territory rather than nationality. In addition, he began to assign Polish priests to non-Polish parishes. He also sought to standardize the education of all candidates for the priesthood by making Chicago's seminary an "engine of Americanization."[20] The real coup de grâce was the mandate to make English the language of instruction in parochial schools. Since the Polish had made a major commitment to parochial schools, every Polish parish had a school that promoted the preservation of the Polish language and culture. Initiatives such as these soured the relationship between Mundelein and Chicago's Polish community, which comprised more than half of the city's Catholics. Polish laity complained that "the Cardinal is not fair to the Polish people," and accused him of being "the greatest enemy of the Polish spirit."[21]

The clergy took the lead in challenging Mundelein's policies and eventually took their complaints to Rome, hoping for support of their demands to strengthen the faith of the immigrants by promoting Polonization. Chicago's Polish clergy, together with Polish priests from across the country, sent a thirteen-page letter to the Vatican strongly criticizing Mundelein and the rest of the American bishops. The clergy were convinced that the bishops were "intent upon destruction of their nationality." To counter this, they wanted more Polish bishops, more Polish parishes, and a curriculum of Polish studies in the seminary. With Mundelein leading the rebuttal, the bishops denied the charges of discrimination against the Polish and strongly defended their Americanization policy:

> It is of the utmost importance to our American nation that the nationalities gathered in the United States should gradually amalga-

mate and fuse into one homogeneous people and, without losing the best traits of their race, become imbued with the one harmonious national thought, sentiment and spirit, which is to be the very soul of the nation. This is the idea of Americanization. This idea has been so strongly developed during the late war that anything opposed to it would be considered as bordering on treason.

They claimed that because of their Americanism "the Church is more respected in America than ever before." Then, in closing they once again underscored the importance of the public image of the church. "It will be a disaster," they wrote, "for the Catholic Church in the United States if it were ever to become known that the Polish Catholics are determined to preserve their Polish nationality and that there is among the clergy and leaders a pronounced movement of Polonization." Such a movement would endanger "the present peaceful and happy relations between the Church and the American people and government." Authorities in Rome accepted the bishops' defense, and no action was ever taken on the clergy's petition.[22]

Defeated in Rome, the Polish prevailed in Chicago. Mundelein's Americanization policy was a failure; in fact, it was "one of his most stinging defeats."[23] Because of their stubborn resistance he no longer tried to assign Polish clergy to non-Polish parishes, and the Polish league of national parishes remained as strong as ever with more than a quarter of a million people belonging to fifty-four congregations. In Chicago the number of Polish parishes actually increased in the 1920s, and so had the number of Polish parochial schools. The school continued to be the key institution in maintaining the Polish language and culture among the second-generation immigrants, with as many as two-thirds of Polonia's youth attending these schools. In trying to Americanize the Polish, Mundelein not only crossed swords with a staunchly nationalistic people, but he also was challenging the centrality of the national parish in the immigrant community. He discovered that the Polish were not about to give up their cultural heritage, and the national parish remained the center of the people's universe. In trying to make them more American and less Polish, he was attempting to sever the bond between religion and culture that had been developed over the centuries. In the 1920s that was too much to ask of Polish Catholics.

The other group that became a target of an intense Americanization campaign was the Mexicans. In the early decades of the twentieth century Mexican migration to the United States increased dramatically. In the 1920s about half a million Mexicans immigrated, most to cities and towns in the Southwest. The 1930 census reported 1,422,533 Mexicans in the United States. The Mexican population of Los Angeles grew from just 30,000 in 1920 to 97,000 by 1930. By 1930, 683,000 Mexicans lived in Texas, almost twice the Mexican-born population of California. Some immigrants traveled to the Midwest, where Mexican barrios began to take shape in cities such as Chicago and Gary. The presence of large numbers of Mexican immigrants served to reinforce the ethnic and foreign complexion of Catholicism. Because the immigration restriction laws of the 1920s did not adversely affect the Mexicans, they continued to immigrate to the United States in succeeding decades. The continued presence of Mexican-born immigrants kept the issue of cultural adaptation alive among this group of immigrants much longer than it did among those from southern and eastern Europe. Because of the proximity of Mexico, Mexican immigrants were able to travel back and forth across the border. This enabled them to stay in touch with the culture of the homeland, thus reinforcing their Mexican identity.

In the 1920s Americanization programs were widespread. Most people viewed them as necessary to maintain the cultural integrity of the nation that seemed so threatened. Their major emphasis was on citizenship classes and English language classes for the foreign born. Their goal, as a leading spokesperson stated, was "to assimilate and amalgamate" the immigrants to the "American race." In the Mexican community proponents of Americanization especially sought to influence the women and the home in order to "save the second generation for America." They promoted "American standards of diet, health, and cleanliness" among Mexican women; through the schools they hoped to influence the children and teach them "a culture different from that of their immigrant parents."[24] In California the Catholic Church, under the leadership of John Cantwell, the bishop of Los Angeles, sponsored an extensive Americanization program among Mexican newcomers. It mirrored what others were doing at this time—civics classes, language instruction, and home economics. But the clergy and laity involved in this work added another dimension to their program—religious instruction. They not only wanted to transform the Mexicans into good citizens, but they also wanted to make Mexican Catholics into American Catholics. To achieve this goal, the church sponsored settlement houses, charitable agencies, religious education programs, and national parishes.

Once again the issue of religion and culture had surfaced. As with the Irish in the 1850s and the Germans in the 1890s, church leaders confronted the question of how American should Catholicism in the United States become. Should the immigrants, in this case the Mexicans, become more American and less foreign? For the American-born clergy, most of whom were of Irish descent, the answer was a resounding yes. The immigrants did not see it that way. To become more American meant abandoning their heritage. It involved casting off part of their culture as well as their religion. In the case of the Mexicans the contrast between their style of Catholicism and that of the English-speaking, American-born Catholic majority was striking, so striking that the clergy looked

upon the religious practices of the Mexicans with suspicion if not disdain. This is what persuaded church leaders to attempt to "Americanize" the religion of the newcomers.

Religion for Mexicans had both a public and private sphere. The home was the center of the private sphere, and the mother of the family was the high priest of this domestic religion. This expression of religion stressed sacramentals such as holy water, candles, rosaries, and medals, along with devotional prayers; many homes prided themselves on having a small altar that served as a domestic shrine complete with statues and candles. The public sphere featured elaborate outdoor neighborhood celebrations of religious feasts with music, processions, and rich symbolism. Regular attendance at Sunday Mass was not part of this tradition, nor were the clergy central figures in the religious culture of the Mexicans. The American style of Catholicism was quite different. For most American priests a good Catholic "attended Sunday Mass, made his or her Easter duty, and supported the parish."[25] This "Mass and sacraments" style of Catholicism was very foreign to the Mexican tradition of Catholicism.

Many priests looked upon the Mexican practice of religion as superstitious and indeed publicly embarrassing. In a letter to a church official, Charles Buddy, the bishop of San Diego, expressed his disgust with the religious customs of the Mexicans as well as "a fear of the Church appearing 'ridiculous' in America."

> A word about Mexican customs... [I] tolerate some, however I have definitely forbidden, for example, opening the Tabernacle during a baptism; dances in the church before a picture of Our Lady of Guadalupe; girls dancing before a procession of the Blessed Sacrament with the thought of driving away the evil spirits; outdoor processions of the Blessed Sacrament through the public streets because there was not

sufficient reverence or devotion to warrant it. After all, this is America, and we must protect the faith of our people. Many Mexicans have an exaggerated cult to certain saints. They do not say, for example, that the Blessed Sacrament is in the Church; but they say the Virgin is in the Church. This after years of Spanish and Mexican administration. I beg to ask is it uplifting to the Mexican to join with them in their meaning-less and senseless shouting re Our Lady of Guadalupe, and at the same time neglect the essential of the Commandments, Easter duty, and valid marriages?[26]

Bishop Buddy's letter reflected the majority opinion of the American clergy. Yet, he expressed a certain ambivalence that was common among many clergy. He acknowledged that he tolerated some Mexican religious customs; in other words, in seeking to provide for their spiritual needs he did support some aspects of their culture and tradition.

The national parish was the major institutional response to the needs of this new immigrant population. In Los Angeles twelve national parishes were founded in a five-year period, 1923–28; by 1936 there were forty-four Mexican parishes in southern California. Similar developments occurred in Texas and in midwestern cities where Mexicans had settled. As was true in other immigrant communities, the parish became a central institution that helped to organize and solidify the sense of group identity. Spanish-speaking priests worked in these parishes. The church also sponsored parochial schools as well as catechetical programs in Spanish and established settlement houses, medical clinics, and nurseries to serve the immigrants. In providing these services, the clergy and laity sought to reconstruct the religious identity of the people by blending together their Mexican traditions with an American Catholic version of Catholicism. They used the parish, the school, and other educational and social service programs as a way to Americanize the Mexicans. In this manner they hoped to make them better Catholics and better citizens. By tolerating some of the religious traditions of the people and grafting them onto the culture of an American Catholicism, they hoped to fashion a Mexican American Catholicism that was more American than Mexican, more clergy-centered and church-centered than what the people had experienced in Mexico. The people did not totally reject the Americanization efforts of the clergy. At home they continued to practice their family-centered devotions, but they also began to adapt to the language and discipline of a Mass and sacramental style of Catholicism. By blending their ethnic traditions with those of the official church they developed a new religious identity as Mexican American Catholics.

As was true with the Polish, the effort to turn Mexican immigrants into American Catholics failed. As the clergy came to realize this, they began to support the efforts of the people to blend the two religious traditions into a Mexican-American style of Catholicism. The Depression of the 1930s and the forced repatriation or deportation of thousands of Mexicans had a decisive impact on the shaping of this new ethnic identity. As historian George Sanchez has noted, it was in this context of economic deprivation and racial discrimination that "parents and children alike forged an ambivalent Americanism—one distinguished by a duality in cultural practices and a marked adaptability in the face of discrimination."[27] This duality shaped their cultural adaptation to the United States and clearly influenced the manner in which they practiced their Catholicism.

In the 1930s the rise of unionism and the triumph of mass politics along with the emergence of a mass culture transformed the ethnically fragmented world of the 1920s. As a result of this transformation a more homogeneous cultural experience tended to Americanize Polish Catholics.[28] Though their identity as Polish did not disappear, they were becoming more American. Like the Mexicans their cultural adaptation to the United States took place in a gradual manner. They, too, evidenced a duality in cultural practices, and they forged this dualism into "an ethnic way of life" in which Catholicism remained a central ingredient.[29] For both Polish and Mexicans being Catholic in America meant practicing a religion forged out of two cultural traditions. The attempt to force them to replace their traditional religious culture with an American style of religion would not succeed.

Public Catholicism

THE EFFORTS OF CHURCH leaders to transform immigrant Catholics into American Catholics was mainly a local church issue that affected working-class Catholics. While this effort was taking place within immigrant, working-class communities, another campaign was under way in the 1920s. Taking place beyond the parish, its main thrust was to persuade Catholics to break out of their "sectarian compound" and become involved in shaping the future of American society.

The advocates of this style of Catholicism were educated, American-born, middle-class laymen and clergy—few women were involved. Like the Americanists who focused on the issue of national identity and wanted immigrants to become more American and less foreign, the primary concern of this group of intellectuals was the relationship between Catholicism and American culture. However, they were not concerned with the issue of nationality. Rather than culture shaping religion, this vision of Catholicism sought to transform American culture. It was a more active and dynamic posture not usually associated with an immigrant community laboring under an outsider, inferiority mentality. Their focus was on the culture of

Catholicism and its insularity. Wanting Catholics to abandon the clannishness that had set them apart from the rest of society, they advocated a public Catholicism, a style of religion engaged in discussing issues related to the welfare of American society and how this society developed. Their major goal was not the conversion of individual Protestants to Catholicism, but as one of them stated, to transform American society "through the influence of the enduring and tested principles of Catholic Christianity."[30] By casting off the outsider mentality and the inferiority complex that went with it, they sought to adopt the mentality of the insider, the cultural critic who possessed the confidence and ability to comment intelligently on the welfare of American society.

As religious outsiders Catholics had not been inclined to become involved in the shaping of the public culture of the United States. Such involvement was a concept foreign to most Catholic immigrants in the nineteenth century. Church leaders were busy with internal affairs. They focused on building up the institutions needed to serve a rapidly growing population. Religion remained a private affair with the spiritual salvation of the individual being the highest priority. Such a posture encouraged the development of the enclave mentality that became a trademark of American Catholicism. When church leaders did become involved in public, it was most often to defend themselves against attacks against their religion and their foreign roots.

In the late nineteenth century Catholics such as John Ireland became more engaged in the public arena and attempted to transform American culture. The rise of the labor movement in the 1870s and '80s persuaded some church leaders to support the right of workers to organize. A key catalyst in this development was the endorsement of the labor organization, the Knights of Labor, by Cardinal Gibbons and other prelates in the mid-1880s. This marked the emergence of a Catholic social gospel or what can be labeled a public style of Catholicism. Catholics also became involved in the progressive reform movement at the turn of the last century. John Ryan, a priest on the faculty of Catholic University, was a key figure in this movement. By the 1920s Ryan had earned a reputation as an important progressive reformer. A strong advocate of a minimum wage, he sought to link ethics and economics. His genius was his ability to merge Catholic social thought with the American reform movement. He was the author of the 1919 document "Bishops' Program of Social Reconstruction." The Catholic plan for the reconstruction of postwar America, it sought to adapt "the principles of charity and justice . . . to the social and industrial conditions and needs" of the times.[31] Described as "the most forward-looking social document ever to have come from an official Catholic agency in the United States," this statement signaled a decisive development in the emergence of a public Catholicism.[32]

Another key moment in the development of this school of thought was the founding of the journal *The Commonweal* in 1924. The catalyst in this endeavor was Michael Williams, a writer who personified the optimism and enthusiasm of a new breed of Catholic intellectual in the 1920s. Like many other Catholics at this time Williams had a passionate desire to reform American society through "the principles of Catholic Christianity." With the financial and moral support of a small group of clergy and laymen, Williams launched the journal in November 1924. For Williams the idea behind the journal was very clear: "How can Catholic thought, the Catholic outlook on life and the Catholic philosophy of living, as distinct from what might be called the Catholic inlook and individual religious experience, be conveyed to the mind of the whole American people?" Carlton J. H. Hayes, a well-known professor of history at Columbia University and a major supporter of the journal, elaborated on this idea. He wrote that there has been "a tendency too marked on the part of Catholic Americans to shut themselves off from the life and thought of their fellow countrymen, to insulate themselves against powerful intellectual and social currents in their own nation." He believed that the United States was at a turning point in its history and that it was imperative for Catholics "to practice their religion publicly as well as privately, and to cooperate on a basis of equality with their fellow Americans." In this manner they would be able to influence the development of American civilization. It would be hard to find a clearer statement on behalf of a public Catholicism.[33]

From its very first issue *The Commonweal* provided a forum for Catholic intellectuals to comment on the major issues of the day. Described by its editor as a "high brow" journal, it appealed to the educated Catholic elite. Distinguished Catholic intellectuals from Europe and the United States wrote for the journal, discussing everything from evolution to the rise of Hitler, always seeking to bring a Catholic perspective to the discussion. George Shuster provided a major voice in the early years. A former English professor at the University of Notre Dame, Shuster started writing for *The Commonweal* shortly after its founding and eventually became the managing editor of the journal. From 1925 to 1937 he was the brains of the journal, writing essays, selecting contributing authors, and always striving to strengthen the bond between Catholic intellectual life and American society. His life goal was "to help Catholics feel intellectually at home in America."[34] This represented a new vision for Catholicism, and Shuster articulated it better than anyone in the 1920s.

Shuster had "a passionate concern for American culture and for Catholic life within it."[35] The most complete expression of this concern was his book *The Catholic Spirit in America*, in which he examined the relationship between Catholicism and American culture. His purpose was to demonstrate that over the centuries this was a harmonious relationship that had enriched both church and culture. By writing the book he hoped to "bring about the day when they [Catholics] can participate more openly, fruitfully and industriously in the nation's political, moral, social and creative business than they can now."[36]

For Shuster a key moment in the emergence of a public Catholicism was the publication of the "Bishops' Program of Social Reconstruction" in 1919. Looking back at that event, Shuster wrote that "it is almost impossible for people who didn't live at that time to realize the emancipating impact of that document. This was as if the Church had learned to talk to modern America." For him it offered Catholics the opportunity "to move into the mainstream of American life."[37]

The founding of *The Commonweal* was one of the first signs of a new consciousness among Catholics. It was a time when Catholicism, as Shuster noted, was "everywhere experiencing an awakening of its creative and intellectual force."[38] Catholic intellectuals called this awakening a Catholic revival or a Catholic renaissance. First noticeable in Europe in the late nineteenth and early twentieth centuries, it surfaced in the United States in the 1920s and endured into the 1950s. By turning the attention of Catholics to the public arena and urging them to take some responsibility for the future direction of the nation, the Catholic renaissance became a defining moment for twentieth-century American Catholicism. Henceforth, numerous Catholics, both lay and clerical, self-consciously sought to shape the future of the nation by applying "the principles of Catholic Christianity" to a culture in need of mending. Indeed, they "believed that the Catholicization of America was very possible."[39] This perspective of engagement rather than withdrawal resembles very much a similar development in American Protestantism in the late nineteenth century, when it split into a two-party system of public and private Protestantism.

This two-party system of a public and private religion also began to define Catholicism in the early twentieth century. On one side was the enclave mentality that nurtured a private style of religion, what Michael Williams called the "Catholic inlook." The Commonweal Catholic encouraged a more outward-looking religious perspective. As with Protestants, a two-party system continues to define, and indeed divide, Catholicism in the United States.

The 1920s and '30s witnessed a great deal of intellectual activity within the Catholic community. In addition to *The Commonweal*, several other journals, more scholarly and academic in focus, were founded. Catholic philosophers, historians, sociologists, and biblical scholars were numerous enough to be able to organize their own professional societies. A literary revival was also under way in the 1920s. Spearheaded by the Jesuits Francis X. Talbot, Daniel A. Lord, and Calvert Alexander, the revival sought to strengthen Catholic intellectual life by promoting Catholic writers and thinkers. It hoped "to develop an articulate laity capable of defending and explaining the Church to a seemingly hostile world and to prove to themselves and the rest of the American intellectual community that Catholicism was an intellectual and cultural force worthy of respect and recognition."[40] Looking back at this period, Catholic publicist Frank Sheed commented on the "euphoria" that "reigned among Catholics." The number of converts was increasing; a brilliant crowd of novelists, poets, philosophers, and theologians appeared on the scene; and Catholic book publishing became a thriving industry. "The intellectual activity was enormous," Sheed recalled, and "we were happy in the Church and confident in its future."[41]

The 1930s had a major impact on the shaping of this public Catholicism. Despite the vision of Shuster and other Commonweal

Catholics, most Catholics were still turned inward in the 1920s and early '30s. The Great Depression of the 1930s forced Catholics to become more concerned about the welfare of American society. Developments in Catholic social thought reinforced this concern by providing people with the intellectual rationale to work on behalf of social justice. Influenced by the work and writings of John Ryan as well as by the writings of Pope Pius XI, clergy and laity became involved in the labor movement. Conferences that sought "to discuss and promote the study and understanding of industrial problems" attracted large crowds. They often became the catalyst for the founding of social action schools for the clergy and labor schools for the laity.[42] A new theology was also taking hold among many Catholic intellectuals. Known as the theology of the Mystical Body, it stressed the unity of humanity over against the individualism championed by modern thought. By heightening the sense of social responsibility, it encouraged Catholics to become involved in shaping the society in which they lived. There was also a heightened sense of crisis that Western civilization was coming apart as the godless ideologies of Fascism and Nazism gained strength in Europe. In the United States secularism and materialism appeared to be destroying the Christian roots of the nation. As Catholics turned outward and became less parochial in their thinking, they sought to integrate their faith with their life in the world. This was a new awakening for many Catholics raised in a subculture that had fenced itself off from the rest of society. Indicative of their confidence and hubris, this new breed of Catholic believed that Catholicism was the only effective remedy for a broken civilization.

Catholics were not alone in their desire to improve society. Many other Americans also sensed a disintegration of society in the 1930s. Some working-class people looked to Communism as the answer. Liberal Protestants adopted a new theology of Christian realism as the most valid way to strengthen the role of religion in the modern world. They attacked the secularism of American society and sought to return it to its Christian roots. For Catholics a system of thought known as neo-Scholasticism became the basis for their confident turn toward the larger society and their desire to transform American culture.

Neo-Scholasticism represented a revival of the medieval philosophy of Thomas Aquinas; it gained widespread popularity in the period between the First and Second World Wars. Endorsed by the papacy, it became the officially sanctioned Catholic system of thought. Neo-Scholasticism enshrined reason and its ability to prove the existence of God. In doing so, it demonstrated not only the power of reason, but also the supremacy of the supernatural. It argued on behalf of order and purpose in the universe placed there by an intelligent supreme being. From this divine plan emerged a natural law. This law consisted of universally binding moral principles that human reason had the power to discern. This way of thinking permeated the culture of Catholicism. As the intellectual foundation of this culture, it shaped the thought of schoolchildren and was enshrined in the college classroom as the one true philosophy. Catholics grew up believing that human reason could discover meaning where there seemed to be chaos and confusion. They learned about the natural law and how it established an objective moral order that stood in opposition to the relativism and subjectivism that they believed had taken hold of modern thought. Armed with this philosophy, Catholics confidently believed they could reform society.

For the new breed of Catholic that emerged in these years, religion was more than just a set of beliefs and rituals. It had become a way of life, a culture that they believed would be able to mend a world that had come apart. Two distinguished intellectuals, the French philosopher Jacques Maritain and the English historian Christopher

Dawson, became major forces in shaping public Catholicism by helping to develop the concept of Catholicism as a culture. Both converts to Catholicism, they were frequent visitors to the United States, lecturing throughout the country and teaching at American universities. In their writings they articulated the crisis confronting the modern world and challenged Catholics to become involved in rebuilding society.

According to most Catholic writers the basic flaw in modern thought was its secularism. Society was drifting from its Christian origins and turning from God. Catholic intellectuals continually hammered this point home throughout the 1930s and '40s. They looked out across the land and saw the spirit of secular humanism taking over. A sense of urgency gripped these thinkers. The trend had to be reversed, they advocated, and the only way for modern society to become fully human was by becoming more Christian. In their minds the richness of the Catholic tradition provided the solution to the transformation of modern culture. Their confidence and optimism convinced them that "the disorder, incoherence, and fragmentation of the modern world could be healed only by a return to Christian truth as taught by the Catholic church."[43] By synthesizing reason and revelation, nature and grace, neo-Scholasticism provided the intellectual system to construct a truly Christian and human culture. By reversing the secular drift and replacing it with a spirit of Christian humanism, Catholicism would become relevant. Once and for all it would abandon its cultural enclave, with neo-Scholastic thought providing the way out.

Dawson, Maritain, and many other intellectuals furnished the rationale and inspiration for the development of a public Catholicism throughout the 1930s, '40s, and '50s. Others made a name for themselves by promoting what they called Catholic action. This was a movement that encouraged active engagement of laypeople working to transform society through the application of Catholic teachings. John LaFarge, S.J., worked in the area of race relations, urging Catholics to become involved in breaking down the barriers separating the races. Catherine de Hueck founded a movement to promote interracial justice. John Ryan and Raymond McGowan, priests identified with the Catholic social action movement, sought to involve people in a campaign for social justice. The most lasting example of Catholic Action was the Catholic Worker movement, founded in 1933 by Dorothy Day and Peter Maurin.

Like other Catholic activists, Day and Maurin adopted a countercultural posture. They found the American industrial-capitalist order wanting because of its homage to the gods of materialism and secularism. A world without God had begotten a civilization without religion. They sought to change this by advocating a more personalist style of faith rooted in the practice of voluntary poverty, love for the distressed, and a gospel of nonviolence. They sought to integrate faith and life, religion and culture, and thus make Catholicism a more relevant religion. Through their newspaper, *The Catholic Worker*, and houses of hospitality located in cities across the country, Day and Maurin promoted their unique vision of a public Catholicism.

Another major figure who promoted public Catholicism was the Jesuit theologian John Courtney Murray. After his ordination to the priesthood in 1933, Murray was sent to Rome to pursue graduate studies in theology. This was a time when Fascism, Nazism, and Communism were tearing apart European society. A sense of crisis was in the air, and Murray could not help but absorb this mentality. While in Rome he had also come into contact with the writings of a number of Catholic intellectuals who were attempting to rethink the role of the church in the world. These included Maritain and Dawson, as well as Teilhard de Chardin, Henri de Lubac, M.-D. Chenu, and Yves Congar, individuals whose writings would eventually influence the agenda of the Second Vatican Council. Upon his return to the United States in 1937, Murray began to teach theology at the Jesuit seminary in Woodstock, Maryland. In the next three decades he emerged as a major Catholic intellectual, whose chief legacy was to initiate a public conversation between the Catholic theological tradition and the American political and cultural experience. "He saw himself as rooted in two worlds—the world of Catholic faith and the world of American democracy—and he believed that these two worlds had to be in conversation with each other constantly, vigorously, and challengingly if the dignity of the human person was to be safeguarded in an increasingly impersonal and technological era."[44]

In a series of lectures given at Loyola University in Baltimore in 1940 Murray spelled out how Catholicism could mend American society. In his opinion "American culture, as it exists, is actually the quintessence of all that is decadent in the culture of the Western Christian world." This was a strong indictment, but it was a common theme among Catholic intellectuals at the time. The reason they gave for such decadence was because American culture denied the primacy of the spiritual over the material and the social over the individual, as well as the reality of the metaphysical. He believed that the businessman, in his business suit, best typified the American, "a person for whom there is no divine transcendence, spirituality or collective responsibility, respectively."[45] To change this, Murray advocated a Christian humanism whose goal was to achieve a spiritual unity of the human community. "It is the Spirit of Christ, indwelling in man," he wrote, "that gives meaning and direction to the whole historical process. . . . The spiritual unity of all men with each, with the Father, through the Son, in the Holy Spirit: that is the goal of history." To be fully human, a person had to be united with God through the Spirit of Christ. Then the restoration of society could begin. This could best come about through Catholic Action in which the church through the laity would transform a decadent culture into a Christian society. To help to rebuild this culture was a "sacred duty" for Catholics. They not only had a personal responsibility for their own salvation, but also a "collective responsibility of all for all."[46] In other words, Catholicism was not just about individual salvation, but it had a public dimension to it.

Drawing heavily on European thinkers, Murray offered a theological rationale for a public Catholicism. Shuster, Day, and others had urged Catholics to become involved in American society so that they could transform it. Murray's contribution was to ground this perspective in the Catholic theological tradition. He offered a well-developed and intellectually compelling rationale for a public Catholicism. John Ryan had also developed a persuasive rationale on behalf of a public Catholicism in the early part of the twentieth century. His focus was on the ethical dimension of the economy and how Catholics could apply the social teachings of the church to American society. Murray's vision was much broader and less pragmatic. But he was not content to limit his concern to the restoration of American society, a rather vast and indeed amorphous challenge. He also wanted to Americanize Catholicism.

The Americanization of Catholic Doctrine

As the controversy over Americanism in the late nineteenth century indicated, the interaction between Catholicism and American culture would eventually touch on issues of Catholic doctrine. In the twentieth century the major issue came to be reconciling the Catholic position on religious freedom with the American tradition of religious freedom. John Courtney Murray was the main protagonist in the effort to reconcile these very different understandings.

In his desire to mend American society, Murray wanted to cooperate with Protestants and Jews. But in advocating such cooperation,
he ran into fierce opposition from individuals who thought that such
an alliance would compromise the integrity of Catholic teaching and
lead Catholics down a slippery slope toward religious indifferentism.
By accusing Murray of endorsing religious indifferentism, his opponents, a few faculty members at Catholic University, raised the
specter of the 1893 Parliament of Religions and Pope Leo XIII's warning to liberal Catholics not to participate in such interfaith gatherings. By associating Murray with the liberals of the nineteenth century, whom the pope had silenced with his condemnation of
Americanism, they sought to tarnish Murray's reputation and
integrity.

Opposition to Murray increased substantially when he shifted his
work from how Catholicism could transform American culture to
how American culture could shape Catholicism. By suggesting that
Catholic doctrine should adapt itself to the American tradition of
religious freedom, he challenged the Catholic position that advocated a union of church and state, where erroneous religions, i.e. those
that were not Catholic, had no rights.

For centuries Catholic teaching had held that church and state, the
spiritual and the temporal, were not distinct and autonomous
spheres. Rather, the temporal sphere, the state, was subject to the primacy of the spiritual or the church. Not only was the state subordinate to the church, but it derived its power from the church. The ideal
situation or model was the medieval Christian society, in which
church and state were united in the person of the Christian ruler.
Since Catholicism was regarded as the one true religion, there was no
place for other religions and the state could repress them. This meant
that the only individuals who enjoyed full religious freedom were
Catholics. Where Catholics were in the minority, such an ideal

arrangement was not possible, and the church would not press its right to legal establishment as the religion of the state. The church then would tolerate this situation. What this meant in practice was "tolerance whenever necessary and intolerance whenever possible."[47]

In the late 1940s and early 1950s Murray took up the cause of demonstrating the compatibility between Catholicism and the American democratic tradition. Grounding his argument in recent papal writings, he believed that it was time to discard the medieval concept of the union of church and state and adopt the American model of the separation of church and state, which guaranteed religious freedom for everyone. By using such terms as "religious freedom" and "separation of church and state" he was invoking ideas that had a very pejorative connotation among the Catholic theologians who associated such concepts with enemies of Catholicism, specifically nineteenth-century anticlerical European liberals intent on destroying the church. By divorcing religion from public life, they wanted to make the state the absolute sovereign power in society. Murray adamantly opposed such thinking, but it did not make much difference to his opponents. His use of the language and concepts of liberalism was enough to convince them of the error of Murray's thought.

Murray explained the core of his thinking in a series of articles published in the Jesuit journal *Theological Studies*. He sought to demonstrate that his ideas concerning the separation of church and state were grounded in the Catholic tradition. In appealing to the writings of the popes, he argued that the traditional teaching regarding the union between church and state was historically conditioned. It was not the ideal for all time, but an idea that made sense in the medieval period when church and society were so closely intertwined. He suggested that the traditional teaching regarding church and state had developed over time. In a modern democratic society in which religious pluralism was the norm, new questions and issues emerged, and it was necessary once again to discern what he called "the growing end" of the tradition. Murray undertook this process of discernment and promoted a Catholic theology of religious freedom that mirrored the American tradition.

According to Murray, every person has a right to religious freedom, which the church should safeguard. By endorsing the separation of church and state, Murray did not support the idea of a secular state immune to religious influence. Church and state should cooperate and be in harmony with each other. In a society where religion is free of state interference, religion should be able to flourish and have a significant influence on public life. The key to this would be the individual citizen who enjoys the free practice of religion not just for personal benefit, but also for the general welfare of society. For Catholics this meant becoming involved in Catholic action so that they could apply "the principles of Catholic Christianity" to a society in need of reform. Murray's new theology of religious freedom, developed in response to the American situation, reinforced his strong belief in the need for a public Catholicism.

Murray's revision of the traditional teaching on church and state met fierce opposition from two theologians on the faculty at Catholic University, Joseph Fenton and Francis Connell. They had not approved of his advocacy of cooperation between Catholics, Protestants, and Jews, accusing him of fostering religious indifference. His efforts to revise Catholic teaching on church and state elicited even more vehement objections. They criticized him severely and informed authorities in the Roman curia of Murray's thinking. They believed that Murray held positions contrary to Catholic teaching as spelled out in the 1890s by Pope Leo XIII in his condemnation of Americanism. By associating Murray with the Americanists of the 1890s, Fenton and Connell linked the two major endeavors that sought to promote the Americanization of Catholicism. Murray's opponents had correctly concluded that both endeavors had a common goal—to demonstrate the compatibility between Catholicism and the American democratic tradition. But in their opinion such an enterprise was riddled with theological error. Church authorities stated this in the 1890s, and it was time, they concluded, once again to speak out and condemn the errors of the new Americanist, John Courtney Murray.

Murray sealed his own fate when he publicly criticized Cardinal Alfredo Ottaviani, a powerful presence in the Vatican who strongly defended the traditional teaching of the church on this issue. Fenton, an ally of Ottaviani, informed the cardinal of Murray's talk. It was only a matter of time before the powerful ecclesiastical machinery was put into motion to silence the Americanist theologian. This took place in July 1955, when Murray's Jesuit superiors in Rome advised him that it was no longer wise for him to write on the church and state issue. They told him that the climate in the Vatican was not conducive to his new ideas about religious freedom and church and state. Murray obeyed the order, hoping for a better day when the atmosphere in Rome would change. That day came ten years later when the Second Vatican Council approved a document on religious liberty that Murray had helped write. In that document the bishops of the world endorsed Murray's view of religious freedom by acknowledging that the "human person has a right to religious freedom."[48]

The debate over the relationship between church and state revealed a fundamental divide in Catholic thought. According to Murray, on one side was what he called the American Catholic Right. This school of thought "believed that the fortunes of the Church—and of the individual soul—are completely divorced from all manner of earthly fortunes." They believe in "the secular separation of Catholics from the main currents of national life." Murray labeled this orientation withdrawal. It seems clear that Murray was referring to Fenton, Connell, and other like-minded individuals who wanted to strengthen the ramparts that surrounded the Catholic enclave. For them the idea of seeking some type of engagement with American culture was but the beginning of the trail that would lead to the corruption of Catholicism. Murray decribed the other orientation as one of participation. He called it an "incarnational humanism" that sought to become engaged in the world in order to bring all things under the headship of Christ. Rather than flee from society, this orientation urged people to transform society so that "there will be a new heaven and a new earth."[49] This was clearly Murray's position, and it put him in line with Commonweal Catholics as well as Maritain, Dawson, and others who wanted to fashion a public Catholicism that was at home in the American civic square.

Murray's contribution went far beyond providing a theological rationale for a public Catholicism. He also challenged the church to think historically by examining its tradition from the perspective of the present in order to discern how Catholic doctrine could be brought up to date. That was a bold challenge, too bold for most Catholics in the 1950s. Most Catholics were not interested in theology. For them Catholic doctrine was fixed, not subject to change, and so they never questioned it. Not so for Murray. In the end the church accepted Murray's position, and in doing so it sanctioned the validity of the development of doctrine. Moreover, it also acknowledged that culture can shape religion, even to the point of reshaping Catholic doctrine. This was a major development in Catholic thought, one that many Catholic intellectuals are still not willing to accept. However, the evidence of history clearly indicates that culture can shape not only the practice of religion, but even Catholic doctrine.

Another area in which a changing culture was challenging traditional Catholic teaching was the public support of birth control. Initially identified with radical feminists, Margaret Sanger in particular, birth control became the centerpiece of a significant reform movement by the 1920s. At first virtually all religious denominations opposed the use of any contraceptives, but by the mid-1930s the more liberal, mainline religious denominations approved artificial birth control. Even though conservative Jews and Protestants together with Catholics remained opposed to the use of contraceptives, the Catholic Church was singled out as the chief enemy of what many regarded as a liberal and enlightened understanding of marriage. The main reason for this view was that Margaret Sanger and other birth-control advocates, capitalizing on the anti-Catholic atmosphere of the 1920s, convinced the American public not only that the Catholic Church's position on birth control was old-fashioned, but also that it was trying to force its morality on the American public. Throughout this period Catholic teaching remained adamantly opposed to the use of contraceptives. A papal encyclical in 1930 reaffirmed the church's position. In the pulpit and in marriage handbooks the clergy hammered home the sanctity of marriage and the sinfulness of any type of artificial contraception. Such strong opposition led to increased hostility toward the church and strengthened the culture of anti-Catholic sentiment.[50] It also increased Catholics' sense of standing apart from mainstream American culture. This meant, as historian Leslie Tentler has suggested, "that the issue of birth control came to loom almost unnaturally large in the mind of the Catholic community. Opposition to birth control was a veritable badge of tribal membership for growing numbers of Catholics, and a touchstone of loyalty to the Church."[51]

Nonetheless, an increasing number of Catholics began to ignore the church's teaching on birth control. Priests acknowledged that Catholic women were practicing birth control, and a 1940 survey claimed that 43 percent of the women questioned used methods of contraception condemned by the church. Another survey done in 1955 concluded that 30 percent of Catholic women practiced birth control. The percent of Catholics who believed that birth control was morally acceptable was even higher. The few historical studies of the Catholic practice of birth control clearly suggest that people's view of sex in marriage was very different from official Catholic teaching. They also suggest that this disparity of judgment increased as birth control became more acceptable among the American public. As was true with the issue of church and state, cultural change was clearly influencing the beliefs of Catholics. Moreover, such disparity between doctrine and practice caused conflict for many married couples as they struggled to come to grips with the opposing demands of church and society. It also created serious division in the Catholic community, a division that would intensify in the 1960s and afterward.[52]

Democracy

THE AMERICAN TRADITION OF democracy had a profound influence on Murray's thought. Like Ireland and Hecker he sought to integrate the democratic ethos with Catholic tradition by reshaping its teaching the issues of church and state. Though he did not complete this reconciliation of seemingly opposite traditions until the early 1960s, his writings sparked substantial interest in this issue, thereby encouraging many Catholics to question critically the church's traditional position on the relationship between church and state.

The democratic experience had influenced Catholic thinking ever since the birth of the republic. Prior to the work of Murray, interest centered on the manner in which decisions were made in the local church. Since the days of John Carroll numbers of clergy and laity had continually sought to democratize the government of the local church. Widespread in the age of Carroll, such efforts declined steadily as the century progressed. By the 1920s the idea of congregational democracy was a dead issue. Some of the more recent Polish and Ukrainian immigrants went against the trend by incorporating some democratic processes, such as elected church councils, into the government of their parishes, but these were infrequent instances at the margin of the community. Clerical control of the local church had become the norm. The status of the priest was never higher than in these post–World War I years. The people put him on a pedestal that seemed unreachable. People seldom challenged his authority, and few would ever dream of questioning the authority of the bishop. Nonetheless, the authoritarian nature of Catholicism, so prominent in this period, did spark a debate on the compatibility of Catholicism and democracy. This time the protagonists were not Catholics, but highly regarded American intellectuals who, like their counterparts in the Know Nothing era, attacked Catholicism because of its authoritarian, antidemocratic tradition.

In the 1930s and '40s American intellectuals engaged in a scholarly discussion that sought to define the meaning of American liberalism. They grounded their thought in a naturalist philosophy in which there was no room for theology or the supernatural. For them the scientific method was the key to unlocking the meaning of the universe. A very positivist and pragmatic school of thought, it was diametrically opposed to the neo-Scholastic Catholic philosophy that upheld the supremacy of the supernatural and endorsed the idea of the natural law as the common ground uniting the human community. Liberal intellectuals were quick to point out the chasm that separated their understanding of American culture and Catholic thought. They championed intellectual freedom and tolerance of religious pluralism; they also encouraged intellectual curiosity and experimentation. For these intellectuals Catholicism was the antithesis of what they understood to be the true meaning of Americanism. It was "a culture," as a *New Republic* editorial stated it, "which is based on absolutism and encourages obedience, uniformity and intellectual subservience" whereas Americanism was "a culture which encourages curiosity, hypotheses, experimentation, verification by facts and a consciousness of the processes of individual and social life as opposed to conclusions about it." Liberal intellectuals also regarded Catholicism as antidemocratic and feared that a rise in Catholic power threatened the future of the nation. For them democracy was the nation's religion. By judging Catholicism to be incompatible with the national ethos, they created an environment that encouraged anti-Catholicism. This is just what occurred in the 1940s, although other events helped to foster this resurgence of anti-Catholicism.[53]

One development was the American Catholic hierarchy's support for General Franco during the course of the Spanish Civil War. Such support aligned Catholicism with the antidemocratic forces of Fascism and served to reinforce the suspicions of American liberals. The strong public opposition of Catholics to Margaret Sanger and her campaign promoting the practice of birth control raised the fear among many Americans that Catholics were attempting to force their own moral code upon the rest of society. Then, in 1939, President Roosevelt appointed Myron C. Taylor as his personal representative at the Vatican. Such official recognition of the papacy created an uproar among Protestants. In 1944 and 1945 a series of articles appeared in the Protestant journal *Christian Century*, entitled "Can Catholicism Win America?" As preposterous as it may now sound, the essays expressed the fear that Catholics were engaged in a plan to take over the United States and overthrow its democratic heritage. In 1947 a Supreme Court decision sanctioned the use of public funds to support the busing of parochial schoolchildren. People across the country attacked the decision as another example of Catholic power and its efforts to weaken American democracy.

In 1949 Paul Blanshard's book *American Freedom and Catholic Power* appeared. It was an immediate best-seller, going through ten printings in less than a year and selling more than 100,000 copies. The book received numerous favorable reviews, and such American icons as Albert Einstein and John Dewey praised Blanshard's work. That Blanshard was a self-acknowledged "anti-Catholic bigot" did not seem to matter. His book articulated what many Americans believed—Catholicism was a power to be feared, and for this reason it must be resisted and held in check. In his opinion the problem with Catholicism was not the people but the hierarchy. "The American Catholic people," he wrote, "have done their best to join the rest of America, but the American Catholic hierarchy…has never been assimilated. It is still fundamentally Roman in its spirit and directives. It is an autocratic moral monarchy in a liberal democracy." He believed that through the hierarchy the Vatican fostered an authoritarian and antidemocratic program that was at odds with a free, democratic culture. According to Blanshard there was no other alternative "for champions of traditional American democracy except to build a resistance movement designed to prevent the hierarchy from imposing its social policies upon our schools, hospitals, government and family organization."[54]

Blanshard's charges offended Catholics, and they angrily attacked him. His name quickly became the synonym for anti-Catholic bigotry. John Courtney Murray offered one of the more substantive rebuttals. For Murray the real problem with Blanshard and his liberal intellectual supporters was their secularism. Labeling this new wave of anti-Catholicism the "new nativism," he attacked it for its naturalist philosophy. By absolutizing democracy, they had transformed it into a secular religion. For Murray the fear of a Catholic takeover of America was nonsense. As he stated, "the peril of a Catholic America is a chimera; the real peril is secularism, as represented by Blanshard."[55]

Though it never entirely disappeared, anti-Catholic sentiment subsided by the mid-1950s. Liberal intellectuals began to praise Catholicism as one of the "three great faiths of democracy." Even though John F. Kennedy's Catholicism was an issue in the 1960 presidential election, his victory seemed to suggest Americans were ready to accept Catholics. Shortly afterward, John Courtney Murray's picture appeared on the cover of *Time* magazine, where a feature essay reviewed his new book, *We Hold These Truths*, and praised Murray's efforts to fashion a public philosophy rooted in the natural law. Murray's book had appeared in the spring and was instrumental in reducing the fear that many people, liberal intellectuals in particular, entertained about the possibility of a Catholic becoming president. After the election *Newsweek* magazine commented that "Murray demonstrated in theory what John F. Kennedy demonstrated in practice: that Americanism and Roman Catholicism need no longer fear each other."[56] Roman Catholicism was no longer viewed as antithetical to American democracy. Indeed, as Murray would suggest, the task of Catholicism was to make democracy safe for the American people by grounding it in moral law.

Devotional Catholicism

THE DEBATE OVER NATIONAL identity, the effort to fashion a public Catholicism, the controversy over religious freedom, and the polemic concerning the compatibility between Catholicism and democracy were the major areas where Catholicism and American culture intersected in this period. Two other aspects of Catholic culture, piety and gender, also raised the issue of the relationship between reli-

gion and culture, but the interaction in these areas was not so explicit nor so pronounced as it had been in the late nineteenth century. Nevertheless, changes taking place in both society and church did indeed influence how Catholics understood the role of women in society as well as the practice of piety in the Catholic community.

In the 1920–1950 era devotional Catholicism reached its high-water mark. The two main features of this style of piety were the widespread practice of a "Mass and sacraments" Catholicism and devotion to Mary. This was the era when Catholics became "more disciplined than ever before when it came to attending Mass and receiving the sacraments."[57] Large crowds of people going and coming from the many Sunday Masses in parish churches were a common sight. A description of St. Nicholas of Tolentine parish in Chicago conveys the centrality of Sunday Mass in the parish:

> There are 1,100 seats in the main sanctuary of St. Nicholas of Tolentine church, and on Sunday morning in 1957, most of them were filled every hour on the hour: at seven o'clock, when the nuns attended and Monsignor Fennessy sometimes presided; at nine, when the parish children filed in and arranged themselves next to their school classmates; at noon, when the stragglers got their final chance to avoid starting the new week on a sinful note. Among the people who lived in the parish and considered themselves Catholic, the vast majority were there at some point on Sunday.[58]

For Catholics the Mass was immutable. As far as most people knew, the Mass had never changed and never would. They sat in church as quiet spectators and said their own private prayers. A holy ritual, and at times a spectacle, the Mass reinforced the trademarks of devotional Catholicism that had emerged in the nineteenth century. The centrality of the priest in the ritual of the Mass underscored his authority in the community. Without him there was no Mass, and without the Mass Catholicism was bankrupt. Since the Mass also emphasized the sinfulness of the human person, only those free of sin could receive Communion. Because of this, Confession, the sacrament of penance, became another major ritual for Catholics. Confession and Communion—these were the major Catholic miracles. At Mass Jesus became present in the midst of the congregation, uniting himself with the devout in Communion. In Confession God forgave the sins of the penitent. In both rituals the priest was the key mediator who escorted the divine into the human community. Authority, sin, ritual, and the miraculous were the key ingredients of the Catholic ethos. This was true in the 1890s and remained so in the 1940s and '50s.

Devotion to Mary was especially popular in this period and was generally identified with women. The recitation of the rosary, the spring ritual of May crownings of Marian statues, and the celebration of Marian feast days occupied a prominent place in the lives of Catholics. A new and popular expression of Marian piety was the novena, a nine-day private or public devotion. One of the most popular was the novena in honor of Our Sorrowful Mother, commonly known as the Sorrowful Mother novena. Inaugurated in Chicago, it spread to other cities, where it met with surprising success. Thousands of people flocked to parish churches to participate in the novena ritual of prayer and song. The Marian apparition at Fatima, Portugal, in 1917 and the papal promotion of new Marian feast days, climaxing with the 1950 papal definition of Mary's Assumption into heaven, also encouraged popular devotion to Mary.

Devotional Catholicism reinforced the countercultural stance of Catholic intellectuals who were promoting a public Catholicism to combat the secular drift of American culture. The increased emphasis on miracles and the growth of shrines that encouraged this focus on the miraculous stood in stark contrast to the modern emphasis on the scientific method and positivism. Thus, there arose the dilemma of promoting a public Catholicism that sought engagement with culture while encouraging a piety that placed Catholics in opposition to the dominant values of that culture. This anomaly has always been a challenge for Christianity—to establish a relationship with culture without succumbing to it in a way that corrupts the Gospel values.

Continuity with patterns of the past, rather than change, was the most noticeable aspect of this resurgence in devotionalism. Nonetheless, some new patterns of piety emerged at this time, reflecting the interests and concerns of a new generation of Catholics who had come of age in the turbulent years of the 1930s and '40s. Studies of some of these developments suggest that cultural and social changes were clearly influencing the religion of the people.

One new devotion centered on St. Jude, the patron saint of hopeless causes. In his study of St. Jude, Robert Orsi has convincingly argued that a new generation of Catholic women took an old saint and reimagined him according to their needs. Though men also were numbered among Jude's devout, women were the most prominent and numerous. The devout women were the American-born children of an immigrant generation that came of age in the 1930s and '40s, when the ethnic enclave was beginning to break up. The influence of the family in the immigrant community was on the wane, and the children of immigrants confronted "new challenges and possibilities in a changing social and economic world." They were caught between two cultures—American and immigrant Catholic—"between competing expectations and needs" and for many this created a sense of hopelessness. To cope with this distress they turned to Jude.[59]

In calling upon Jude, their prayers "were situated precisely at the point where personal, intimate experience intersected with the greater impersonal forces of history under way outside the door."

Orsi examined four areas or intersections "in order to enter more deeply into the social history of hopelessness." These were the Depression of the 1930s, World War II, work, and childbearing. As the devout sought to navigate their way amid the conflicting expectations of two cultures, one or more of these experiences caused a sense of hopelessness in their lives. They then called upon Jude for help.[60]

As Orsi's study suggests, devotional Catholicism was undergoing change as the social situation of the devout changed. People's prayer life was hardly immune to cultural influence. This would become more clear in the post-1960 era when a new style of devotionalism replaced the devotional Catholicism of the immigrant church.

Developments within Catholicism were also challenging the primacy of devotional Catholicism. A major challenge came from the liturgical movement. Rooted in nineteenth-century Europe, this was an effort to renew Catholic worship, principally in the celebration of the Mass and in the reception of the sacraments. By the 1930s this movement had spread to the United States. Throughout the 1940s and '50s gatherings of Catholics interested in liturgical reform took place each year. These meetings became the center of liturgical reform in the church. Meeting in a different city each year, they served as a catalyst for liturgical renewal in the host city and its environs. These liturgical weeks reached their peak in the late 1950s, when liturgical reform became a widely popular issue. The goal of the movement was to gain greater involvement of the people in the celebration of public worship in the church. By emphasizing the participation of the devout in the public liturgy of the church, it was implicitly devaluing private, individual devotions so central to devotional Catholicism.

National gatherings of Catholics, such as the annual liturgical weeks, become more commonplace in the 1930s and '40s. Centered on some aspect of spiritual life, they encouraged Catholics to look beyond their parochial boundaries to gain a broader, more national perspective on the relation between religion and culture. Most of these movements, such as spiritual retreat leagues for men and women, the young people's sodality organization, the catechetical program known as the Confraternity of the Christian Doctrine, as well as the liturgical movement, were grounded in the theology of the Mystical Body, which sought to shape Catholic sensibility by reminding people of their intimate link with the larger human community. This public-oriented theology expanded the horizons of people beyond the parish, thus weakening the parochialism and individualism of devotional Catholicism.

Another new development emerging at this time was the promotion of scripture reading. The Bible had never held a prominent place in the prayer life of Catholics. This began to change in this era. The liturgical movement encouraged the link between the liturgy and scripture. So too did catechetical programs that were becoming quite popular. As a result Bible study groups became more commonplace. This emphasis on the Bible subtly but decisively began to change the patterns of prayer among many Catholics, most especially among the younger generation who were not so strongly linked to the devotional Catholicism of the immigrant era. These significant developments prepared the groundwork for more sweeping changes in the devotional life of Catholics that would occur in the 1960s and '70s. While the practices associated with devotional Catholicism still remained the trademark of Catholic piety, the widespread support given to these other movements suggested that the "praying patterns of an earlier Church were coming to an end."[61]

Gender

IN THE FIRST HALF of the twentieth century the role of women in American society was undergoing substantial change. The "new women" of the progressive period had bonded together to gain the right to vote in 1920. However, once the vote was won, the women's movement stalled, and by the end of the decade it was "in the doldrums." Economic independence rather than politics became "the new frontier of feminism." Because of this development more women entered the labor force as teachers, nurses, and social workers.[62] The working single woman had finally become accepted. Attitudes toward sexuality also began to change as new norms of sexual behavior replaced Victorian standards. A new mood of sexual emancipation took over, evidenced by rising support for birth control. The 1920s were a time when the flapper emerged as an icon of the age. Young, vivacious, and daring, she challenged the traditions and customs of the past.

Despite such changes, the domestic ideal remained strong. Even though the number of working women increased during the Depression and again during World War II, the domestic ideal of the home as the woman's proper place remained strong. As one historian wrote, "Two decades of crisis only underlined a desire for stable and secure American families, with pay-checked fathers and caring mothers who devoted themselves to domestic life. Throughout the 1930s and 1940s, domestic ideals showed tremendous resilience. Vindicated in Depression and retained through the war, they emerged full-blown and stronger than ever in the postwar era."[63]

The Catholic community was a major force in promoting the traditional domestic ideal. During this era Catholics became concerned about the "moral crisis" threatening the family. By the 1930s this concern had reached "hysteric proportions." The alarm over the disintegration of the family was linked with the larger issue of the secular drift that Catholic intellectuals feared was overtaking Western civilization. In 1947 the hierarchy issued a pastoral letter condemning secularism as "the root of the world's travail today," an ideology that

reduced the family to a human institution, rather than one of divine origin, with disastrous effects. Two years later, the bishops issued a statement on the Christian family in which they described the crisis threatening the family as a "danger more fearsome than the atomic bomb."[64] Catholic sociologists shared the bishops' sense of alarm and published articles documenting this concern. A marriage textbook widely used in Catholic colleges supported the alarmist thesis and the fear that the family was on the brink of disintegration. According to Catholic scholars an ideological revolution was taking place that attempted "to substitute pagan ideals for Christian ones."[65] Short stories published in Catholic magazines upheld the domestic ideal in which "housekeeping and childrearing ... gave the woman the highest sense of fulfillment imaginable."[66] Sermons also promoted such an ideal with Mother's Day sermons especially sentimental and tradition-bound.

Bishop Fulton J. Sheen was an enormously popular preacher. From 1952 to 1957 his television show, *Life Is Worth Living*, transformed him into a national icon. A Gallup poll named him as one of the ten most admired men in the United States. In his sermons he sought to relate Catholic thought to the larger American culture. "Crafting a Catholic identity intended to speak to broad popular television audiences, Sheen relocated traditional Catholic thought and values beyond the Catholic subculture of the early twentieth century and into a new postwar national cultural context that transcended denominational lines. In particular, Sheen suggested how a Catholic philosophy of moral law could provide the structure and purpose for a postwar America seeking to understand its role in the world and maintain peace and unity at home. He consistently promoted traditional Catholic values and sought to adapt them to a larger American audience. High on his list was domesticity. He presented true womanhood in terms of women's capacity to suffer and share the pain of others. Moreover, he offered the model of Catholic domesticity "as a resource for all Americans seeking happy homes."[67]

This theme of suffering and sacrifice permeated women's devotional literature. In his study of Catholic women in the 1950s historian Timothy Kelly concluded, "The idea of life as a sacrifice underlay the education of young women and justified both the demands made and the rewards denied. Self-denial was offered as a model of holiness, especially for Catholic women. A wife sacrificed for her husband, a mother for her children. Nuns were sacrificing all over the place for everybody."[68]

Another popular devotion of this time honored the "Little Flower," Thérèse of Lisieux. When in 1925 the church declared Thérèse, a French Carmelite nun, a saint, popular devotion to the Little Flower flourished. Described as "everybody's sweetheart," she had a special appeal to women. Indeed, she became a cherished icon of Catholic womanhood. Her secret was described as following the little way in which she performed the ordinary chores of daily life in a saintly manner. This was portrayed as the way of female sanctity— accepting the daily trials of marriage and motherhood. Thérèse provided the model of sanctity for these women—a model of suffering and self-denial. Devotion to the Little Flower freed the devout from the tribulations encountered in their domestic shrine. Such devotions enabled the devout to reconcile the ideal world of the Catholic family with the real-life situations that women encountered. They also empowered women to contend with the social changes that were challenging the domestic ideal.[69]

After World War II the domestic ideal continued to gain ground. It was "reinforced by the dominant trends of postwar life—a consumer economy, an expanding middle class, a tremendous spurt of suburban growth, and a fifteen-year baby boom."[70]

While the traditional domestic ideology was enjoying a resurgence of popularity, a contradictory development was occurring. More and more women were leaving the home to go to work. For single women this had been going on since the 1920s. A new trend was the increase in the number of married working women. By 1940 they represented 35 percent of female wage earners. With the outbreak of war, over six million women entered the workforce, "increasing the size of the female labor force by over 50 percent." This "marked a watershed in the history of women at work."[71] After the war women continued to work, and by the end of the 1940s they made up 31 percent of the workforce. The woman wage earner had become an accepted feature of American culture. Also on the increase was the working wife. By 1950 one out of two working women was married; this represented 21 percent of married women. By 1960 the number climbed to 30 percent.[72] What these figures suggest is that two contradictory developments were taking place in this era. Although the domestic ideal was as strong as ever, more and more women were leaving home to go to work. This presented a dilemma for the American woman as she confronted two opposing cultural expectations—become a suburban housewife or enter the job market. The dilemma became more acute in the post-1960 era when the tradition of the home as the woman's shrine began to lose appeal.

The dilemma of opposing expectations confronted all American women, Catholics included. They had entered the workforce in this period in increasing numbers while being continually warned that the proper role for women was marriage and motherhood. As the trend of working women grew stronger, the objections to it from Catholic voices became louder, intensifying the contrast between the ideal and the reality.

Another development that heightened the dilemma for Catholic women was the emergence of Catholic action. Promoted by the papacy, it encouraged laypeople to become active apostles who would seek to advance the kingdom of God on earth, to "restore all things in Christ." Through Catholic action a new breed of layperson emerged in the community. This person became more involved in the world beyond the home and the parish. He or she was an activist who manifested a more public, less inward, style of Catholicism. New organizations sprang up, the Young Catholic Workers and Young Catholic Students, whose thrust was action, not education. They sought to change their environment at work or school through a specific action program. Another group organized at this time was the Christian Family Movement; its focus on the family also featured a social action orientation that sought to promote social justice in the world beyond the home. Women not only belonged to all of these organizations, but they also won key leadership roles in them. Other reform movements that attracted the new breed of laywoman included the Catholic Worker movement, led by Dorothy Day; Friendship House, founded by Catherine de Hueck; and the Grail, an organization led by women that sought to train women apostles to go forth to Christianize the world "with a womanly charity."[73]

These reform movements were manifestations of the new style of Catholicism emerging in the 1930s and 1940s. More public in its orientation and nurtured by a more active participation in the liturgy, it encouraged a new breed of Catholic woman, a descendant of the new Catholic woman that had emerged by the turn of the previous century. Heir to this tradition that sought to broaden the sphere of women's activity, she was "middle-class, college-educated, devoutly Catholic, activist in spirit and articulate."[74] Clearly visible by the 1950s, her emergence indicated how far removed the ideology of domesticity was from the real world where women were no longer content to be housewife and mother. Yet, raised in a culture and a religion that still championed a domestic ideology, Catholic women were reluctant to challenge tradition. Thus they struggled to balance opposing expectations placed on them by the church as well as by society. The challenge women faced in the 1950s resembled that of the 1890s. At that time Catholic women were coping with the emergence of the "new woman" and seeking to reconcile this shift in thinking with the Catholic tradition. By the 1950s changes in society once again forced Catholics to re-evaluate the traditional view of woman.

Looking back into the past it becomes clear that the first half of the twentieth century was a key transition era in the history of American Catholicism. Though this was the golden age of the immigrant church, it was also a time of decisive change as a modern American culture began to develop. As society changed, so did Catholicism as it sought to come to terms with modern America. Nationality was becoming less of a major issue as immigration dropped sharply. The ethnic provincialism of the 1920s was giving way to "more homogeneous cultural experiences brought about by the triumph of mass culture, mass consumption, mass unionization, and mass politics."[75] Slowly but surely the suburban parish replaced the national parish as the key social institution in the American Catholic community. Though still very popular and widespread, devotional Catholicism was being reshaped by social and cultural changes. It would not be long before new patterns of prayer would replace the style of piety identified with the era of the immigrant church. World War II had a major influence on transforming the role of women in society. This would seriously challenge the supremacy of the domestic ideal that had been so prominent in the Catholic community. The sexual revolution associated with the rise of birth control also began to alter the relationship between women and the church. Democracy in church government was an outdated relic of times past. Nonetheless, as Catholics became better educated and moved up the socioeconomic ladder, they began to chafe against the authoritarian nature of Catholicism and increasingly sought out a more independent sphere of action and thought within the Catholic community. Finally, a key development in this period was the emergence of a public Catholicism, a style of religion that sought to break free from the insularity and sectarianism of the immigrant church. Thus, many Catholics were ready for change by the 1950s, a key transitional decade in the history of American Catholicism. The trends that had been slowly developing in the post–World War I era gained momentum in this decade and would ultimately usher in an era of change unimagined in the 1940s.

The Decade of the Fifties

THE 1950S WAS A boom time for religion in America. The nation was undergoing a postwar religious awakening that some observers have compared to the great awakenings of the eighteenth and nineteenth centuries. Though some commentators questioned the genuineness of the revival, few questioned the widespread interest in religion. Church attendance rose to record levels. Just about every denomination was expanding, and by 1959, 63 percent of the nation's population belonged to a church. In that year the American people spent $935 million in the construction of new churches. As one writer noted, "We did not need the evidence of polls or church attendance to confirm what we could so easily observe—the walls of new churches rising in town and countryside wherever we went."[76] During this decade the evangelist Billy Graham stepped onto the national stage and became a religious folk hero for many Americans. Norman Vincent Peale, another prominent preacher, saw his 1952 book, *The Power of Positive Thinking*, became a runaway best-seller. Hollywood tapped into this revival by producing such religious favorites as *Quo Vadis?*, *The Ten Commandments*, and *Ben-Hur*.[77]

In the vanguard of this cultural and religious awakening was the

Catholic Church. Its expansion during this decade was remarkable. The number of Catholics increased dramatically, doubling between 1940 and 1960. By the end of the 1950s Catholics numbered forty million, close to one-quarter of the nation's population. Across the country four to five new churches opened each week. By 1959 more than four million children attended Catholic elementary schools, more than twice the number in 1945. The archdiocese of Chicago alone built 75 new elementary schools at the cost of $85 million over the course of eighteen years, 1939–58. The number of Catholic high schools was also on the rise. The 1950s was also a decade of intense interest in religious life. More than 21,000 women entered the convent in the 1950s. Seminaries were forced to expand as record numbers of young men chose to study for the priesthood. The number of priests increased 25 percent, reaching an all-time high of 53,746 in 1960. The contemplative life became especially attractive to men. The writings of Trappist monk Thomas Merton, especially his best-seller *The Seven Storey Mountain*, provided people with a glimpse of life in the monastery. One clear result of his writings was an increase in the number of men entering the Trappists. By the mid-'50s over 1,000 monks were crowded into eleven Trappist monasteries in the United States. This development was unprecedented in the history of American Catholicism.

A new breed of bishops emerged to guide the church in the postwar period. Richard Cushing of Boston, Francis Spellman of New York, Edward Mooney of Detroit, Samuel Stritch of Chicago, and Joseph Ritter of St. Louis were the most prominent of this group. Educated and articulate, they became spokesmen for the church in their city and region. Spellman became a national figure and a symbol, a pugnacious one at that, of Catholicism's rapid rise to wealth and power. His patriotism was remarkable, reminding people of how American and loyal Catholics were.

Catholics seemed to sit at the top of the world during these years. Every index suggested that they had embraced the American way of life and still remained staunchly Catholic. Will Herberg, a noted sociologist, observed in 1955 that "the Catholic church is recognized as a genuinely American religious community." He noted that along with Protestantism and Judaism, "it has become one of the three great 'religions of democracy.'"[78] The age of the immigrant church appeared to be over, and Catholicism, at least to observers like Herberg, finally seemed at home in America.

As American as they appeared, however, Catholics were still very much tied to the religious culture of the immigrant church. While changes were indeed taking place in several key areas of Catholic life, the religious lives of most people in the pew remained much the same. For them "change" was not a word associated with their religion. Priests were giving the same advice that their predecessors had given forty years earlier; in fact, some parish bulletins reprinted verbatim pastoral advice that was sixty years old. In her memoir of growing up in the 1950s in Rockville Centre, Long Island, Doris Kearns Goodwin captured the centrality of religion in her childhood years. An ardent Brooklyn Dodgers fan, she wrote that her "early years were happily governed by the dual calendars of the Brooklyn Dodgers and the Catholic Church." The "great festivals of the Catholic Church" guided her life throughout the year. She recalled the beauty of the church with its imported stained glass windows, "the serene darkness of the interior, with its colorful banners and its white marble altar and its enormous crucifix suspended on chains from the canopy." Her accounts of her First Communion and Confession underscore how central they were to this young girl growing up Catholic in the 1950s. She recalled how important the Legion of Decency was in the Catholic community in its efforts to protect Catholics from the bad influence of what were labeled immoral movies. The church in which

Goodwin grew up was little different from the church of her parents' youth in the early twentieth century. She was a product of devotional Catholicism, the old-time religion of the immigrant church that was still very much alive in the 1950s.[79]

Another study of the 1950s confirmed Goodwin's recollections. In his study of Chicago Alan Ehrenhalt wrote about St. Nicholas of Tolentine parish. He described the parish as a "world unto itself," where the vast majority of Catholics "attended mass at St. Nick's every Sunday and sent their children to the parish elementary school, where fewer than twenty nuns taught a thousand pupils." Fifties Catholicism in St. Nicholas was a carbon copy of 1920s Catholicism. The Holy Name Society was the prominent men's society, and women enrolled in the Altar and Rosary Society. Marian devotion was very popular, and many parishioners regularly prayed the rosary. The Legion of Decency continued to shape the movie preferences of Catholics. The pastor of the parish was Monsignor Fennessy. By the 1950s he had become "an ancient monsignor," who was a "dominant presence at St. Nicholas of Tolentine." Much like Father Peter Yorke of San Francisco's St. Peter's parish in the 1920s and countless other pastors of this era, Fennessey projected an image of "lordly spirituality." Like Yorke, he "had walked the neighborhood day and night, dressed in a black cassock that reached down to his shoe tops. He greeted people on their front stoops and handed out dimes to children. On Sunday nights he would knock on parishioners' doors and stop in for conversation.... He would appear everywhere. It was his personal fiefdom.... He was lord of the manor, and there was no mistaking who was in charge." He represented the authority of the church, and few questioned his role as the parish chieftain.[80]

Ehrenhalt captured the confidence and optimism that inspired Catholics in the 1950s. "The church at the parish level in the Chicago of the 1950s was no dinosaur limping dejectedly toward its appointment with Vatican II," he wrote. "It was a thriving, self-confident institution at the peak of its influence. It was not searching for a new identity. It was simply not interested in change. It cared about tradition and authority."[81]

Nevertheless, as Ehrenhalt has wisely pointed out, the 1950s "were not a period of stasis but of rapid and bewildering change: nuclear tension, population explosion, the creation of a new world in the suburbs, the sudden emergence of a prosperity and materialism that scarcely anyone had expected and few knew how to handle."[82] Such changes clearly affected the culture of Catholicism. The move to the suburbs was but one clear example of such influence.

The development of suburban America had been occurring for some time, but in the 1950s it accelerated. The modern shopping center became popular, acting as a magnet drawing people and businesses away from "downtown." The government expanded its home loan policy to veterans, and this program fueled construction in new suburban developments. Federal support for new highways strengthened the American love affair with the automobile, making the move to suburbia more feasible. Catholics joined the exodus to the suburbs. Cardinal Stritch of Chicago described this population shift that was taking place throughout the nation. "Chicago," he said, "is emptying out into its suburbs. Thousands and thousands are going out into little homes in the suburban areas.... New parishes are needed, new schools are needed and of course priests are needed."[83]

The migration to the suburbs was one major result of the economic bonanza that changed the American landscape. World War II had ushered in an age of prosperity as wages and salaries more than doubled by the end of the war. This new age of prosperity continued into the 1950s. Such astonishing economic growth "represented the single most impressive development of the postwar years.... As a result of the postwar boom, nearly 60 percent of the American people had achieved a middle-class standard of living by the mid-1950s."[84] Large numbers of Catholics joined this new middle class, and a new type of Catholic appeared on the scene—the Catholic suburbanite. These suburbanites were better educated than their parents and had become members of the rapidly emerging professional and managerial class that had taken hold in the 1950s. Their move into the suburbs signaled the arrival of Catholics into the mainstream of American society. "For in the suburb," noted Andrew Greeley in his 1959 study of the suburban church, "the Catholic is regarded, at last, as a full-fledged American."[85]

The move to the suburbs signaled the beginning of the end of the European immigrant era of Catholicism. New immigrants from Latin America and Asia would usher in another era of immigrant Catholicism in subsequent decades, but in the 1950s commentators frequently wrote about the demise of the immigrant church that had been such a central feature of Catholicism in the United States. Greeley wrote, "The ghetto walls are crumbling. The old national parishes are breaking up."[86]

A major reason for the breakup of the old national parishes was race and the urban crisis that transformed the nation's cities. The post–World War II era was a time of large-scale African-American migration out of the South to the urban North. The newcomers chose to settle in neighborhoods located on the fringe of the old immigrant enclaves. As the Black Belts of these northern cities expanded, white Protestants and Jews fled the old neighborhoods. Catholics stayed put longer because of their deeply rooted ties to the parish and its sacred turf. As the 1950s progressed, however, more and more Catholics began to put their houses up for sale in order to relocate to the expanding suburbs. What began as a slow but steady trickle in the 1950s reached flood-tide levels by the 1960s.

The suburbs became the home of a new breed of Catholic intellectuals. Heirs of the Commonweal Catholics of the 1920s and '30s, they wanted to leave behind the religious culture of the immigrant church. Many of these college-educated, middle-class individuals were involved in one or more Catholic action groups that had developed in the postwar period. This was a time when great emphasis was put on the laity. Popes, bishops, and clergy had been encouraging laypeople to become more involved in the life of the church since the 1930s. By the 1950s it was clear that the laity had responded to the challenge. By promoting a public Catholicism, they hoped to transform the church as well as Christianize society.

In 1959 Leo Ward, C.S.C., a priest on the faculty of the University of Notre Dame, wrote a book on contemporary lay movements. He believed that "the brick and mortar era of the Church in America had passed its peak and we must begin to think of a new era with new opportunities and new questions." The question he posed was, "How is the layman as well as the bishop and the priest to take a vital and intimate part in the forward movement of the Church in America?" He answered his own question by describing the many activities in which laymen and women were involved. For him "the most important recent religious development" was "the increase of liturgical life in America."[87] The liturgical movement that had been challenging the popularity of devotional Catholicism in the United States since the 1930s found its most ardent supporters in the new breed of Catholic layperson that emerged in the 1940s and '50s. These were the men and women who joined the many Catholic action groups that emerged at this time. They attended the national gatherings of these organizations, formed Bible study groups, and began to dream about a more pubic, less parochial, sectarian Catholicism. For them the liturgy was the wellspring of this public Catholicism that they hoped would bring about the reform of both church and society. Ward's study examined several of these Catholic action groups and portrayed them as visible signs of a church come of age, a church in which laypeople and not just the clergy were major actors.

Catholic nuns merited inclusion in Ward's study because they, too, were in the midst of reform. In the twentieth century life in the convent was comparable to living in a closed society. Sisters lived in two separate worlds—"the world of the medieval monastery and that of the competitive twentieth-century marketplace." The tension that this produced surfaced in the 1950s as more and more sisters, the vast majority of whom were engaged in teaching, began to further their education in order to meet the professional demands placed on teachers at this time. Further education led to personal and professional development, and this fostered a new orientation to the world, one that threatened to break down the walls of the cloister culture that had kept the sisters the mystery women of Catholicism. Like the liturgical reformers and the Catholic suburbanites, they too began to question the institution and many of its cherished traditions. Patricia Byrne has studied this critical change, demonstrating how tensions developed in the 1950s "over the conflict between professional demands in school and an outdated conventual spirituality." By the end of the decade, that conflict had grown, as one sister expressed it, "almost ... to the point of absurdity."[88] Such conflict would become a powerful force for change in the years ahead.

One group that Ward did not examine was the clergy. A large number of priests had also joined the vanguard for change. They promoted a new vision of the church that advocated the involvement of the laity in the life of the church. In doing so, they sought to cast aside the immigrant church's "Father knows best" syndrome. Some of these priests began to meet on a regular basis and, as one of them remarked, they would "exchange thoughts and chew over our mutual interests as kindred spirits in the priesthood of Christ and the Apostolate." Their hope was to affirm a public style of Catholicism that would influence the future direction of American society. They sought to overcome what one described as "the defensive ghetto, fortresslike mentality which has been dominant in the church, U.S.A." Through such meetings these priests "prepared for Vatican II without knowing it."[89]

Another sign of unrest within the Catholic community was the tide of self-criticism that was beginning to crest in the middle of the decade. One source of this change came in an essay published in 1955 by church historian John Tracy Ellis. "American Catholics and the Intellectual Life" was a powerful indictment of Catholicism's failure to develop a strong intellectual life in the United States. After marshaling a host of evidence to demonstrate the poor intellectual achievement of Catholics, Ellis then discussed a number of social, cultural, and educational reasons for such inferiority. In concluding the essay he pointed squarely at Catholics themselves. "The chief blame, I firmly believe, lies with Catholics themselves. It lies in their frequently self-imposed ghetto mentality which prevents them from mingling as they should with their non-Catholic colleagues, and in their lack of industry and habits of work."[90] George Shuster and others had made much the same observations in the 1920s and 30s, but few Catholics had paid any attention. American Catholics were at a different place in 1955, however, and Ellis's essay touched a vital nerve within the Catholic community. Like Ellis, the new breed of Catholic was inclined to adopt a more critical view of the immigrant Catholic culture, most especially its clericalism and its anti-intellectualism. Ellis's essay sparked a prolonged debate on Catholic intellectual life. This peaked to some degree in 1958 with the publication of Thomas O'Dea's *American Catholic Dilemma*. The book became a best-seller among Catholics who were interested in shaping a new Catholicism in harmony with post-immigrant, postwar America. O'Dea reinforced Ellis's thesis that the Catholic mentality was the real culprit. In order for Catholicism to come of age at this moment in its history, a major reordering of Catholic life was necessary. "In fact," as historian Philip Gleason has noted, "the overall impression conveyed by his discussion was that practically everything historically associated with American Catholic life, intellectual and otherwise, would have to be scrapped." That is an extreme judgment, but it underscores how deep-seated and radical was the call for change in the late 1950s.[91]

In the 1950s Catholicism exhibited a Janus-like appearance. One of its faces was most visible at the parish level and was more widespread in the early years of the decade. This was the "thriving, self-confident institution" that Alan Ehrenhalt wrote about. It was the old immigrant church "at the peak of its influence." As he noted, "It was not searching for a new identity. It was simply not interested in change. It cared about tradition and authority."[92] As the decade progressed, this face of Catholicism began to lose its luster and magnetism. The other face of Catholicism was associated with the new breed of Catholic who emerged in postwar America. Clergy and lay, male and female, they were in search of a Catholicism more in tune with American culture. What this would look like they were not sure. What they were sure of, however, was that change was necessary. A new age and a new breed of Catholic demanded a new Catholicism. As the decade progressed, the call for reform grew louder and louder. The election of a new pope in 1958 and his intention to have a church council suggested that change might be on the way. However, even if Vatican II had never happened, the renewal of Catholicism would still have taken place in the United States. That is because the social and cultural transformation of the post–World War II era proved to be as important if not indeed more important for American Catholics than Vatican II. Catholicism was indeed ripe for change, and change it would in a manner that would have been totally unexpected in 1960.

CHAPTER FIVE

An American Religion
and a Roman Church, 1960–2001

    THE "1960S" CONJURES UP many images—astro-
nauts walking on the moon, the Beatles, race riots and burning cities,
Russian missiles in Cuba, the Fifth Dimension, *Hair*, napalm bombs,
My Lai massacre, the March on Washington, Freedom Rides, "We
Shall Overcome," Woodstock. But for Americans who lived through
the decade the one image they will never forget was the assassination
of President John F. Kennedy. People still recall where they were and
what they were doing when they first heard the news. Time stopped
on that fateful Friday, November 22, 1963, and a nation mourned for
days as Americans honored their fallen leader.

In the years since his death the aura surrounding President
Kennedy has lost much of its glitter. Historians have re-examined the
Camelot era and stripped away the myth surrounding JFK. As a result
Kennedy is now viewed as being equally flawed as other presidents,
maybe even more so. Yet, there is no denying that in the early 1960s
he captured the popular imagination. He was young, vigorous, hand-
some, and sophisticated. Norman Mailer described him as "our leading man." Born to wealth and politics, he married an equally charm-
ing and sophisticated woman. At his inauguration he spoke about a
New Frontier and eloquently appealed to the idealism of young
Americans who had come of age in the 1950s. Just as people note
Lincoln's Gettysburg Address, they still quote Kennedy's inaugural
speech and his call for sacrifice on behalf of the nation.

Kennedy's election to the presidency was also a high point for Catholics. It was a symbolic moment that appeared to mark the end of people's bias against Catholics. As Martin Marty noted, "His inauguration symbolized the end of 'Protestant America.'" A Catholic was in the White House, and the nation survived. His victory had finally put to rest the idea that a Catholic could not be elected president. Catholics basked in the glow of the Catholic Kennedy in the White House. His popularity enabled Catholics to stand a little taller. One of their own had made it and done so with style. John Cogley observed that "his poise, sophistication, the modernity worn as casually as his London-tailored clothes, suggested more than any proclamation could that Catholics at long last were comfortably integrated into American society."[1]

Catholics had another reason to stand tall. They had a new pope, John XXIII. Elected in 1958, he too brought a new style to his office. Unlike his predecessor, Pius XII, John was an outgoing, gregarious individual. He could charm heads of state as well as common people. John did away with many of the imperial trappings of the papacy; he abandoned the papal tiara, a medieval symbol of papal power. Not willing to remain a prisoner of the Vatican like his predecessors, he left the Vatican and drove through the streets of Rome in his limousine, waving to people astonished to see the pope in their midst. His visits to Rome's hospitals and prisons became the talk of the town. He was the people's pope, whose warmth, humor, and openness captured the world's attention. His modern, urbane style was much like that of John F. Kennedy. People even began to speak of the two Johns as if they had a common destiny. The death of both of them in 1963 sealed this connection.

John XXIII's election created a sense of excitement among Catholics. In January 1959 he shocked the world when he announced that he would convoke an ecumenical council. In his opening address to the council on October 11, 1962, surely one of the most important documents of twentieth-century religious history, Pope John explained his reasons for calling the council. He wanted to bring the church up to date, and to gain this goal he sought to establish a dialogue with people of other religions, with fellow Catholics, and with the world beyond the church.

When the council ended in December 1965, it had charted a new course for Roman Catholicism. Breaking with a four-hundred-year tradition, it abandoned its defensive posture toward modern society and sought engagement with the world. In assessing the changes that have taken place as a result of the council, several deserve special mention. First, the council launched a new era of worship in church. By 1970 a new rite of the Catholic Mass was in place. Modern languages replaced the use of Latin, and people were encouraged to participate in the liturgy. The goals of the liturgical movement that reformers had promoted since the 1930s were finally realized. What seemed unchangeable suddenly changed. For some Catholics the shock of change was too much. For others it was long overdue. Public dissent and conflict soon became routine in a religious community that had stifled dissent for so long. A new understanding of the church also emerged from the council. Abandoning the triumphal posture of the past, the council articulated a new self-understanding of Catholicism. Describing the church as the people of God, it sought to underline the important place of the laity in the church. The council also encouraged a spirit of collegiality between bishops and pope, clergy and laity. Pope John also wanted to breach the chasm that separated Catholics from Protestants and people of other religions. Following his lead, the council ushered in a new era of Catholic-Protestant relations. As an ecumenical spirit swept through the American Catholic community, interfaith dialogues became commonplace by the end of the 1960s.

Another significant change affected theology. The ahistorical approach of traditional Scholastic theology with its emphasis on the immutability of Catholic dogma gave way to a methodology that emphasized the historical conditioning of religious truths. Scholars acknowledged that culture can indeed shape religion and the manner in which doctrine is expressed and understood. Another momentous change for Catholics was the endorsement of religious liberty. This took place in the final session of the council and vindicated the work of John Courtney Murray. By affirming a person's right to religious freedom, the council proclaimed that coercion in matters religious had no place in modern society. This was a significant change from the days of John Ireland when official Catholic teaching proclaimed that in matters religious, error had no rights.

Finally, the council articulated a new posture for the church in the modern world. Spelled out in a council document appropriately titled *Pastoral Constitution on the Church in the Modern World*, it represented the crowning achievement of years of theological development. Incorporating the social teachings of the popes since the late nineteenth century and most especially the work of theologians in the post–World War II era, the document provided a theological rationale for a public Catholicism that had been the goal of numerous American Catholics since the early twentieth century. It not only recognized the importance of culture in shaping religion, but it also underscored the need for religion to transform culture. As a result, dialogue between Catholicism and modern culture began. No longer was the church a community turned inward on itself. Its mission was to be a servant church that would reach out to the larger society living beyond the Catholic sanctuary. This new attitude would have significant implications in the United States, where Catholicism did an about-face, abandoned its sectarian posture, and sought to become a major force in American public life.

The euphoria and optimism that marked the early 1960s began to evaporate as the war in Vietnam, race riots, and assassinations of popular heroes drained the spirit of the nation. Hope turned into rage. Nonetheless, the social revolution of the 1960s reshaped American society. As Todd Gitlin wrote, "The genies that the Sixties loosed are still abroad in the land, inspiring and unsettling and offending, making trouble. For the civil rights and antiwar and countercultural and women's and the rest of that decade's movements forced upon us central issues for Western civilization—fundamental questions of value, fundamental divides of culture, fundamental debates about the nature of the good life."[2] Much the same can be said about the changes that took place within the Catholic community. The decade began in an atmosphere of optimism and hope and ended in anger and confusion as the change sweeping through the institution unsettled many people.

In the 1960s "change" entered the lexicon of Catholics, and many were uncomfortable with such an idea. As Garry Wills noted, the Council "let out the dirty little secret. It forced upon Catholics, in the most startling symbolic way, the fact that the church changes."[3] Scores of Catholics resented change in what they believed was an unchanging institution. Others wanted more change and were disappointed with Pope John's successor, Paul VI, for what they believed was a too hesitant and cautious endorsement of reform. Conflict has never been absent from the history of American Catholicism, but the conflict that emerged in the 1960s was unprecedented in its scope. It spread through the entire community, dividing families and parishes, bishops and priests. The American Catholic community continues to be conflicted because the genies that the council loosed are still abroad.

Much has been written about what has happened in the American Catholic community since the 1960s. The story is a familiar one:

decline in the number of clergy, women religious, parochial schools, and Catholic colleges. Along with a decline in church attendance, there has been a massive increase in the number of Catholics living on the margin of the church. Indeed, a recent study has suggested that as many as one-third of the Catholic population, about twenty million people, are not affiliated with a parish.[4] They consider themselves Catholic, but are unaffiliated with the institutional church. In addition to such quantifiable changes, the beliefs and morals of Catholics have also changed so that there is much more diversity of belief among Catholics than is generally assumed to have been the case in the pre–Vatican II era. Conflict has riddled the community, and dissent from official church teaching became public and commonplace. Nonetheless, interest in religion remains very high. Numerous vibrant parishes dot the landscape; laymen and laywomen have assumed key leadership roles in many areas of institutional Catholicism; volunteerism has become commonplace; and the church continues to be one of the most important social service agencies in the nation.

There is no simple explanation for such contrasting developments. Change has taken place to be sure, but decline has not set in. Rather, a restructuring of religion has taken place, ushering in a new era in the history of American Catholicism. It is an era of fewer priests and more lay ministers, fewer Mass and sacraments Catholics as well as more dynamic parish communities, widespread dissent on issues of doctrine along with intense commitment to religion. The reasons behind such restructuring can be located both in society and in the church.

Robert Wuthnow has studied recent developments in American religion and convincingly argues that the changes that swept through American society in the post–World War II era have transformed religion in America, Protestant as well as Catholic. "The period since

World War II has been a time of momentous social change. New developments in technology, the changing character of international relations, shifts in the composition of the population, the tremendous expansion of higher education and in the role of government, new policies and new administrative systems all attest to the seriousness of these changes. To the extent that American religion is a social instiution, embedded in and always exposed to the broader social environment, it could not help but have been affected by these changes."[5] In addition to such social changes that have affected all religions in the United States, Catholicism has also experienced its own internal, religious changes. Vatican II was the primary force behind these changes, but they had been developing for some time prior to the 1960s. Taken together these social and religious changes have transformed Catholicism.

A new Catholicism is taking shape in the United States, and it is not yet clear what it will look like. Once again, people are asking what it means to be Catholic in modern America. Catholics have asked this question time and again over the past two hundred years. This time the questioning is much more widespread, much more revolutionary. Like Pope John XXIII, many Catholics want to bring the church up to date. The pope first raised the idea, and the council endorsed it. In the United States Catholics have accepted the challenge of fashioning a new Catholicism. To achieve this goal, they are trying to form a religious identity that is no longer linked to cultural separatism. Instead, they want to forge a religious identity that is faithful to the Catholic tradition and at the same time is rooted in American culture.

Interaction between Catholicism and American culture has been common throughout the past two hundred years. But the post–World War II period has been special. More so than before, Catholics have sought to fashion a Catholicism that is in tune with modern America. As they became more American and left behind the immigrant church of the nineteenth and early twentieth centuries, the search for an American Catholicism became more intense, with consequences far more revolutionary than previously. But before considering how American culture has shaped Catholicism in this period, it would be helpful to discuss the emergence of a public style of Catholicism that has become such an important development in the twentieth century.

Public Catholicism

SINCE THE EARLY PART of the twentieth century Catholics had increasingly become more engaged in the public arena. The more American they became, the more Catholics began to take moral and political positions that they believed would benefit the welfare of the nation. The hierarchy frequently published statements that addressed the nation's moral climate. Clergy and laity also became involved in numerous efforts to improve the quality of life in their neighborhoods. In the 1960s these efforts to shape the moral fiber of the nation intensified. Issues of social justice took center stage in the 1960s as crusades on behalf of civil rights, women's rights, and peace swept across the landscape. These social movements for reform attracted many Catholics, and before long the Catholic religious community became a major player in the reform movements of the 1960s. This was a significant development in the history of American Catholicism.

In his study of the Catholic encounter with race in the urban North, John McGreevy demonstrated the influence of the civil rights movement on Catholics. He also documented how the new under-standing of the church and its relation to the world articulated at Vatican II influenced Catholics to become involved in such public issues as civil rights. "A renewed focus on social justice" reshaped the relationship between Catholics and modern society and, noted McGreevy, "as Catholics reevaluated their roles in contemporary society, the national focus on racial issues and urban poverty provided a mechanism for engagement with the world."[6] Much the same pattern took place with the peace movement. A new understanding of the role of the church in the world and the consequent destruction of the barrier separating the sacred from the secular inspired many Catholics to join the peace movement. Indeed, by the end of the 1960s Catholics were in the forefront of the movement to stop the war in Vietnam. Other issues related to social justice also provided Catholics the opportunity to become major actors in the public square. Most notable would be their involvement with Cesar Chavez and the farm workers' movement as well as the urban renewal movement that sought more affordable housing for the nation's city dwellers.

In all of these areas religion and culture were interacting and influencing each other. As the demands for social justice increased, Catholics responded in an unprecedented manner. A social gospel has now become a trademark of the Catholic religious community. In the 1970s and '80s this trend toward a social gospel, or what could be called a public religion, gained momentum when the American hierarchy mounted the national pulpit and spoke out on issues of national concern. What was so special about their intervention in these years was the strong sense of collegiality that the bishops had achieved in the post–Vatican II era. A strong episcopal conference headquartered in Washington, D.C., and forceful leadership from such individuals as Cardinal John Dearden and Cardinal Joseph Bernardin strengthened this collegial dimension. Thus, when the hierarchy officially spoke out on issues of public concern, they did so with a strong consensus. Though the bishops have spoken out on many issues in the past thirty years, three issues in particular attracted more attention than others and clearly illustrate the emergence of a public Catholicism.

One concern was the threat of nuclear war. This resulted in a 1983 pastoral letter on nuclear war, *The Challenge of Peace: God's Promise and Our Response*. One commentator claimed that it was the "most significant event in the American Catholic Church, and perhaps in the international church, since the Second Vatican Council."[7] The reasons for such a claim are clear. The cold war environment was still prevalent in the early 1980s, and the build-up of nuclear arms posed the threat of nuclear holocaust. The bishops believed that they had a moral responsibility to address the critical issue of war in a nuclear age. In addition, the process followed in the drafting of the letter was unprecedented. Over the course of three years numerous consultations took place with foreign policy experts, ethicists, and other authorities on issues related to war and peace. Such consultation on the part of the bishops was very unusual. Normally, when they published a pastoral letter, as they did many times in the twentieth century, it was the work of a single individual or at best just a few individuals, and the work was done privately with no public consultation. The bishops also debated the issue as the letter went through four drafts. When it was finally put to a vote, 238 bishops voted for it and only nine dissented.

This pastoral letter took an historical approach to the issue. It sought to read the "signs of the times," namely, the political realities of a nuclear age in which the arms race threatened the universal desire for peace. In doing so, the bishops acknowledged that culture does indeed influence religion, that the church does not live in a vacuum or cultural enclave, but in a society with which it is always interacting. The bishops also recognized that as leaders of the Catholic religious community they had "both the obligation and opportunity to share and interpret the moral and religious wisdom of the Catholic tradition

by applying it to the problems of war and peace.... "[8] In other words, religion can and indeed should shape the moral fiber of the nation.

Another key aspect of this pastoral letter was that it was addressed to people of other religions as well as to Catholics. It was a statement addressed to the entire nation. The threat of a nuclear holocaust was not a merely Catholic issue; it was an issue of national importance. Such a strategy indicated how far Catholics had come in terms of their own self-confidence about their role in American society. They were no longer outsiders, but loyal Americans who were able to offer a critique of the nation's defense policy in a forceful and unapologetic manner.

In addition, the letter was a sign of the new era in American Catholicism, an era when issues of social justice became paramount. Between 1966 and 1988 the American hierarchy issued 188 official statements and letters and more than half of these addressed issues of social justice.[9] The influence of Vatican II was decisive in shaping this perspective. In fact, "the influence of the council, particularly of the *Pastoral Constitution on the Church in the Modern World*, could be seen on virtually every page of the bishops' letter" on peace. J. Bryan Hehir, the principal author of the letter, did indeed acknowledge that the letter was "both a product of and a response to the pastoral constitution."[10]

A second concern of the bishops was the national economy and how it "touches human life and whether it protects or undermines the dignity of the human person."[11] This was the issue addressed in their 1986 pastoral letter, *Economic Justice for All*. Since the late nineteenth century the Catholic Church in the person of the pope has been issuing pastoral letters on economic issues. Taking their cue from the pope and seeing the need for speaking out on social issues, the American hierarchy had also established a tradition of issuing pastoral statements on the economy. The most notable of these was the 1919 statement drafted by John Ryan, "Bishops' Program of

Social Reconstruction." Thus, the 1986 letter was able to draw on a rich tradition of Catholic social teaching. However, it was quite different from earlier statements. Like the peace pastoral it was addressed both to Catholics and to people of other religions. Once again the writing of the pastoral letter took place in public over the course of two years. The committee charged with drafting the letter consulted more than two hundred experts in various fields related to the economy. In addition, the letter went through three drafts before the entire hierarchy finally approved it.

The American public was no longer inclined to view such statements as parochial Catholic documents. The religious climate of the nation had changed, and the sense of denominationalism had declined. As a result, a much better atmosphere of interdenominational cooperation and respect held sway. Another key point of this document was the emphasis on the dignity of all human persons. Like the threat of war, the economy was not a Catholic concern, but a human concern. This was the main principle of the letter from which all else flowed. "We judge any economic system by what it does for and to people, and by how it permits all to participate in it," the bishops declared. They further reminded Americans that "the economy should serve people and not the other way around."[12]

A third concern of the bishops was abortion. For the past thirty years the hierarchy has continually and resolutely addressed this ethical issue. Like the issues of peace and the economy, abortion was a topic discussed at Vatican II, specifically in the *Pastoral Constitution on the Church in the Modern World*, which described abortion and infanticide as "unspeakable crimes."[13] Though abortion was only briefly alluded to in this council document, it has become a major concern in the Catholic community since the late 1960s, when abortion began to become more legally acceptable. In response to increasing efforts to legalize abortion at the state level, the bishops addressed the issue in

a 1968 pastoral letter, *Human Life in Our Day*. In this letter they repeated the long-standing Catholic tradition opposing abortion. In opposing the practice of abortion, they appealed not just to a Catholic tradition but also adopted a broader perspective stating, "that abortion
was contrary to Judeo-Christian traditions inspired by love for life,
and Anglo-Saxon legal traditions protective of life and the person."[14]
In 1973 when the Supreme Court legalized abortion in *Roe v. Wade* the
bishops undertook a more aggressive antiabortion campaign. They
adopted a national pastoral plan in 1975 that was aimed at gathering
public support for a constitutional amendment that would outlaw
abortion. Their hope was to gain grassroots support for such an
amendment. Since the *Roe v. Wade* decision, abortion has become a
major social issue throughout the country, the subject of heated
debate, not just among Catholics. Catholic clergy and laity as well as
the hierarchy are involved in this debate. In the 1976 presidential election Catholic bishops spoke out against the Democratic platform
because of its pro-choice position. In the 1984 presidential election a
major controversy arose when both the governor of New York, Mario
Cuomo, and the Democratic vice-presidential candidate, Geraldine
Ferraro, both of whom are Catholic, supported legal abortion. When
the archbishop of New York, John O'Connor, publicly condemned
their position, a prolonged discussion ensued in the national media.
Some Catholics supported Cuomo and Ferraro, while others stood
behind Archbishop O'Connor.

While the issue of nuclear war has faded with the end of the cold
war, abortion continues to be a topic of national discussion, and
Catholics have become major players in this public conversation.
Although the abortion debate has divided Catholics, they still expect
their religious leaders to speak out on public issues. As one writer
stated, "They want Catholicism to be a public religion."[15]

From the perspective of history the emergence of Catholics into the public sphere in the 1960s and afterward was not surprising. Since the early twentieth century many Catholics had been urging others to break out of the enclave and, in the words of a noted Catholic of the 1920s, Carlton J. H. Hayes, "practice their religion publicly as well as privately."[16] Although they had been moving in this direction for some time, Catholics took a major leap into the public arena in the 1960s. This set the trend for what followed in the 1970s and '80s. Clearly, the American Catholic community had entered a new stage in its history and more specifically, a new era in its relationship with American society. While these changes were transforming the public presence of Catholicism, the culture of Catholicism was undergoing other changes that would reshape the beliefs and practices of the faithful. These, too, had a long history, and what has happened in these spheres of Catholic life in the past thirty years has been the result of historical developments that go back for decades, indeed in some instances for more than two hundred years.

Democracy

THE DEMOCRATIC IMPULSE HAS been present in the American Catholic community since the late eighteenth century. At that time it took the form of lay trusteeism, a model of local church government that stressed the central role of the laity in the governance of the local parish. Such a style of democracy met with stiff opposition and eventually gave way to clerical control of the local church. Nonetheless, the democratic impulse remained strong with new immigrant groups and thus persisted throughout the nineteenth century. By the early twentieth century, however, democracy in the church was all but extinct. The clergy were in control, and the laity were left to pay, pray, and obey. This style of local church governance fit very well with the prevailing understanding of church as a hierarchical organization ruled by the pope, bishops, and clergy. In the 1960s this system began to change for two principal reasons.

A major reason for such change was the understanding of church articulated at the Second Vatican Council. In the document on the church, *Lumen Gentium*, a more social and biblical idea of church emerged that described the church as the people of God. Such a description gave much greater attention to the role of the laity in the church and emphasized their responsibility for the welfare of the church. In addition, at the council itself a great deal of collaboration took place in the decision-making process. Bishops, theologians, and consultors collaborated in drafting the final council documents. The council also endorsed the concept of collegiality, in which the bishops throughout the world, together with the pope as their head, share supreme authority for the church. All of these developments at the highest level of church government fostered a climate in which cooperation and consultation between clergy and laity at the parish level became increasingly common and indeed expected.

This new understanding of church shaped the new code of canon law that appeared in 1983. For the first time church law recommended that pastoral councils be established in the parish; such parish councils reflected the concept, endorsed by Vatican II, of clergy and laity sharing responsibility for the welfare of the parish. At this level of local church government the idea of democracy once again entered the vocabulary of American Catholicism. To be sure, church law does not speak of democracy or endorse the idea of majority rule; rather it uses the word *consultative* in referring to the role of the laity in the parish council. Nonetheless, in an American environment in which democracy and the democratic process is a cultural given, the popular expectation is that *consultative* is very close to, if not synonymous with, *democratic*.

Another reason behind the return of the democratic impulse was the cultural awakening of the 1960s that encouraged a great deal of democratic activity. Citizens became involved in neighborhood organizations, and participatory democracy became a popular concept for many Americans, both young and old. Sit-ins and demonstrations became commonplace. As Catholics moved out of their enclave and felt more at home with such American traditions of freedom, shared decision making, and open communication, they sought to bring these concepts into the Catholic religious community.

Added to these influences was the emergence of a new type of clergy. Just as Catholic laity began to take on more responsibility for the welfare of Catholicism, a new breed of clergy emerged who wanted to share ownership and responsibility for the welfare of the parish with the congregation. A Jesuit priest in Holy Trinity parish in Washington, D.C., described his parish ministry as one of "colleagueship." Like many of his contemporaries he was "determined to make the laity full partners in governing their church." The parish of St. Brigid in Westbury, New York, entered the post–Vatican II era when a new pastor arrived in 1975. As one observer noted, this priest "very much embraced Vatican II. . . . He was really the one who brought to the attention of the laity that St. Brigid's was not his church; it was their church." Such a mentality contrasted dramatically with the pastor barons of the pre–Vatican II period who never dreamed of collaborating with the laity in administering the parish. In the past thirty years collaboration between clergy and laity has become the new model of parish governance. A new pastor expressed this idea in one of his first homilies to his parishioners. "I come with no agenda except that of the Lord Jesus Christ," he said. "I have no sense of who we shall hire in the future until together we discern in what direction you want the parish to go, and I have no intention of putting in kneelers or additional stained glass, as some of you fear. I intend to minister collaboratively."[17]

Catholics have now come to expect a more democratic style of management in their parishes. They expect that their voices will be heard when it comes to making major decisions in the parish. The key to this new model of government is the parish council, described by one historian as "the most significant parochial development in recent times."[18]

A study of Catholic parishes in the early 1980s concluded that 75 percent had parish councils or their equivalent. Some of these councils operate in a very democratic fashion. Annual elections take place to select council members, and those elected serve for a specified period of time. Council meetings are run in a democratic manner with majority rule operative. In such instances priest and people work together to reach a consensus to which all can agree. The priest has more of an advisory role in such a situation. Other parish councils are more consultative. This is the model spelled out in church law. The elected lay members of the council vote, but their judgment is not binding on the pastor. The decision of the priest is more definitive than advisory in this instance. A third model is more reminiscent of the pre–Vatican II church. The parish council exists, but it is more for show than for real. Acting in a more traditional authoritarian manner, the pastor retains complete control over the government of the parish. All three models are operative in the Catholic community, but in recent years most parishioners have come to expect a more consultative or indeed democratic style of government.[19]

In addition to the parish council, Catholic congregations have adopted a style of operation that includes numerous committees. Indeed, the post–Vatican II parish has become a very complex organization, with committees for worship services, religious education, finances, social action endeavors, family life, and other similar concerns. The modern parish also includes full-time staff personnel; in some parishes as many as a dozen laypeople are on the parish payroll.

Since such a large staff necessitates more meetings and planning, consultation between clergy and laity has become commonplace. At all levels decision making has become more democratic, more collegial than in the past. What took place at St. Vincent de Paul parish in Baltimore in the 1980s illustrates the impact of the democratic impulse in Catholic congregational life.

Founded in 1841, St. Vincent's parish has experienced a long and varied history. In 1973 a new pastor arrived who wanted the people to share in his ministry. Within a year he had organized a parish council, boasting to the parishioners in his first annual report that "Our Council has been elected, our Constitution ratified, our Committees established and the work has begun in earnest: we have stepped into collegial government." It soon became clear that major renovation was needed in the church, and the manner in which this took place reflected the parish's commitment to collegial government. After much planning and discussion, the parish council undertook the task of renovating the church. Their mandate was that the parishioners were to be "the principal architects in the church renovation." Town meetings were held to discuss the proposed designs; surveys of the parishioners were taken to determine what should be included in the renovation. As a result, the parishioners had defined "their requirements and expectations very carefully," knowing exactly what they wanted in the renovation program. This planning process took place over five years. Finally, a referendum was held to decide if the parish should proceed with the renovation. The response was overwhelmingly positive, and the renovation took place as the people had planned it. It would be hard to find a more democratic process. Indeed, the drafting of the Constitution of the United States and its subsequent ratification did not take as long![20]

The key to fostering democracy in the parish is the pastor, who ultimately determines the spirit of the parish. If he is a new breed of priest inspired by the vision of Vatican II and seeks to share his authority with the people, then a more democratic model of parish will emerge. If he is jealous of sharing his authority and acts in an arbitrary and authoritarian manner, then, as historian Jeffrey Burns wrote, he will "face stiff opposition and unrest among his parishioners, or his unhappy parishioners will simply attend another parish. The pastor is now expected to consult his parishioners prior to important decisions … the domineering pastor is a thing of the past."[21]

The democratization of the Catholic parish is not a uniquely American development. Parish councils have become part of the post–Vatican II church in other countries. Nonetheless, in the United States democracy is so ingrained in the culture that it cannot but reinforce the democratic impulse emerging within the Catholic community. Indeed, it has complemented the new vision of church that emerged at Vatican II to the point where American Catholics now expect a style of leadership that is more collaborative between clergy and people. Growing up in a democratic culture and in the shadow of Vatican II, people now expect the government of the local church to be more democratic.

The democratic impulse was also manifest in the drafting of the pastoral letters published by the hierarchy in the 1980s. Bishops consulted numerous experts, and only after several drafts and a final vote were the documents approved. Such collaboration and consultation were unusual, indeed unprecedented, and it reflected the desire for a more democratic decision-making process among the bishops. Even monasteries and convents have entered the age of democratic decision making. As a result they have passed from an era of blind obedience to the mandates of a superior to one of responsible participation in decision making.

The democratic culture fostered in the local congregation and in other areas of church life has raised the expectations of all Catholics.

The experience of collaboration and consultation has conditioned a generation of Catholics to think that their religion nurtures a democratic spirit among its people. This expectation comes into direct conflict with an opposing model of church that envisions Catholicism as a hierarchical institution in which the clergy are the sole decision makers. Both of these visions of church were present at Vatican II and were apparent in the council document about the church. At the council sessions the more collegial model of church became the normative, operational theology that most council fathers endorsed. The hierarchical model soon fell into disfavor.

Over the course of the past thirty years, however, the hierarchical model has made a resurgence. This has become especially evident during the pontificate of Pope John Paul II (1978–). He has increasingly endorsed a more monarchical model of church in which the pope is the boss and the boss, of course, is always right. Many American bishops appointed by John Paul II have adopted a similar style, allowing for very little consultation or collaboration in the exercise of their authority. This development has led to increased tensions within the American Catholic community. Such tensions have produced conflicts quite reminiscent of the trustee conflicts of the early nineteenth century. As historian Patrick Carey observed, they "generally involve objections to the transfer of priests without consultation with the laity, refusal to remove unwanted priests, closing or selling churches and schools without parish participation in the decision, lack of authoritative lay voice on parish councils or meaningful consultative voice in the selection of priests and bishops, and general objections to the unrestrained hierarchical powers in the church and resulting lack of fiscal accountability."[22]

These competing visions of church have divided the Catholic community. On one side is the local congregation that experiences a process of decision making that is collaborative and democratic. On the other side is a hierarchy that exercises power in a very authoritarian manner. Such division is inevitable when two different visions of church are competing with each other. This conflict is not peculiarly American; it is evident throughout the Catholic world. Nonetheless, in the United States it appears to be more deeply rooted in the Catholic community because of the intensely democratic culture that is so much a part of the American experience. Polls taken in the 1990s suggest not only that a majority of Catholics do indeed want more democracy in church affairs, but also that the percentage of those seeking such a democratization of Catholicism has increased in recent years.[23]

Every Catholic knows that the church is not a democracy. The Catholic credo is not the result of a popular vote. It is rooted in scripture and tradition. But when it comes to decision making in the governance of the church, people expect more consultation and collaboration. The challenge will be to blend the American love of democracy with the Catholic tradition of authority. To the degree that such blending takes place, Catholicism will become a much stronger community of faith.

National Identity

THE UNITED STATES ENTRY into World War II marked the beginning of a new chapter in the nation's self-understanding. "Indeed it would be difficult to exaggerate the importance of the war as the central event in shaping Americans' understanding of their national identity for the next generation."[24] The war was a great common experience not only for the millions of young men and women who served in the armed forces, but also for the entire nation. On the battlefields of Europe, Italians, Polish, Irish, and Norwegian young men fought side by side in a crucible of war that melted away the ethnic differences that once had divided them from one another. On the home front war bond rallies, air raid drills, and scrap drives instilled a sense of national purpose as well as unity within local communities. "The war years saw a heightened interest in American history, tradition, and culture, a search for common roots that would provide a means of collective identification."[25] It was a time when people emphasized that what united them was more important than what divided them. The rise of Nazism and its racial intolerance underscored the importance and value of democracy. A nationalist ideology that had been operative since the birth of the new nation was reaffirmed. It stressed the ideals of democracy, the equality of all people, and the toleration of diversity. Ethnicity was clearly on the decline as an important element in defining the nation's identity. Although ethnic differences hardly disappeared, more importance was attached to the ideal of Americanization rather than to ethnic persistence. The melting pot still remained the dominant metaphor to explain the process of cultural assimilation by which many diverse peoples were blended into one people.

In the 1950s relatively fewer immigrants came to the United States. As a result "by 1960 the percentage of foreign-born in the population had dropped to a new twentieth-century low of 5.4 percent."[26] In 1955 Ellis Island, the preeminent symbol of immigration, closed. The era of immigration was over, or so it seemed, and ethnic consciousness was at an ebb. The 1955 publication of Will Herberg's *Protestant–Catholic–Jew* confirmed this state of affairs by proclaiming that with the drying-up of immigration religion had replaced ethnicity as the preeminent badge of self-identity. As he wrote, "Religious association now became the primary context of self-identification and social location for . . . the American people."[27] Citing studies that showed an increase in ethnic intermarriage with no corresponding increase in religious intermarriage, Herberg argued that a triple melting pot of religion had replaced the single melting pot theory of the immigrant era. "America," he wrote, "is the land of the 'triple melting pot,' for it is within these three religious communities [Catholics, Protestants, and Jews] that the process of ethnic and cultural integration so characteristic of American life takes place."[28] Though Herberg had clearly exaggerated the decline of ethnic distinctions, in the assimilationist atmosphere of the 1950s his analysis was persuasive. Ethnic differences still remained, but few paid much attention to them. This would change in the 1960s.

The 1960s was an era of reform, a time when the nation began to embrace more fully the ideals of social justice. A key indicator of this change was the Civil Rights Act of 1964. Its passage in Congress marked the culmination of a civil rights movement that had gripped the country for more than a decade. The legislation barred racial discrimination in restaurants, theaters, hotels, and other places of public accommodation. It also sought to eliminate racial segregation in public schools and other public places. In 1965 President Lyndon Johnson signed into law the Voting Rights Act. This act guaranteed the right to vote for blacks living in the southern states, where they had been disenfranchised for decades. Both of these legislative decisions endeavored to make the nation a more just society by eliminating racial discrimination. Another impulse for reform focused on gender and the rights of women. President Kennedy appointed a Presidential Commission on the Status of Women in 1961. Their 1963 report urged the government to abolish sex discrimination. Prodded by the committee's report, Kennedy signed an Equal Pay Act into law that would guarantee women equal pay for equal work. The Civil Rights Act of 1964 also outlawed discrimination based on gender. Such legislation represented the first fruits of a women's liberation movement that was gaining momentum throughout the 1960s and would flourish in the decades that followed. Both the civil rights

movement and the women's movement embraced the ideal of equality, equal rights for women as well as for men, for blacks as well as for
whites. They represented the beginnings of what historian James
Patterson has called a "rights revolution."

Another key piece of this social revolution was the Immigration
and Nationality Act of 1965. Signed into law by President Johnson
at the Statue of Liberty, it eliminated racial and ethnic discrimination from the nation's immigration policy. Such discrimination had
been in effect since the National Origins Act of 1924, which discriminated against southern and eastern Europeans as well as
Asians. The 1965 legislation ushered in a new chapter in the nation's
history of immigration. Although it was amended in the 1980s and
again in the 1990s, the fundamental principles of the 1965 legislation have remained intact. In place of the national quota system,
which favored some nations over others, the new policy opened the
nation's gates to all the countries of the world. Each country would
have the same annual immigration quota of people allowed into the
United States. In place of a preference system based on racial discrimination, the 1965 legislation introduced a preference system
based on family unification.

When the members of Congress debated this legislation in the
1960s, they never envisioned its consequences. The stream of immigration changed dramatically as Asian and Hispanic immigrants far
surpassed the number of immigrants coming from Europe. In addition, the overall number of immigrants skyrocketed. Between 1966
and 1993 over 17 million immigrants have come to the United States.
In the 1990s close to one million immigrants a year entered the
country, a level of immigration undreamed of in 1965 when the new
immigration policy became law.

Together with the civil rights movement, which stressed the
importance of group consciousness, the arrival of so many people

from diverse cultures fueled the sense of ethnic awareness that had been dormant during the 1950s. Immigrants arrived in the United States with a strong sense of ethnic awareness. Ethnicity now mattered more than ever. The continual stream of immigration has sustained this heightened awareness. In the 1960s scholars cast aside the melting pot ideology, and in its place they promoted the idea of cultural pluralism, which stressed the persistence of ethnicity rather than the inevitability of assimilation. In the late 1960s and early '70s a white ethnic revival occurred among the descendants of the European immigrants. Taking a cue from the black power movement, white ethnics began to emphasize their heritage. Like black Americans they did not want to disappear into the American melting pot. Suddenly, it was fashionable to be Irish, Italian, or Polish. For the first time the U.S. Census even began to ask people to identify themselves by their ethnic origin. "Evidence of a new ethnic awareness could be found everywhere in the late 1960s and early '70s: in the stream of books offering step-by-step instructions in how to trace one's ethnic roots; in the popularity of visits to ancestral homelands; in the tendency to give children ethnically derived names. It could be found, too, in the activities of organizations formed to advance ethnic interests." Congress sanctioned the ethnic revival in 1972 with the passage of the Ethnic Heritage Studies Act, designed to inaugurate "a new federal effort to legitimize ethnicity and pluralism in America."[29]

The shift from the ideal of the melting pot to a pluralist vision was a major cultural and intellectual transformation. It ushered in a new way of thinking. This shift to cultural pluralism had major implications for the Catholic Church as it sought to minister to the new immigrants arriving in the United States. In the 1920s and '30s church leaders followed the trends in American society and pushed for the Americanization of its immigrant people, most especially the Polish and Mexicans. As the culture changed and a new mode of thinking emerged, Catholics also changed the way they thought. The immigrant church of the European era was indeed gone, but a new immigrant church composed of Asian and Hispanic Catholics was taking shape. Among these new immigrants a heightened sense of ethnic consciousness was developing that would shape their identity as Catholics in an American church. Once again, the issue of national identity challenged church leaders.

As a group, Hispanics provided the major catalyst for change within the Catholic community. For most of their history in the United States Hispanics were second-class citizens in the Catholic Church. If they wanted to be full-fledged members of the church, they had to cast aside their particular Hispanic heritage, be it Mexican, Puerto Rican, or Cuban. This situation began to change in the post-1960 era as their numbers greatly increased and respect for cultural diversity gained wider support. In 1960 the Hispanic population in the United States hovered around the seven million mark. Once the gates opened wider in the late 1960s, thousands of immigrants from Latin America settled in the United States with the result that by 1990 their numbers had increased to 22.4 million or about 9 percent of the nation's population. They came from many different countries in Latin America, but Mexicans far outnumbered the rest of the Hispanic population.

As the ethnic awakening developed in the late 1960s, Hispanic Catholics began to reevaluate their status in the church and the nation. They sought to recover the culture that, as Moises Sandoval expressed it, they had once "tried to reject in their unsuccessful efforts to enter the mainstream."[30] By the late 1960s they had launched their own civil rights movement, determined to remove the barriers of discrimination against Hispanics in the church as well as in the nation. An important aspect of this movement among Mexican Americans was the recovery of their historical roots in the ancient Aztec past. In recapturing their past, they strengthened their sense of ethnic identity. Cultural assimilation was no longer an option as far as Hispanics were concerned. The national symbol for this new sense of group consciousness in the late 1960s and early '70s was Cesar Chavez, the labor leader of the United Farm Workers' movement.

In this atmosphere of ethnic militancy a new mission emerged within the Catholic community, Hispanic ministry. A national office was set up in Washington, D.C., for Spanish-speaking Catholics. Regional offices were also established across the country to encourage and strengthen Hispanic ministry. These offices "generally shared the same priorities and concerns. In the social arena, they lobbied for social justice for immigrants, migrants, farmworkers, and the urban poor. They also sought to improve education for Hispanics. In the Church they sought to organize pastoral plans, develop leaders, train ministers, and establish basic Christian communities.... They helped communities organize behind important issues: jobs, health, education, justice. They provided a steady flow of information on immigration and political, social, and economic issues, such as the struggle of farm workers."[31] But the major development in the Hispanic Catholic awakening was the emergence of the *encuentro*, a national movement for equal rights in the American church.

The first encuentro took place in Washington, D.C., in 1972. About 250 clergy and laity attended, and a key theme of the gathering was "the Church had to change from a policy of assimilation to one of pluralism."[32] Hispanics confronted church leaders at this gathering and aired their "grievances stored over many generations." One bishop characterized their list of demands, drawn up at the conclusion of the meeting, as "the Magna Carta of Hispanic Catholics." Five years later, a second encuentro took place. Less confrontational than the first, it included over 1,200 delegates from all parts of the country. A key part of the encuentro process was the local meetings involving over 100,000 people. Those never consulted before were now able to voice their views about their place in the Catholic Church and how its leaders could meet their needs. Such meetings not only encouraged a sense of group consciousness, they also helped to strengthen the Hispanic awakening taking place within the American Catholic Church. At the encuentro itself the people gave notice "that Hispanic culture can no longer be ignored in teaching the Catholic faith."[33]

A decade and more of militant demands for recognition of the Hispanic presence in the church finally persuaded the nation's bishops that they should take a more active leadership role in the Hispanic awakening. Such initiative led to the publication of a pastoral letter in 1983, *The Hispanic Presence: Challenge and Commitment*, that once and for all cast aside the ideal of the melting pot and endorsed cultural pluralism as the guiding spirit for Hispanic ministry.

The very first sentence of the document set the tone for what followed. The bishops recognized "the Hispanic community . . . as a blessing from God" rather than a problem. They acknowledged that Hispanic Catholics brought "special gifts" to the church. Then, stating that "respect for culture is rooted in the dignity of people made in God's image," they went on to say that the "Church shows its esteem for this dignity by working to ensure that pluralism, not assimilation and uniformity, should be the guiding principle" in church and society. This was a far cry from the 1920s and indeed the 1950s, when church leaders wanted to make American Catholics out of Hispanic Catholics. Toleration and respect for cultural diversity now became an important ideal, replacing past attitudes of "cultural and ethnic dominance."[34]

Two years after the publication of the pastoral letter, a third national encuentro took place, even grander and larger than the previous two. One of its major accomplishments was the publication in

1987 of a national pastoral plan for Hispanic ministry. The entire thrust of the plan was to respect the "cultural values and religious traditions" of the Hispanic people by promoting a model of church "incarnate in the reality of the Hispanic people and open to the diversity of cultures."[35] The implementation of the plan would affect the entirety of church life—its worship, preaching, catechesis, formation of lay ministers, schools, and the education of clergy. A major thrust of both the bishops' letter and the pastoral plan was the emphasis on social justice, especially "those social concerns which most directly affect the Hispanic community, among them voting rights, discrimination, immigration rights, the status of farm workers, bilingualism and pluralism."[36]

The recognition of cultural pluralism had also permeated other segments of the Catholic community. Developments within American society surely had an influence on this transformation, but the impact of the Second Vatican Council cannot be discounted. As a result of the council, Catholicism was no longer viewed as a European religion exported to other parts of the globe. Such an awareness was most evident in the council's statement on the role of the church in the world, which stated that the Church "is not bound exclusively and indissolubly to any race or nation, nor to any particular way of life or any customary pattern of living, ancient or recent."[37] Such universalist thinking was visible in the deliberations of an American church gathering convened to commemorate the nation's bicentennial in 1976. One of its recommendations stated that Catholics must "recognize that our society is not a melting pot, but is composed of a rich diversity of ethnic, racial, and cultural groups...." It went on to recommend that "church leadership at all levels clearly assert its commitment to a unity of faith in a pluralism which recognizes and appreciates the right of diverse ethnic, racial, and cultural groups to maintain and develop their traditional culture...."[38] Four years later, the national office of the Catholic hierarchy issued a statement on cultural pluralism, urging "our Catholic people and all others as well to welcome wholeheartedly the new expressions of ethnic diversity, not as a sign of division, but one of recognition of the richness of the American heritage."[39]

The civil rights awakening among black Americans ignited a similar movement within the Catholic Church. Like Hispanics, black Catholics wanted not only an end to discrimination in the church, they also wanted their unique cultural traditions to be acknowledged. A key moment in this awakening took place in 1984, when the ten black Catholic bishops of the United States issued a pastoral letter stressing the importance of recognizing African-American culture in the church's worship services. The church in the United States must "reflect the richness of African-American history and its heritage." Rather than try to mold African Americans into an ideal white Catholic type, the church "must preserve its multicultural identity."[40] By the 1980s blacks had begun to incorporate art, music, and symbols from African-American history and culture into the Catholic liturgy. This black Catholic consciousness continued to develop during the next few years as people across the country prepared for a national Black Catholic Congress. At this congress held in 1987, a national pastoral plan was drawn up. Reflecting the ethnic awakening that had occurred within the black Catholic community, it articulated the unique gifts and aspirations of this people. In the 1990s other national gatherings took place reaffirming the importance and uniqueness of African-American culture within the Catholic Church.

Since the passage of the 1965 immigration act, scores of Asian immigrants have settled in the United States. In 1960 fewer than one million Asians lived in the United States, but by 1990 their numbers had increased to over seven million. Asians, like Hispanics, come from many different countries, each of which has a unique culture.

The Chinese are the largest Asian community in the country, but very few of them are Catholic. The Filipinos are the next largest group, and a good number are Catholic. In fact, by 1990 as many as one-fourth of the Catholic population of the San Francisco archdiocese was Filipino. Vietnamese are another large Catholic immigrant group. About one million Vietnamese live in the United States, of whom about one-quarter are Catholic, with the largest number living in California. There are more than four hundred Vietnamese priests working in the United States, along with a number of religious orders of men as well as women. Vietnamese Catholics promote the use of their native language in religious instruction and celebrate their own religious feasts, and they have developed a number of religious publications.

The immigration of so many Asians coupled with the influx of Hispanics has intensified the multicultural dimension of American Catholicism. This development is seen most clearly in California, the favored destination of immigrants in recent years. From 1985 to 1995 close to four million immigrants arrived in California. They came predominantly from Mexico, as well as Latin America and Asia. The church in California has once again become an immigrant church, serving the needs of an incredibly diverse number of cultural communities. In Los Angeles there are as many as seventy-two different ethnic groups within the Catholic Church; on any Sunday the Catholic Mass is celebrated in forty-seven languages. The national parish (now called the personal parish) has come back into vogue after a long period dating back to the post–World War I era when it was regarded as an obstacle in the Americanization process. It is now once again viewed as an essential institution in the evangelization of the new immigrants. Pastoral plans detailing how the church can best minister to the new immigrants have become commonplace. Reflecting the unusual diversity of the new immigration, the multiethnic parish has become a common phenomenon throughout the country. St. Brigid's parish, located in Westbury, New York, is typical of this new type of parish. Every Sunday the Mass is celebrated in four different languages—English, Spanish, Italian, and Creole. Multicultural liturgies on major feast days are also common. On such occasions the priest even preaches in four different languages.[41] In Daly City, California, St. Andrew's parish established a Cultural Exchange Committee in order to promote greater understanding of the various cultures present in the parish; representatives from eight different nationalities are on the committee. St. Thomas parish in Los Angeles ministers to Hispanic Catholics, but they come from several different Latin American countries, each with their own religious traditions.[42]

Ethnic diversity has been a trademark of American Catholicism. This was true in the immigrant era of the nineteenth and early twentieth centuries, but it is much more pronounced as the church enters the twenty-first century. Along with such diversity is found a new attitude toward the newcomers. In 1915, when George Mundelein was appointed archbishop of Chicago, the local newspaper noted that "he is fitted for the Archbishop of Chicago where the Gospel is preached in twenty-five languages, but where Catholics are all Americans in the making."[43] Today in a city such as Los Angeles the gospel is preached in as many as forty-seven languages. More significant, church leaders are much more open to the richness and vitality of the many different cultures that make up the Catholic mosaic. The Americanization model of Mundelein's era is no longer operative. The pope himself made this point in 1987, when he visited Los Angeles. "Today in the church in Los Angeles," he said, "Christ is Anglo and Hispanic, Christ is Chinese and black, Christ is Vietnamese and Irish, Christ is Korean and Italian, Christ is Japanese and Filipino, Christ is Native American, Croatian, Samoan, and many other ethnic groups." He urged Catholics to have a "keen sensitivity to authentic cultures" and to proclaim the gospel in the language of the people and incorporate into its ministry the distinctive traditions of the various ethnic groups in the city.[44]

As a result of the new wave of immigration Americans have celebrated the cultural pluralism that now defines the nation more than ever before. A major shift has taken place from the nativist 1920s and 1950s, when ethnic discrimination and intolerance were commonplace. People now search for a new definition of what it means to be American in a multicultural society. An integral element in that definition must be ethnicity. However, there must also be a unifying ingredient that binds the society together. *E pluribus unum* still remains the challenge facing the nation. How it negotiates and bridges the distance between the one and the many, American and ethnic, will be a major challenge of the twenty-first century. As American society has changed, so has the church. The same challenge of the one and the many also faces the Catholic Church. It continually advocates unity, a unity of faith, but it must do so within a multicultural society that respects diversity not only among cultures but also among the religious traditions of these various cultures. One faith but many cultures will become the trademark of Catholicism in the coming century. This will mean that the expression of Catholicism among Hispanics, Filipinos, Vietnamese, Anglos, and the many other groups that make up the Catholic mosaic will indeed be different. Diversity rather than homogeneity in the practice of religion will become common. The Catholic faith will become grounded in the many diverse cultures of the people. What separates them will become as important as what unites them as each ethnic group seeks to find its place within the nation and the church.

At the dawn of the twenty-first century immigration to the United States will continue on a large scale. Among the immigrants ethnicity will continue to provide an important cultural defense as they adjust to life in a new cultural environment. A key element shaping their sense of ethnic identity will be religion. Throughout the first age of the immigrant church, the European phase in the nineteenth and early twentieth centuries, ethnicity and religion defined the immigrant church, which became an anchor of stability for the newcomers to America. It was the one institution that they could readily identify with during a period of transition from one cultural milieu to another. For this reason religion took on an importance that in some instances it did not have in the old country. This was certainly the case with the Irish in the mid-nineteenth century. They became better practicing Catholics in the United States than they were in Ireland because of the close bond between religion and ethnicity that developed within the immigrant Irish community. As long as immigration continues to shape the nation and the church, Catholicism will continue to acquire strength and vitality because of its central role in shaping the ethnic identity of the newcomers. By endorsing a cultural pluralism that recognizes the unique richness of each ethnic group, the church and its leaders have acknowledged the importance of the ethnic dynamic in defining what it means to be Catholic in the United States. This major shift in thinking occurred in the closing decades of the twentieth century. Without question, it will continue to shape the future of American Catholicism, the vitality of which will be closely linked to how well the church serves the immigrant communities that make up the Catholic mosaic.

Gender

THE SPIRIT OF REFORM unleashed in the 1960s radically changed the role of women in American society. Looking back with almost a half century of perspective, the differences between the

1950s and the 1990s appear dramatic. In the 1950s "the image of woman as homemaker and child rearer, more passive, less competitive, and somewhat dimmer than man" was the ideal.[45] This domestic ideology permeated society and appeared timeless and unchanging. A woman's place was in the home as faithful wife and nurturing mother. Asked what he sought in the woman he would marry, a Princeton student in the class of 1955 replied, "Although an Ivy League type, she will also be centered in the home, a housewife. Perhaps at forty-five, with the children grown up, she will go in for hospital work and so on."[46] In his mind and the mind of his classmates all a woman needed to be happy was a husband and a few children. The advertising industry promoted this image and together with an emerging television industry brought such ideas into the home every day of the week.

Certain trends were developing in the 1950s, however, that were slowly but steadily challenging the domestic ideal. More married women worked outside the home. In 1950 only 21 percent of married women worked; by 1960 the number had risen to 30 percent, and it reached 40 percent by the end of the decade. By the 1980s the working wife had become commonplace, with one of every two wives working.

A second major trend was the increasing number of women going to college. This trend was noticeable in the 1950s, but it exploded in the 1960s, when the number of women college students doubled. These were the women who would provide the leadership in the women's movement—"a core of young women with egalitarian ideals, high expectations, and little investment in traditional roles."[47] The publication of *The Feminine Mystique* in 1963 tapped into these developments by exposing the myth of domesticity.

Betty Friedan's *The Feminine Mystique* is justly linked to the resurgence of the women's movement in the 1960s. In her reflections on the women's movement, Sheila Tobias wrote that "almost every woman of my generation can remember where she was the day she first came across Betty Friedan's book." One woman recalled her experience of reading the book for a college class. "I couldn't put the book down," she said. "I almost forgot I was supposed to read it for a course. It was riveting. . . . My sense of life's possibilities changed that day, and they have never been the same." Friedan demonstrated that the ideology of domesticity, or what she called the feminine mystique, was historically conditioned. It did not have to be. According to Tobias, "Her analysis actually changed the course of American women's history, first by identifying a phenomenon—the feminine mystique—no one had previously isolated or described, then by providing an analysis of how such a set of beliefs came into being, and finally, by giving the feminine mystique a limited place in history."[48] It soon became one of the most widely read books of the 1960s, selling over five million copies by 1970.

Another key turning point in the development of the women's movement was President Kennedy's appointment of a Presidential Commission on the Status of Women in 1961. Their report, issued in 1963, created "a new agenda of women's demands." Many of their recommendations, such as government-funded day-care programs, paid maternity leaves, and promotion of women to upper-level federal jobs, eventually became accepted practices. Prodded by the committee's report, Kennedy signed an Equal Pay Act into law in 1963, which sought to guarantee women equal pay for equal work. Once the presidential commission disbanded, similar state commissions were established to continue the work of the presidential commission. These committees not only kept the women's issue alive across the country, they also tended to serve as "a consciousness-raising experience for most of the women involved."[49] Members of these state committees eventually became leaders in the women's movement.

The third turning point that separated the 1950s and the ideology of domesticity from the feminist revival of the 1960s was the civil rights movement. The issue of civil rights for African Americans was a crusade that touched every American during the 1960s. It sparked a rights revolution that sought equality for all people regardless of race, gender, or religion. The Civil Rights Act of 1964 and the Voting Rights Act of 1965 were the legislative foundations for the movement. The 1964 legislation was especially pertinent to the feminist revival because it included a section that outlawed discrimination in employment based on sex as well as on race or religion. This law provided the basis for the transformation of the workplace that would occur in the coming years.

By the 1970s there was widespread public support for the idea of gender equality. As a result of this shift in thinking, large numbers of women began to pursue careers in areas previously closed to them, such as law, medicine, and business. The idea of gender equality also permeated the religious sphere. Women began to enroll in the nation's theological schools in record numbers. In the 1970s the number of female theology students increased more than 200 percent. By the 1990s about one-third of the students in these schools were women. In some denominations the figure was 50 percent or higher.[50] During this period the issue of gender equality became linked with women's ordination, with the result that the ordination of women became more common among the nation's denominations. Once again the 1970s was a decisive time in this trend. As Mark Chaves noted, "More denominations began to ordain women during the 1970s than during any other decade in the past 140 years." Although women made up only 3 percent of the clergy in 1970, by the 1990s 12 percent of the clergy were female. Half of all the Protestant denominations in the country now ordain women, as well as most of the branches of Judaism. Moreover, by the mid-1990s women had reached the highest positions of authority in some major denominations. Lutherans had elected two female bishops, the Methodists had elected eight, and the Episcopalians in the United States had four women bishops. Among the Presbyterians numerous women occupied key positions in their presbyteries.[51]

A key catalyst in this development was the feminist revival of the 1960s and '70s. According to Mark Chaves in his study of women's ordination, "The most prominent proponents of women's ordination were connected to and influenced by the secular women's movement."[52]

Catholic Church authorities strongly opposed the ordination of women, chiefly because Jesus chose only men to be his apostles. For this reason a male priesthood has remained the normative tradition for centuries, and church authorities are not likely to change it any time soon. Nevertheless, the ordination of women has become a topic of debate among Catholics since the 1970s. Indeed, it remains one of the most divisive issues confronting American Catholicism. As was true within the Protestant churches, the leading proponents of women's ordination were linked to the secular women's movement. The debate over the ordination of women, however, was just one phase of the gender revolution that took place among Catholics.

Traditionally, women were heavily involved in religion. As one woman noted, "Religion is a woman's job."[53] Within the Catholic community women were the backbone of parish life. Women's sodalities were prominent in parishes throughout the nineteenth and early twentieth centuries. Parish missions attracted more women than men. Devotions to female saints were very popular, underscoring the strong feminine quality of Catholic devotionalism. Women regularly outnumbered men at Sunday Mass. The number of women who entered the convent far exceeded the number of men who became priests. By 1965 there were three women religious for every priest, and these sisters served as the backbone of the parochial school system. They also administered numerous Catholic hospitals located throughout the country. Women's involvement in the life of the church was not something new in the post–1960s era. What was new was the type of involvement and the rising chorus of support for gender equality.

Up until the 1960s the ideology of domesticity shaped the role of women in the church. The home was their sanctuary, and they were called to be "saints in aprons." The women's movement challenged such thinking, and eventually a more public, career-oriented model became a popular alternative to the domestic ideal. The Second Vatican Council was another major impulse for change. Though it did not address the issue of gender equality in the church, it did encourage women to "participate more widely in the various fields of the Church's apostolate."[54] Its major influence was to open the church to the world by encouraging Catholics to take a more active and public role in society. By encouraging the development of a more public Catholicism, it was urging women as well as men to become more engaged in the public arena. Many Catholic women did just that by becoming involved in the civil rights movement as well as the peace movement. They also became major actors in the new style of Catholicism that was emerging in the 1960s and '70s.

Post–Vatican II Catholicism has largely become the church of the laity. Laypeople have become much more involved in parish ministry since the 1960s, taking on new roles previously reserved to the priest, such as ministers of the Eucharist at Mass, readers of the scriptures, and directors of worship. By 1999 as many as 29,146 laypeople and religious were working as paid parish ministers in the nation's Catholic parishes. Eighty-two percent of these parish ministers were women, and seven out of ten were laypeople. Such a development has been described as "a virtual revolution in pastoral ministry." Not only are the laity taking over work traditionally associated with the priest, but the preponderance of women in pastoral ministry has reshaped this ministry. Parishes are now much more "engaged in the kinds of support and nurturing activities that have been characteristically associated with women."[55] Women have also emerged as influential leaders in the local parish. Beyond the parish women now are serving as chaplains in hospitals and colleges. A revision of church law in 1983 allowed women to become officials in the administration of the Catholic diocese. It was not long before women emerged as diocesan chancellors and judges in ecclesiastical courts of law. By 1998 women held close to half (47 percent) of the nation's diocesan administrative and professional positions.[56]

Even though the Roman Catholic Church does not allow women to be ordained as priests, in recent years church authorities have permitted women to be pastors of parishes. This is a rather odd compromise, but the reasons are clear. While the Catholic population has steadily increased since the 1960s, the number of clergy has declined. This trend has created a shortage of priests to administer parishes, resulting in an increasing number of parishes without priests. At the same time the feminist revival of the past four decades has transformed the role of women in the church. Among Catholics in particular women are much more accepted as leaders in the parish, and studies done in the 1990s indicate that close to two-thirds of the Catholics surveyed approve of female priests.[57] This has been a very dramatic change in the thinking of Catholics. Acknowledging the priest shortage, the new code of church law allowed a person who is not a priest to be pastor of a parish. All of these developments came together by the late 1980s and early '90s and made possible a new phenomenon in the Catholic Church, the woman pastor.

Studies of priestless parishes in the United States suggest that there are more than 2,000 parishes without a resident priest. An increasing number of these, at last count 437, have a person who is not a priest in charge of the pastoral ministry of the parish.[58] Many of these pastors are women. Initially, most women pastors were members of religious orders, but in recent years more laywomen have become pastors of priestless parishes. In his study of American Catholics, Charles Morris included a profile of Sister Honora Remes, pastor of St. Mary's Cathedral parish in Saginaw, Michigan. She "does everything a pastor does, except say Mass and administer the sacraments. She hires the staff, manages the finances and budget, provides counseling and advice to parishioners, oversees the liturgies and supervises the religious, social, and educational programs." As one parishioner said, "She's the pastor.... She's in charge of everything, except that Fr. Groh comes in to say Mass." This has drastically changed the role of the priest. In St. Mary's, as in most priestless parishes, the priest is "a special guest star, a visiting shaman who does his routine and is gone."[59]

This transformation is a far cry from the 1940s and '50s, when the parish was so intimately identified with the priest. In those days laypeople were the pastor's helpers, and no one bothered to ask who was boss. The priest was the patriarch of the parish, and his word was law. Though many reasons can account for the changes that have taken place in parish ministry in the closing decades of the twentieth century, the feminist revival clearly stands out as a major force in this transformation.

The women's movement also provided a major catalyst of change among women religious. Indeed, the changes that have taken place among women religious in recent years have been one of the most dramatic developments in modern American Catholicism. In the 1950s the cloister culture that had shaped the lives of American sisters began to crack. A key reason was the educational and professional development taking place among the sisters. Then, in the

1960s, a major upheaval transformed the cloister culture. The two principal forces behind this upheaval were, like so much in U.S. Catholicism, grounded in both religion and culture, namely Vatican II and the women's movement.

In her study of Catholic religious orders Patricia Wittberg argues convincingly that two council documents on the church "would deeply affect religious communities." The first was the *Dogmatic Constitution on the Church*. This document democratized the church in that it emphasized the egalitarian nature of the church as the people of God in which "all members of the Church had received an equal call 'to the fullness of the Christian life and the perfection of charity' simply by virtue of their baptism." Wittberg goes on to say that "the importance of this seemingly innocuous statement cannot be stressed enough. *In one stroke, it nullified the basic ideological foundation for eighteen centuries of Roman Catholic religious life*." (her italics) In attacking the "very definition of religious life" it undermined the elitist tradition that put clergy and religious on a pedestal above the laity. Furthermore, since they were not ordained, women religious were now on the same level as the laity, sharing the same call to holiness by virtue of their baptism. The council's *Pastoral Constitution on the Church in the Modern World* sought to end the separation of church and society by urging Catholics "to be in solidarity with the very world its religious orders had so long shunned."[60] This statement signaled the end of the cloister culture by dissolving the boundaries that set women religious apart from the rest of society. "Whether perceived as capitulation or commitment," wrote historian Patricia Byrne, this "new orientation toward the world was the most profound reality underlying all change in convent life during the 60s and it had concrete effects in the works sisters chose to do."[61]

The new thinking about the place of women religious in church and society had been developing for a number of years. By the time the

Vatican Council was under way, the status of women religious was ripe for change. One telling indication was the popularity of the book *The Nun in the World*, written by Cardinal Suenens of Belgium. It appeared just as the council was starting. Suenens, a major supporter of the council and its reform agenda, opened his book by acknowledging the advancement of women that had taken place in recent years. He went on to urge sisters to renew their mission in society by becoming more engaged in the world beyond the cloister. His book became a best-seller. As Patricia Byrne noted, "It was devoured by sisters."[62]

At the very moment that sisters were re-evaluating their self-identity as women religious, a resurgence of the women's movement was beginning in the United States. This movement and the consciousness raising it inspired had a major impact on women religious. They now began to think of themselves as women as well as sisters. Their dress changed, and they began to "present themselves as women in appearance." In acquiring a new self-identity as women, they "have come to understand that part of their struggle for meaning involves coming to terms with the implications, personal and public, of being women." The women's movement not only transformed the self-identity of individual sisters, it also affected the manner in which religious communities of women functioned. One study concluded that the feminist movement has impacted the "majority of communities . . . in styles of worshipping, gathering, ministering, and governing." Moreover, it has done so in a very American manner. Communities of women religious appeal to American culture to support many of the changes that have taken place in their communities. As one sister said, "Our American culture is a very alive culture and religious life in the United States must be an ongoing living expression of our reality." As a result, the manner in which communities make decisions has become more participatory, more democratic.[63]

The Leadership Conference of Women Religious, a national association of the leaders of American women religious communities, has also undergone a process of Americanization since the 1970s. Their members "adopted distinctly American strategies—joining in public discourse and dissent, calling for equal access to power, championing the cause of the excluded, and advocating policies to guarantee due process." In previous years women religious had ignored culture in their analysis of the human condition. Now they consciously incorporate American culture as pertinent to their religious identity both as individuals and as corporate bodies.[64]

Through much of the twentieth century women religious followed a Roman model of religious life. Since the 1960s they have adopted a model that is deeply rooted in American culture, grounded in freedom of speech, due process, open deliberations, and participation in policy making. Such values are at odds with the authoritarian and hierarchical Roman model that emerged in the early twentieth century. This has led to conflict between American women religious and church authorities both in Rome and in the United States. Such areas of conflict include the change in the dress of women religious, the political involvement of sisters, and the democratization of governance in religious orders of women.

The women's movement has touched other areas of Catholic life. As many as one-third of the students studying in Catholic schools of theology are female.[65] In addition, a good number of distinguished theologians are women. They have brought a new agenda to the study of theology by incorporating gender as a key analytical tool in their work, resulting in a reinterpretation of scripture, theology, and history. In fact, according to historian Susan Hill Lindley, "Some of the most creative and influential feminist theologians" come from the Roman Catholic tradition.[66] The feminist revival has also reshaped the spiritual lives of many women. Theologian Elisabeth

Schussler Fiorenza wrote that "at the heart of the spiritual feminist quest is the quest for women's power, freedom and independence." It is most often in small gatherings of women where such searching takes place. This is where many women pray, study, and celebrate their faith. Some find their freedom and independence by reinterpreting the tradition from a feminist perspective and by looking differently at the female saints. Others have found this tradition inadequate and seek alternatives to the classical expressions of spirituality. Such alternatives include goddess worship as well as a political spirituality rooted in liberation theology and the desire for social justice.[67]

Numbers of women, both religious and lay, began to gather in informal groups to celebrate the Eucharist without including a priest as their celebrant. This is a fairly widespread phenomenon found throughout the country. Generally, they meet monthly, and many are still active in their local parish, but the informal gatherings for Eucharist provide support as well as the experience of worship for women who feel alienated from the church's official worship services. As one woman said, "We must attend liturgy with intellectual, emotional and spiritual blinders on in order to remain practicing members of a faith community. To pray with people whom we love and know as faith-family, we must ignore excluding language, insensitive homilies, poor liturgy. The pervasive nature of sexism in the church ... is a burden of stone strapped to the backs of women."[68]

Another major development among Catholic women is the founding of feminist organizations that seek church reform and offer mutual support of women. Two of the more prominent groups are the Women's Ordination Conference and Woman Church. The Women's Ordination Conference held their first national gathering in 1975, and they have been meeting regularly since then. It seeks "to advance women's rights, equality, and leadership both within and outside church doors in the U.S. and in collaboration with the world-wide women's movement."[69] This organization helped to found Woman Church in 1983. This is a loosely organized group of Catholic women who want a future church free of patriarchy and sexism. In addition to their occasional national gatherings, members of Woman Church also gather in small groups to celebrate Eucharist.

The formation of these and many other feminist organizations reflects the anger and frustration of many Catholic women with an institution that they view as riddled with patriarchal authoritarianism. Several studies have concluded that Catholic women are quite angry with their church. "More women feel alienated in the Catholic Church than in any other denomination," noted one study.[70] The alienation is so intense that many women leave the church, while others just drop out, joining one of the largest religious communities in the United States, the 20 million Catholics who do not belong to a parish. Such a development was one of the reasons why, after several years of discussion, the nation's bishops decided in 1983 to write a pastoral letter addressing the concerns of women.

After consulting more than 75,000 women throughout the country, a first draft of the pastoral letter appeared in 1988. It sparked a storm of controversy. Conservative Catholic women did not like it because it did not fully address their concerns about family, the distinctiveness of female nature, and respect for the teaching authority of the pope. Liberals did not approve of the draft because while proclaiming gender equality the pastoral letter nevertheless still denied women access to the priesthood and to equal decision-making power in the church. This was a fundamental contradiction that would never be overcome throughout the process of writing the pastoral letter. As one analysis stated, "The question of ordination remains the Achilles' heel of the document... The exclusion of women from ordination remains and continues to draw into question all the efforts of the bishops to repudiate the sin and structures of sexism."[71] In the next four years the pastoral went through three more drafts. The process of discussion and revision continued to generate controversy among Catholics about the role of women in the church. Vatican authorities sought to bring the document more in line with traditional teaching about the role of women in the church and society. Along with many American bishops, Vatican officials "insisted on expansion of the sections on the ordination of women, birth control, sexual ethics and respect for the authority of the magisterium. As each draft became more acceptable to Rome, it became less acceptable to many U.S. Catholic women." At their annual meeting in fall 1992 the majority of bishops voted to accept the fourth and final draft of the letter, but the required two-thirds majority for approval did not materialize. This was the first time that a pastoral letter of the hierarchy was "defeated on the floor of the conference."[72] The entire nine-year process proved to be very divisive. Even the committee writing the letter was divided between those stressing more traditional values and those who supported the final version of the letter. The most critical issue remained the application of the principle of gender equality, specifically "the participation of women in ministry in the church and especially the discussion on the ordination of women." One bishop stated that the vote on the document "became a referendum on women's ordination and the teaching office of bishops rather than on the content of the letter."[73]

It is no surprise that the women's movement has affected the Catholic Church; what is surprising is how much controversy this has caused. Without a doubt one of the most painful issues within the American Catholic community is the relationship of the church to women. The Catholic Church's rejection of the ordination of women remains a critical problem as the church moves into the new millennium.

One reason for this continuing controversy is that women's ordination has a symbolic meaning that goes beyond women in the pulpit and at the altar. Because it is linked with gender equality, the refusal to allow the ordination of women means resistance to modernity. Mark Chaves writes, "Rules about women's ordination largely serve as symbolic display to the outside world, and they point to (or away from) a broader liberal agenda associated with modernity and religious accommodation to the spirit of the age. From this perspective, a denomination's formal policy about women's ordination is less an indicator of women's literal status within the denomination and more an enactment of its position vis-à-vis the liberal and modern agenda of institutionalizing individual rights."[74] The archbishop of Milwaukee, Rembert Weakland, in an op-ed essay in the *New York Times*, expressed much the same idea when he wrote that in its relation to the modern world "the church is at a turning point and the role of women could be its new Galileo."[75]

Devotional Catholicism

ONE OF THE MOST revolutionary changes in Roman Catholicism since the 1960s has been the overhaul of the church's rituals of worship. The Second Vatican Council centered its first efforts at reform on the liturgy. The chief focus of this reform was the Mass. In the pre–Vatican II era "rigid uniformity," as the council stated, characterized the church's liturgy. The Mass was the same throughout the world. Whether it was Calcutta or New York, Saigon or Bogotá, the priest silently prayed the prayers of the Mass in Latin with his back to the people. There was a certain charm to such uniformity that Catholics never ceased to mention. Wherever a Catholic went in the world, the Mass was the same. A Latin language and a uniform, standardized ritual united worshiping Catholics regardless of their nationality. No one was an outsider at the Catholic Mass. The council changed all that. Not only did it encourage the active participation of the people in the liturgy, it also encouraged the adaptation of the church's liturgy to different cultures. It abandoned the idea of "rigid uniformity," and in its place endorsed the idea of adaptation or what would become recognized as acculturation. This would prove to be a most revolutionary decision, the full implications of which the bishops at the council never fully realized.

A key decision of the council was to allow the Mass to be celebrated in the language of the people rather than in Latin. In one momentous act the council abandoned an ancient tradition. Gone was the uniformity of the Mass. Cultural adaptation, in this instance the use of the vernacular, replaced the tradition of sameness and uniformity. Many other aspects of the Mass also changed. Piece by piece, ritual by ritual, a new Mass gradually took shape. By the end of the 1960s most of the changes were in place and a new Catholic Mass had replaced the old-style Latin Mass. Though Mass is still occasionally celebrated in Latin, the Mass in the vernacular has become the norm throughout the world.

A major consequence of the revision of the liturgy was a decline in many of the devotions that had become so normative and popular among Catholics. By emphasizing the Mass as the summit and source of the Christian life, the council focused all attention on the new Mass. The clergy encouraged people, in some instances even commanded them, to put aside any private devotions they were accustomed to practice during Mass. They were now to become more active participants in the celebration of the liturgy. The Mass was to be the center of their prayer life. With such an increased attention given to the Mass, popular devotions like the rosary, novenas in honor of the saints, benediction of the Blessed Sacrament, Forty Hours, and stations of the cross were not strongly promoted. Though never prohibited in the post–Vatican II era, they were pushed to the margins of Catholic life. These devotions consequently underwent a dramatic decline in popularity as the new Mass became the center of Catholic worship. A 1968 Pittsburgh survey, just a few years after the council, clearly indicated that many devotions central to the life of the immigrant church had declined in popularity. More than 40 percent of the parishes surveyed reported that such devotions as Forty Hours, novenas, and First Friday Mass attendance were in decline. A more recent national study discovered that beyond the practice of weekly prayer "only a minority of parishioners engage in other pre–Vatican II practices. Only 35 percent practice devotions to Mary or a special saint at least once a week; only 27 percent of Catholics pray the rosary at least once a week; and even fewer (25 percent) go to private confession several times a year." An even more telling indication of the sea change in the prayer life of Catholics is that Catholics "who experienced their formative years either during or after Vatican II are much less likely to believe in and practice traditional Catholicism."[76]

The reasons for this decline are not as obvious as the decline itself. Certainly many reasons were related to the changes taking place within Catholicism. Promoted as the summit and source of the Christian life, the new Mass became the center of attention and pushed other devotions to the margins of Catholic life. The use of English in the Mass made it more comprehensible and accessible to the people. This undermined the uniqueness of the English-language devotions and subsequently weakened their popularity. New devotional practices were encouraged, such as reading the Bible and participating in small prayer groups. Though they have never reached the popularity that the traditional devotional practices enjoyed in the pre–Vatican II era, their endorsement by the clergy weakened the status of traditional devotional practices. Another reason for the decline was the emergence of a new breed of priest in the 1960s. Inspired by the new style of Catholicism articulated at the council, these priests not only endorsed the new liturgy, they also discouraged devotional practices associated with the "old" pre–Vatican II church. Organizations that promoted traditional religious practices began to decline in popularity. Their decline meant that the religious practices associated with devotional Catholicism lost a major booster. Another major reason for the decline was the emergence of a new religious sensibility. Identified with the style of public Catholicism that emerged in the early twentieth century and subsequently endorsed at the council, this type of religion encouraged the pursuit of holiness in the world, not apart from it. Church leaders encouraged Catholics to become involved in such issues as the crusade for racial justice, the war against poverty, and urban renewal. For many Catholics involvement in these issues replaced participation in traditional devotional practices that tended to be much more oriented to an individual pursuit of holiness apart from the world and its concerns.

Cultural reasons also help to explain the demise of devotional Catholicism. One key influence was the changing understanding of the role of women in society and in the church. Without question the new model of women articulated by the feminist revival of the 1960s served to undermine women's attachment to many of the old-time devotions. Surely, many women still pray the rosary, visit Marian shrines, and honor the saints, but they have invested these practices with a new understanding of self that stands in opposition to the model of woman that was traditionally associated with devotional Catholicism. The old devotional rituals with their traditional model of femininity have lost their appeal to women who came of age in the post–1960 era. Their search for holiness takes them along paths different from those of their grandmothers.

The spread of television throughout domestic America since the 1960s has also presented a challenge to evening-scheduled rituals of devotion. The emergence of pop culture that is visual, electronic, and experiential has undermined rituals fixed on the dull recitation of set prayers. Other cultural influences may also be at work, such as the economic advancement of Catholics and their move to the suburbs. Without question, more study is needed before a definitive analysis can be offered for such a dramatic decline. Nonetheless, one point is clear—changes within American culture have had a decisive impact in the shaping of a new Catholicism.

In recent years, however, a resurgence of devotional practices associated with the pre–Vatican II era has taken place. As one writer stated, "Rumors of an increasing interest in the once popular post-Tridentine devotions circulate widely, even though little hard data have been collected to support the claims. Still, anecdotal and unscientific reports are numerous enough that liturgists cannot afford to ignore them."[77] Adoration of the Eucharist has once again become popular with some Catholics. The public recitation of the rosary and the popularity of private revelations centered on apparitions of Mary are other examples of a resurgence of the old-time religion. Visitors to shrines are on the increase as well. One reason for this resurgence is that intense emphasis on the new Catholic Mass as the summit and source of the Christian life together with the virtual disappearance of the traditional devotions has created a void in the spiritual lives of people. People found they needed more than the celebration of the Eucharist to satisfy their spiritual needs. New devotions such as Bible reading and Bible vigils were just not that successful among the people in the pew. Because of the lack of appealing new rituals of devotion, some Catholics have turned to the traditional devotions associated with pre–Vatican II Catholicism. Another reason for this resurgence may well be the restorationist movement taking place within Catholicism. Some Catholics are clearly dissatisfied with many developments that have taken place within the church since the

1960s. They urge a return to a more traditional style of Catholicism, in which order and uniformity prevail. They want to put the clergy back on a pedestal and increase respect for papal authority. As a sign of their turn to the past and its traditions, they have encouraged the re-establishment of the time-honored devotions.

Without question, devotions are an important part of an individual's religion. "In fact, to the extent that devotions can emerge with new religious symbols and reinterpret old ones, they will be meaningful and authentic. In their proper context and good use, devotions can be a means of connecting the past with the present in order to face the future. The necessity still remains of forging authentic devotional forms which will be expressive of contemporary and inculturated religious identity. Within American society, the search for identity continues. If devotions can be forged that will speak to the people of a new generation, then they will reflect the genius of the American culture and further the mission of the American church."[78] Until that happens the old-time devotions will remain an option for some Catholics.

The Vatican Council's document on the liturgy has been called "the Magna Charta of liturgical adaptation." By endorsing the idea of cultural adaptation, it encouraged Catholic communities throughout the world to adapt the new Catholic Mass and other aspects of liturgy to their cultures. In doing so, they have acknowledged the intimate bond that links religion with culture.

In the United States efforts at cultural adaptation have been most pronounced in the African-American and Hispanic communities. A key person in the African-American community was Fr. Clarence Joseph Rivers. In the 1960s he emerged as a major advocate of adapting Catholic worship to African-American culture. He "inaugurated a revolution in liturgical music ... and brought new hope, joy, and spirit to millions of Black Americans when he introduced the melodies, rhythms, harmonies, symbols and rituals of African American Sacred Song into Roman Catholic worship."[79] Throughout the 1970s African-American Catholics continued to seek ways to adapt their worship to their African-American culture. Parishes introduced elements of African-American culture such as spirituals, spontaneity, and emotive expression into their Sunday liturgies. Such elements were acknowledged as the very heart of the people. Bishop James P. Lyke, a strong advocate of an African-American liturgy, wrote, "As in jazz so in worship: spontaneity and emotive expression embody the 'genius' of black people."[80] Gospel choirs became especially popular. In 1984 the black bishops of the United States issued a pastoral letter on evangelization. They underscored the unique gifts of the black experience. "These are gifts that are part of an African past," they wrote. "For we have heard with Black ears and we have seen with Black eyes and we have understood with an African heart. We thank God for the gifts of our Catholic faith and we give thanks for the gifts of our Blackness." They went on to discuss the importance of the black cultural heritage in shaping the liturgy in the African-American community, a liturgy that "should be authentically Black . . . [and] truly Catholic." Acknowledging the principle of cultural adaptation sanctioned by the Second Vatican Council, the bishops recognized that now "there is a splendid opportunity for the vast richness of African-American culture to be expressed in our liturgy." Moreover, they encouraged clergy and laity to work to introduce "the African-American idiom into the expression of the Roman liturgy."[81]

An important step in this direction was the publication of the African-American Catholic hymnal, *Lead Me Guide Me*, in 1987. This hymnal sought to reflect both the African-American heritage and the Catholic faith. A year later, the hierarchy's subcommittee on black liturgy published a brief document, *In Spirit and Truth: Black Catholic Reflections on the Order of Mass*, which outlined the possible options for blending expressions of African-American culture with the Roman Catholic Mass. Both of these publications sought to provide some guidelines to an African-American Catholic liturgy that was exploding in many different directions. In 1990 a companion document was published, *Plenty Good Room: The Spirit and Truth of African American Catholic Worship*. A substantive theological essay, it offered a solid explanation of the principle of cultural adaptation in the liturgy and how the application of this principle could lead to an authentic African-American Catholic worship.

A poll taken in 1995 among African-American Catholics revealed that nearly two-thirds of the survey's respondents "strongly supported an increased African-American cultural emphasis in the liturgy."[82] Not only do the laity endorse the cultural adaptation of the church's worship, but black Catholic clergy are also committed to such an endeavor and together with the laity have made significant steps in that direction. In the past thirty years especially, African-American culture has had a decisive impact in shaping the way Catholics pray. In doing so, it has introduced an entirely new chapter in the history and development of Catholic spirituality.

Another equally distinctive cultural expression of Catholic life has emerged in the Hispanic community. Prior to the Vatican II era Hispanic Catholics, Mexicans in particular, were not known for their practice of the official style of Catholicism that stressed attendance at Mass and frequent reception of the sacraments. Their religion was centered in the home and around major feast days honoring Mary or one of the saints. Thus, within the Hispanic community two expressions of religion coexisted—the official Mass and sacraments religion of the institutional church, and the popular religion of the people. Fashioned in medieval Spain and carried to Spanish America, this popular religion was deeply rooted in the history of the people. Arturo J. Perez describes this religious expression:

Popular religiosity is the ritual expression of the spiritual life of the Hispanic people. It is an expression of how the Hispanic community belongs to the Church. In conjunction with official worship, the faith life of the community is nourished through these devotions. Within popular religiosity are contained the symbols and rituals that are accepted as the right/rite way of celebrating a birth, joining two persons in marriage, bringing our beloved dead to their final place of rest, as well as initiating young women into the community through the Quinceanera (fifteenth birthday) celebration, protecting our children from evil through blessings, and acting out our prayer through promises and processions.[83]

In America this popular religion encountered the official style of Catholicism that had emerged in Europe in the sixteenth century as a result of the Council of Trent. By the early twentieth century these two expressions of religion coexisted side by side in Mexican communities in the United States. Part of the Americanization program of the Catholic hierarchy in the early twentieth century included turning Mexicans into Mass and sacraments Catholics. In this manner the clergy hoped to reduce the influence and practice of the popular religious devotions. This never happened to any large degree. Popular religion survived and continued to define and shape the religious world of the Hispanic people. As Perez noted, "Popular religiosity is the primary way the mestizo people of the Americas prayed, and still pray today."[84]

When the Second Vatican Council encouraged the cultural adaptation of the church's worship, Hispanic Catholics took up the challenge of weaving together the people's religion and the official Roman liturgy. In this manner they hoped to achieve the acculturation of the liturgy from the Hispanic perspective. This desire to reshape the Roman liturgy became part of the larger awakening taking place among Hispanic Catholics in the United States in the post–Vatican II era. Not only did Hispanics want a larger voice in the church, they also wanted to fashion a style of worship that was a creative blend of "the liturgical tradition of the Church and Hispanic traditions of popular religiosity."[85] In 1972 the Mexican American Cultural Center was founded in San Antonio, and two years later it was designated as a center for liturgical research and study. In 1979 the *Instituto de Liturgia Hispana* was founded to promote the liturgical life of the Hispanic communities. Throughout the 1980s it sponsored several national liturgical conferences. It also encouraged the continued Hispanicization of the liturgy. Spanish-language texts were prepared so that Spanish-language liturgies could be celebrated. Eventually, church authorities in Rome recognized Spanish as an official liturgical language in the United States. This was deemed a "breakthrough." It was not long before "New texts reflecting the reality of Hispanic life, the affirmation of Hispanic traditions of prayer as authentic sources of spirituality, and liturgical organizations accepting Hispanic persons as advisors and consultants . . . moved Hispanic liturgy more into the mainstream of Church life."[86]

As in the African-American community, music helped to shape the liturgy among Hispanics. Parishes organized choirs complete with guitars, percussion, and other instruments "more proper to the different Hispanic ethnic groups."[87] Spanish music defined the new liturgy in these parishes. An entire new industry of music publishing emerged as a result of the increase in Spanish liturgical music. *La danza*, or liturgical gestures and movements, was also introduced into the liturgy. More than just dance, *la danza* includes processions on feast days, the acting out of biblical stories such as the crucifixion of Jesus on Good Friday, and the Last Supper. Each year on Good Friday in Chicago's Pilsen neighborhood Mexican Catholics process through the streets as live actors selected from the community re-enact the stations of the cross. Thousands of people participate in this ritual, which ends in the neighborhood park with the dramatic re-enactment of the crucifixion and burial of Jesus. Similar Good Friday processions take place in New York and Miami.

As is true among African Americans, culture is shaping religion in the Hispanic Catholic community. Inspired by the Vatican Council's sanctioning of the cultural adaptation of the Roman liturgy, Hispanic Catholics continue to search "for a new liturgical expression of their cultural heritage and Christian experience, one that is in keeping with their way of thinking and their way of feeling the presence of grace in their lives."[88]

What has taken place among African Americans and Hispanics has also transformed the style of worship in the many diverse communities of Asian Catholics as well as among Native Americans. This recognition of the principle of acculturation in the church's worship has transformed American Catholicism into a multicultural mosaic of religion.

Acculturation has reshaped the devotional life of Catholics. Without the ethnic awakening of the 1960s this would have never happened. Surely the influence of the Second Vatican Council and its endorsement of the idea of cultural adaptation in the liturgical life of the church was a powerful force in the transformation of the religious practices of the people. However, without the cultural influence of the ethnic awakening that had taken place in the past thirty to forty years, such a transformation would not have been as sweeping and swift. As a result of this development, the devotional life of Catholics is no longer modeled on the principle of rigid uniformity or, as it is often called—the principle of "one size fits all." Rather it comprises a diversity of traditions that strikingly underscores the multicultural character of Catholicism as it enters the new millennium.

The Americanization of Catholic Doctrine

ANOTHER CLEAR EXAMPLE OF how culture has trans-
formed Catholicism is seen in the area of sexual ethics, most particularly the practice of birth control. By the 1960s the practice of artificial contraception had become widely accepted within the United
States. The official approval of a contraceptive pill by the Food and
Drug Administration in 1960 made the practice of birth control even
more feasible for women. Among Catholic women the use of forms
of birth control not approved by the church began to increase significantly. Andrew Greeley estimated that the use of such unapproved
forms of birth control had increased between 1960 and 1965 "from
38 percent to 51 percent, with almost all of the change during these
years being accounted for by the invention of the pill."[89] While the
laity were changing their thinking about birth control, Catholic theologians were also revising their thoughts on this issue. Given the
changes taking place in both church and society, Pope John XXIII
appointed a special commission to study the question of birth control. In 1967 the majority report of the commission recommended
that contraception no longer be considered intrinsically evil and married couples could if necessary practice birth control. Pope Paul VI
rejected the report and issued an encyclical in 1968, *Humanae Vitae*, in
which he upheld the church's traditional condemnation of any form
of artificial contraception. Pope John Paul II has also reaffirmed this
teaching.

Despite the church's official stance on the issue of artificial contraception, the number of Catholics who approve of birth control has
increased over the years. By 1993 more than 85 percent of American
Catholics approve of birth control, an increase of about 45 percent
since 1967. Among those Catholics born after 1960, as many as 90
percent of them believe that the practice of artificial birth control

should be a decision left "entirely up to the individual."[90] Simply put, the vast majority of American Catholics, both clergy and laity, does not believe that the practice of birth control is sinful. A moral development has taken place among the community of believers, and what was once prohibited is now regarded as permissible. Whether or not such widespread opposition to official church teaching will persuade church authorities to re-examine the church's teaching on this issue remains to be seen. Nonetheless, the acceptance of artificial contraception within American society has transformed the belief of Catholics. For the vast majority of them birth control is no longer an issue worthy of debate.

Another example of culture reshaping the beliefs of Catholics is observed in the area of religious freedom. In this instance, unlike the issue of birth control, changing cultural values also changed the church's teaching. This reversal took place at the Second Vatican Council when the council fathers endorsed the principle of religious freedom. In doing so, they acknowledged that culture does indeed shape religion.

The repressive intellectual climate that led to the silencing of John Courtney Murray in 1955 subsided in the early 1960s with the election of a new pope. The opening of the Second Vatican Council in fall 1962 symbolized the beginning of this new era. Discussion and debate became the mantra of the council rather than contempt for intellectual freedom and the silencing of dissenting voices. One of the topics proposed for consideration at the council was the issue that had consumed Murray for more than a decade—the relation between religion and the state. Since Murray was recognized as a leading authority on this issue, he was invited in 1963 to take part in the council's deliberations as a theological expert. The sentence of silence had ended. In the next two years he emerged as one of the key authors of the council's declaration on religious freedom.

Throughout his writings Murray referred to the importance of history in shaping the human consciousness. By the middle of the twentieth century "man," to use his phrase, had become "more and more conscious of his own dignity, personal and civil." The rise of Fascism, Nazism, and Communism in the 1930s and '40s had raised the scepter of totalitarianism. Reacting against these forces of evil, politicians and popes began to champion the rights of the human person. In 1948 the United Nations issued the Universal Declaration of Human Rights, which affirmed freedom of religion as one such right. The World Council of Churches also spoke out on behalf of religious freedom. In Murray's opinion it was now time for the Catholic Church to recognize this fundamental principle that "is accepted by the common consciousness of men and civilized nations."[91]

A small but powerful group of bishops and theologians at the council opposed the idea of the church endorsing religious freedom. Such an endorsement would mean rejecting the prevailing theory of church and state relations. According to this theory only Catholics would enjoy complete religious freedom. Other religions would be tolerated when necessary and not tolerated whenever possible. More was at stake, however, than endorsing the principle of religious freedom. As Murray wrote on numerous occasions, to reject the prevailing doctrine was to acknowledge that Catholic doctrine can change and develop over time. This is what made this declaration so controversial. "The notion of development," wrote Murray, "not the notion of religious freedom, was the real sticking-point for many of those who opposed the Declaration even to the very end."[92] The opposition, led by Murray's aging nemesis, Cardinal Ottaviani, was able to stall final passage of the declaration for two years. But after considerable debate, the sixth and final draft of the declaration was overwhelmingly approved at the fourth and final session of the council in December 1965.

What Murray did, together with the American bishops, was to persuade the bishops at the council to endorse the American idea of the *"free exercise* of religion in society." Moreover, his influence is visible in the document itself, which he helped write. In a very real sense the council endorsed the idea of the Americanization of Catholic doctrine by endorsing the principle of religious freedom. As John Noonan wrote, "free exercise ... is an American invention."[93] When American bishops spoke at the council on behalf of religious freedom, they did not apologize for the American system of government. They stood shoulder to shoulder with John Carroll, John Ireland, and countless others American Catholics who affirmed and indeed celebrated the American proposition of religious freedom for all people. Taking their cue from Murray, who coached them throughout the debate, the American bishops supported the American constitutional system and its guarantee of the free exercise of religion. They wanted to make this tradition part of Catholic teaching. When the council fathers accepted their argument, they were accepting an "American invention" that in the course of the twentieth century had become widely accepted throughout the world.

In his book on the American experience of religious freedom, John Noonan examined the influence of this principle in France, Japan, Russia, and the Catholic Church. In concluding the chapter on the Catholic Church, where he traces the influence of Murray and the American idea of the free exercise of religion at the Second Vatican Council, he noted that "the Council proclaimed that the Church learned from human experience." He went on to state, "The learning had been largely from the United States: from its Constitution of such extraordinary importance ... and from the Virginian Declaration ...; from its bishops who kept the issue alive as 'the American *issue*' in the Council; from its theologian John Courtney Murray, who poured his energy and insight into the shaping of the new teaching. Impossible without the recent European experience and the support of bishops from around the world and the receptivity of Italian popes, the Declaration on Religious Freedom would not have come into existence without the American contribution and the experiment that began with Madison."[94]

FROM 1960 TO THE turn of the century the American Catholic community has undergone substantial and rapid change. For a church in which change was an oxymoron, change has entered with the swiftness of a tornado and redesigned the Catholic landscape. A key reason for such change has been the transforming influence of culture on Catholicism. Immigration has refashioned the profile of the American Catholic community. The immigrant church of the European era is gone, replaced by a Latin-Asian immigrant church. The women's movement of the past forty years has had a truly revolutionary impact on the church. Within a single generation an entirely new consciousness has permeated the Catholic community, and it is clear that this will change the future of the church. A new style of devotional Catholicism has also taken hold. Along with this is a change in Catholic doctrine, chiefly the endorsement of religious freedom. In addition, more and more people are challenging the official teaching of the church on such moral issues as birth control. Another issue is democracy in the church. Without question, the American idea of democracy has permeated the community. This development poses a challenge for the bishops and their priests. How will they together with the laity reconcile the authoritarian tradition of Catholicism with the American democratic tradition?

The history of American Catholicism is the study of change. This has been especially true for these past forty years, 1960–2000. Much of this change has resulted from the interaction of the American and Catholic cultures. Religion cannot escape the influence of history, nor can it avoid the impact of culture. This change has brought new life to Catholicism. Like any living institution, it needs to change and change it did. But opposition to change has intensified in the recent past, most especially during the pontificate of John Paul II. Elected pope in 1978, John Paul II has gained superstar status through his unprecedented travel throughout the world. The sight of him kissing the tarmac at airports across the globe has become a familiar scene. Thousands of people turn out for the papal masses celebrated at each visit. Nonetheless, his pontificate has also been a period of intense controversy.

John Paul II will be known not just for his world travels, but also for his efforts to control the changes that are sweeping through the church. The pope has sought to restore discipline and order to an international community of believers that has tasted change and found it satisfying. In his pontificate the church has become more centralized in the Vatican, embracing a more monarchical and less collegial model of Catholicism. Vatican authorities have become less sensitive to the cultural diversities that distinguish Catholicism across the globe and have sought to impose a one-size-fits-all brand of Catholicism. This concern for order and control has sparked a good deal of debate as well as outright opposition. In the area of theology the repressive intellectual climate of the 1950s has reappeared as the Vatican has believed it necessary to censure the work of several theologians, even without satisfactory explanation. Most recently, the Vatican forced the American hierarchy to inaugurate a litmus test of orthodoxy for all college professors of Catholic theology. Since Pope John Paul II has appointed most of the bishops throughout the world, they tend to mirror his concern for order and control. This is the mandate given to them; loyalty to the papacy is the mantra of these bishops. Any thought of dissent, at least in public, is anathema. Like the pope they must condemn birth control and oppose the idea of a married clergy or women priests. This hierarchical church represents one dimension of Catholicism, a very bureaucratic aspect, and one that gains the headlines in the evening news. However, there is another aspect of Catholicism, a church within the church, that is more attuned to the cultural influences of the past half century. This is the people's church, rooted in the parish community. These two expressions of Catholicism, the people's church and the bureaucratic church, are like two ships passing in the night, each traveling in a different direction.

In the United States a very vibrant expression of Catholicism exists at the local parish level. Surely not all parishes fit this description, but many do. In these communities the future of Catholicism is being shaped. This is where American culture is shaping the future of Catholicism. A spirit of democracy is evident in these parishes. They also manifest a lively, public worship in which laymen and laywomen play central roles. Such liturgies mirror the culture of the people in language and song. The Vatican issues its edicts, but they do not seem to have much impact at this local level. The people are not disloyal to the pope or their local bishop. They just have other concerns—to strengthen and sustain the spiritual life of themselves and their families.

As these two ships, these two expressions of Catholicism, travel into the future, what awaits them? Will they eventually follow the same course and support each other, or will they continue to go their separate ways? If they continue on their separate paths, what will be the consequences of such division? For the bureaucratic church the prospect of a new pope may change the direction of the journey and bring the people's church closer to the bureaucratic church. The romance with modernity may then be resumed once more. For the local church the challenges are formidable. One of the foremost challenges is the decline of clergy. As the number of priests, sisters, and brothers decline, the laity must take on more responsibility. But only the priest can celebrate the eucharistic liturgy. Will there be enough priests to minister to the thousands of local churches? If celibacy remains a requirement for ordination to the priesthood, most likely there will not be a sufficient number. This poses a pastoral crisis that is becoming more significant each year. Sunday without Mass may become a too frequent occurrence in many parishes. Will such a crisis lead to the ordination of women or married men? Or will it force thousands of Catholics to look to other denominations for their Sunday worship? With the increase of immigration from Asia and South America, the church has taken on a multicultural dimension. Will there be enough clergy to minister to these newcomers in their language and according to their culture? As the laity take over more responsibility in the local church, how will this impact the role of the parish priest? Finally, how will the local bishop preside over these many parish communities that seem to take on a life quite removed from what goes on in the bureaucratic church? Will the bishop be able to bridge the gap that separates the two churches and fashion them into one community of believers, or will he try to impose a bureaucratic model of church on the people's church?

The resolution of these issues will undoubtedly create conflict. Nonetheless, the Catholic church must continue its dialogue with American culture. As change reshapes American society, the church must adapt. It has no choice. Otherwise it will become a lifeless relic of a mythic past. The future challenge for Catholicism in the United States will be to remain faithful to the Catholic tradition as it adapts to a modern American culture. The result will be a genuine American Catholicism, fully American and authentically Catholic. To achieve this goal will be the challenge of the twenty-first century.

POSTSCRIPT

∾ SINCE I COMPLETED WORK on this book in the fall of 2001, a major scandal has torn apart the American Catholic community. In January 2002 allegations that a priest had sexually abused children over a number of years in different parishes created turmoil in Boston's Catholic community. As the number of accusations against other priests in the Boston archdiocese and across the country grew, the crisis deepened with the revelation that church officials, seemingly more worried about the negative effects of a public scandal than about the well-being of those in their care, had often reassigned accused priests to other parishes without restricting those priests' interaction with children. In April Pope John Paul II took the unusual measure of calling the American cardinals to the Vatican. The magnitude of the crisis is clear, and there is no question, whatever the ultimate outcome of the Vatican meetings, that it will take time and great effort to restore the hierarchy's credibility.

As a historian and a Catholic I believe I have a responsibility to comment on this crisis that has gravely wounded a community of believers, a church that I love. There has been nothing like this in the history of American Catholicism. Regardless of how much good the church has done—and its good works are remarkable—this scandal of abuse and cover-up has shaken to its foundation the sacred trust between priests and their parishioners. The Catholic community's sadness, confusion, and sense of betrayal are profound.

But even if unprecedented, the crisis of 2002 reveals some of the tensions between religion and culture that I have discussed in this book. For almost two hundred years Catholics have been arguing about what type of church Catholicism should become. Many wanted a more democratic church, while others demanded a monarchical model of church. The monarchical model prevailed. But as this recent scandal has shown, the monarchical model has lost its efficacy in the modern world. By fostering a clerical culture of arrogance and secrecy, the church has failed to respond to the needs—spiritual and social—of the people in the pew. Now, more than ever before, American Catholics want a church open to the spirit of democracy where their views can make a difference.

As Catholicism has become a more public, less insular religion, church leaders have addressed such topics as war and peace, the economy, abortion, and the death penalty. By speaking out, they assumed an important moral authority in the public discussion of these critical social issues. The duplicity and cover-up on the part of many bishops has severely damaged, if not destroyed, that authority, and it will take more than just apologies to restore the credibility lost in the revelations of the winter and spring of 2002. The church needs better leaders who are more accountable to the people they serve. Ensuring accountability by involving the laity in the selection of future bishops and the appointment of local pastors may be one way of restoring confidence in the church's leadership.

This crisis in the church has necessitated a painful and difficult examination of deeper issues affecting the Catholic community and revealed the need for far-reaching change. Most crucially, the American Catholic church is running out of priests, and the shortage is wearing out the many excellent priests who are not only overworked but also deeply troubled by the sexual abuse scandal. The church has tried to fill the gap by importing clergy from other countries, but this is a shameful admission that after three hundred years on American soil, the church cannot recruit an American-born clergy. I believe that the answer to this dilemma is to open the priesthood to men who wish to be married as well as to women who want to be ordained. During the course of the past century the women's movement has transformed many religious denominations. In the Catholic church the impact has been significant, but women are still seeking gender equality. A place at the altar would be an important step in this direction.

A celibate, male, clerical culture impervious to outside scrutiny has created the worst scandal in the history of American Catholicism. It is time for change. My hope is that change will occur.

NOTES

INTRODUCTION

1. Jay P. Dolan, "A Catholic Romance With Modernity," *The Wilson Quarterly* 5, no. 4 (Autumn 1981), 120–33.

2. W.E.B. Du Bois, *The Souls of Black Folk*, ed. David W. Blight and Robert Gooding-Williams (Boston: Bedford Books, 1997), 38.

3. John T. Noonan, Jr., "On the Development of Doctrine," *America* 180, no. 11 (April 3, 1999), 6.

4. Jay P. Dolan, *The American Catholic Experience: A History From Colonial Times to the Present* (Garden City, N.Y.: Doubleday, 1985), 101–24.

CHAPTER ONE

1. This data was taken from Ronin John Murtha, "The Life of the Most Reverend Ambrose Marechal Third Archbishop of Baltimore, 1768–1828" (Ph.D. diss., Catholic University of America, 1965), 97–99; see also Gerald Shaughnessy, *Has the Immigrant Kept the Faith?* (New York: Macmillan, 1925), 69–73, for a different set of population figures.

2. Mathew Carey, *Autobiography* (New York: E.L. Schwaab, 1942), 9–10.

3. Archives, The Historical Society of Pennsylvania, *Diary of Mathew Carey*, Jan. 1, 1787; Carey, *Autobiography*, 1; see also another diary of Carey for frequent references to classical authors, Rare Book Room, University of Pennsylvania, *Diary of Mathew Carey*, Nov. 2, 1825, et passim; Edward C. Carter II, "The Political Activities of Mathew Carey, Nationalist 1760–1814" (Ph.D. diss., Bryn Mawr College, 1962), 7; Catalogue of the Library of Mathew Carey (Philadelphia: Joseph R.A. Skerrett, 1822).

4. Carter, "The Political Activities of Mathew Carey," 25, 116.

5. Rare Book Room, University of Pennsylvania, *Carey Diary*, Dec. 1, 1824; Nov.

2, 1825; and Nov. 15, 1825; *Niles National Register*, 5th series, no. 4, 7, Baltimore, Sept. 21, 1839; David Kaser, "The Retirement Income of Mathew Carey," *The Pennsylvania Magazine of History and Biography*, 80, no. 4 (Oct. 1956), 410–15.

6. Mathew Carey, *An Address to the Roman Catholics of the United States by a Layman of St. Mary's Congregation*, July 1821, 7.

7. Mathew Carey, *Plan for the Publication of Religious Books*, Nov. 7, 1791.

8. Rare Book Room, University of Pennsylvania, *Carey Diary*, Dec. 1, 1824.

9. See James Turner, *Without God, Without Creed: The Origins of Unbelief in America* (Baltimore: Johns Hopkins University Press, 1985), 35ff.

10. Henry F. May, *The Enlightenment in America* (New York: Oxford University Press, 1976), 210.

11. Ibid., 197–98; in his study of trusteeism Patrick W. Carey notes that many Catholic trustees evidenced an Enlightenment style of religion, *People, Priests, and Prelates: Ecclesiastical Democracy and the Tensions of Trusteeism* (Notre Dame, Ind.: University of Notre Dame Press, 1987), 148–49. See also Dale B. Light, *Rome and the New Republic: Conflict and Community in Philadelphia Catholicism Between the Revolution and the Civil War* (Notre Dame, Ind.: University of Notre Dame Press, 1996). Also Ronald H. Bayor and Timothy J. Meagher, eds., *The New York Irish* (Baltimore: Johns Hopkins University Press, 1996).

12. Ronald Hoffman, *Princes of Ireland, Planters of Maryland: A Carroll Saga 1500–1782* (Chapel Hill: University of North Carolina Press, 2000), 155–56.

13. Ronald Hoffman, "A Worthy Heir: The Role of Religion in the Development of Charles Carroll of Carrollton, 1748–1764," Cushwa Center for the Study of American Catholicism, Working Paper Series, Fall 1982, 2, 42–44, 60.

14. Thomas O'Brien Hanley, ed., *The John Carroll Papers* (Notre Dame, Ind.: University of Notre Dame Press, 1976), I, 53, 81; Robert Emmett Curran, S.J., ed., *American Jesuit Spirituality: The Maryland Tradition, 1634–1900* (New York: Paulist Press, 1988), 133.

15. Joseph P. Chinnici, O.F.M., "American Catholics and Religious Pluralism, 1775–1820," *Journal of Ecumenical Studies* 16 (Fall 1979), 733–36; Joseph P. Chinnici, *Living Stones: The History and Structure of Catholic Spiritual Life in the United States* (New York: Macmillan, 1989), 13; Curran, S.J., *American Jesuit Spirituality: The Maryland Tradition*, 16–18.

16. Thomas W. Spalding, *The Premier See: A History of the Archdiocese of Baltimore, 1789–1989* (Baltimore: Johns Hopkins University Press, 1989), 59–60.

17. See Chinnici, "American Catholics and Religious Pluralism," 736.

18. Joseph P. Chinnici, "Politics and Theology: From Enlightenment Catholicism to the Condemnation of Americanism," Cushwa Center for the Study of American Catholicism, Working Paper Series 9, no. 3 (Spring 1981), 22; see also Owen Chadwick, *The Popes and European Revolution* (Oxford: Clarendon Press, 1981), 3–95.

19. Chinnici, *Living Stones*, 2.

20. Chinnici, "Politics and Theology," 24–25; Chinnici, *Living Stones*, 6; Curran, *American Jesuit Spirituality*, 136.

21. Chadwick, *The Popes and European Revolution*, 406.

22. See Joseph P. Chinnici, O.F.M., *The English Catholic Enlightenment, John Lingard and the Cisalpine Movement 1780–1850* (Shepherdstown, W. Va.: Patmos, 1980), 173–74.

23. Rhys Isaacs, *The Transformation of Virginia 1740–1790* (Chapel Hill: University of North Carolina Press, 1982), 64.

24. Sean Wilentz, *Chants Democratic: New York City and the Rise of the American Working Class, 1788–1950* (New York: Oxford University Press, 1984), 61.

25. Nathan O. Hatch, *The Democratization of American Christianity* (New Haven, Conn.: Yale University Press, 1989), 9.

26. Edwin Scott Gaustad, *Historical Atlas of Religion in America* (New York: Harper and Row, 1962), 43 for the number of churches.

27. P. Carey, *People, Priests, and Prelates*, 108; I have relied on Carey for the history of the trustee system in the United States.

28. M. Carey, *Address to the Rt. Rev. Bishop Conwell and the Members of St. Mary's Congregation*, Feb. 14, 1821, 3–4; *Address to the Right Rev. The Bishop of Pennsylvania and the Members of St. Mary's Congregation, Philadelphia*, Dec. 21, 1820, 3; *Address to the Rt. Rev. The Bishop of Pennsylvania, The Catholic Clergy of Philadelphia and the Congregation of St. Mary in this City by a Catholic Layman* 1822, v.

29. Quoted in Patrick W. Carey, "Republicanism Within American Catholicism, 1785–1860," *Journal of the Early Republic* 3, no. 4 (Winter 1983), 416.

30. Ibid., 417.

31. The phrase "American Republicans" appears in the *Documents Relative to the Present Distressed State of the Roman Catholic Church in the City of Charleston, State of South Carolina*, Charleston, South Carolina, 1818, 5; this document was found in the collection at the Library Company of Philadelphia.

32. P. Carey, *People, Priests, and Prelates*, 165.

33. *Address to the Rt. Rev. The Bishop of Philadelphia, The Catholic Clergy of Philadelphia and the Congregation of St. Mary's in this City By a Catholic Layman*, 1822, 30–31.

34. P. Carey, *People, Priests, and Prelates*, 161.

35. Ibid., 163.

36. Sr. Mary Ramona Mattingly, *The Catholic Church on the Kentucky Frontier 1795–1812* (Washington, D.C.: Catholic University of America Press, 1936), 139.

37. Quoted in Thomas T. McAvoy, *A History of the Catholic Church in the United States* (Notre Dame, Ind.: University of Notre Dame Press, 1969), 130.

38. Thomas Bokenkotter, *A Concise History of the Catholic Church* (Garden City, N.Y.: Image Books, 1979), 285.

39. Chadwick, *The Popes and European Revolution*, 481.

40. Spalding, *The Premier See*, 93.

41. "Archbishop Marechal's Report to Propaganda, October 16, 1818," in *Documents of American Catholic History*, ed. John Tracy Ellis (Chicago: Henry Regnery Co., 1967), 1: 214.

42. Clyde F. Crews, *An American Holy Land: A History of the Archdiocese of Louisville* (Wilmington, Del.: Michael Glazier, 1987), 64.

43. Ibid., 73–75.

44. Ibid., 102; Dolan, *The American Catholic Experience*, 119–120.

45. Ibid., 121.

46. Light, *Rome and the New Republic*, 241.

47. P. Carey, *People and Prelates*, 214.

CHAPTER 2

1. *Address of the Committee of Saint Mary's Church of Philadelphia to Their Brethren of the Roman Catholic Faith Throughout the United States of America on the Subject of a Reform of Sundry Abuses in the Administration of Our Church Discipline* (Philadelphia, 1821), 3–4, 11; Dale B. Light discusses this pamphlet in *Rome and the New Republic: Conflict and Community in Philadelphia Catholicism between the Revolution and the Civil War* (Notre Dame, Ind.: University of Notre Dame Press, 1996), 127–31.

2. Quoted in Light, *Rome and the New Republic*, 105.

3. Hugh J. Nolan, *The Most Reverend Francis Patrick Kenrick Third Bishop of*

Philadelphia 1830–1851 (Philadelphia, 1948), 118ff; Light discusses this at great length, *Rome and the New Republic*, 259ff.

4. Quoted in Henry J. Browne, "The Archdiocese of New York A Century Ago: A Memoir of Archbishop Hughes, 1838–1858," *Historical Records and Studies* 39–40 (1952), 139, 183.mar

5. Quoted in Lawrence Kehoe, ed., *Complete Works of the Most Rev. John Hughes* (New York: Lawrence Kehoe, 1865), 1: 323; quoted in Jay P. Dolan, *The Immigrant Church: New York's Irish and German Catholics, 1815–1865* (Baltimore: Johns Hopkins University Press, 1975), 164–65.

6. Quoted in Jay P. Dolan, *The American Catholic Experience: A History From Colonial Times to the Present* (Garden City, N.Y.: Doubleday, 1985), 208–9.

7. Joseph P. Chinnici O.F.M., *Living Stones: The History and Structure of Catholic Spiritual Life in the United States* (New York: Macmillan, 1989), 75.

8. See Dolan, *The American Catholic Experience*, 211–213.

9. Ibid.

10. Robert Emmett Curran, S.J., *American Jesuit Spirituality: The Maryland Tradition, 1634–1900* (New York: Paulist Press, 1988), 272, 293, 282, 288.

11. Walter J. Walsh, "Religion, Ethnicity, and History: Clues to the Cultural Construction of Law," in *The New York Irish*, ed. Ronald H. Bayor and Timothy J. Meagher (Baltimore: Johns Hopkins University Press, 1996), 49.

12. Ibid., 60–65; Paul A. Gilje, *The Road to Mobocracy: Popular Disorder in New York City, 1763–1834* (Chapel Hill: University of North Carolina Press, 1987), 134.

13. See David A. Gerber, *The Making of an American Pluralism: Buffalo, New York 1825–60* (Urbana: University of Illinois Press, 1989), 113–14.

14. Quoted in Robert Emmett Curran, S.J., *The Bicentennial History of Georgetown University: From Academy to University 1789–1889* (Washington, D.C.: Georgetown University Press, 1993), 125; see also Ray Allen Billington, *The Protestant Crusade 1800–1860* (New York: Macmillan, 1938), 345, and Tyler Anbinder, *Nativism and Slavery: The Northern Know Nothings and the Politics of the 1850s* (New York: Oxford University Press, 1992), 103.

15. Quoted in ibid., 266.

16. Quoted in William LeRoy Portier, "Providential Nation: An Historical-Theological Study of Isaac Hecker's Americanism" (Ph.D. diss., University of St. Michael's College, Canada, 1980), 300.

17. Ann Taves, *The Household of Faith: Roman Catholic Devotions in Mid-Nineteenth-*

Century America (Notre Dame, Ind.: University of Notre Dame Press, 1986), 128.

18. Quoted in J.L. Spalding, *The Life of the Most Rev. M.J. Spalding, Archbishop of Baltimore* (New York: The Catholic Publication Society, 1873), 383.

19. Quoted in Dolan, *The American Catholic Experience*, 195.

20. Jenny Franchot, *Roads to Rome: The Antebellum Protestant Encounter with Catholicism* (Berkeley: University of California Press, 1994), 281.

21. O.A. Brownson, *The Convert: or Leaves From My Experience* (New York: Edward Dunigan and Brother, 1857), 359–60.

22. Quoted in Dolan, *The American Catholic Experience*, 296.

23. Orestes A. Brownson, "Mission of America," in *The Works of Orestes A. Brownson*, ed. Henry F. Brownson (Detroit: T. Nourse, 1884), 11: 567.

24. Ibid., 556–57, 576, 584.

25. Quoted in Thomas R. Ryan, *Orestes A. Brownson: A Definitive Biography* (Huntington, Ind.: Our Sunday Visitor Press, 1976), 534.

26. Quoted in Henry F. Brownson, *Orestes A. Brownson's Latter Life: From 1856–1876* (Detroit: H.F. Brownson, 1900), 71.

27. Lawrence Kehoe, ed., *Complete Works of the Most Rev. John Hughes, D.D.* (New York: Lawrence Kehoe, 1865), 2:688.

28. Ibid.

29. Ibid., 71–72; a very important essay of Hughes on this topic was written in November 1856, "Reflections and Suggestions in Regard to What Is Called the Catholic Press in the United States," see Lawrence Kehoe, ed., *Complete Works of the Most Rev. John Hughes, D.D.*, 2: 686–701.

30. Brownson, "Mission of America," 559.

31. Henry F. Brownson, *The Works of Orestes A. Brownson* (Detroit: Thorndike Nourse, 1884), 14: 565–68; David J. O'Brien, *Isaac Hecker: An American Catholic* (New York: Paulist Press, 1992), 121–23.

32. Hughes, "Reflections and Suggestions," 688; see Portier, "Providential Nation," 306–19 for detailed discussion of this group.

33. Robert Emmett Curran, S.J. "Prelude to 'Americanism': The New York Accademia and Clerical Radicalism in the Late Nineteenth Century," *Church History* 47 (March 1978), 54; Portier, "Providential Nation," 306–19 discusses the 1850s group which seems clearly linked to the Accademia of the 1860s.

34. Portier, 363–64.

35. Portier, 363–64; quoted in Dolan, *The American Catholic Experience*, 308, and O'Brien, *Hecker*, 154.

36. Quoted in O'Brien, *Hecker*, 154, and Portier, "Providential Nation," 324.

37. Quoted in O'Brien, *Hecker*, 316.

CHAPTER 3

1. *Three Great Events in the History of the Catholic Church in the United States* (Detroit: William H. Hughes, 1889), xv.

2. Ibid., 13–16.

3. Till Van Rahden, "Beyond Ambivalence: Variations of Catholic Anti-Semitism in Turn of the Century Baltimore," *American Jewish History* 82 (1994), 13–14.

4. *Three Great Events*, 17, 90.

5. See Glen Janus, "Bishop Bernard McQuaid: On 'True' and 'False' Americanism," *U.S. Catholic Historian* 11, no. 3 (Summer 1993), 53–76.

6. Quoted in Frederick J. Zwierlein, *The Life and Letters of Bishop McQuaid* (Rochester, N.Y.: Art Print Shop, 1927), 3: 234.

7. James Turner, *Without God, Without Creed: The Origins of Unbelief in America* (Baltimore: Johns Hopkins University Press, 1985), xii–xiii, 179.

8. Martin E. Marty, *Righteous Empire: The Protestant Experience in America* (New York: Dial, 1970), 179.

9. There are many instances among many different ethnic groups, both Catholic and Protestant, of this desire for a more democratic form of parish government; see, for example, Jon Gjerde, *The Minds of the West* (Chapel Hill: University of North Carolina Press, 1997), 115–31.

10. Quoted in Jay P. Dolan, *The American Catholic Experience: A History From Colonial Times to the Present* (Garden City, N.Y.: Doubleday, 1985), 181.

11. Quoted in Dolan, *The American Catholic Experience*, 182.

12. Ibid., 183.

13. Ibid.

14. Quoted in Dolan, *The American Catholic Experience*, 185.

15. Quoted in ibid., 181.

16. Alexis de Tocqueville, *Democracy in America* (New York: Vintage Books, 1945) 1: 311–12.

17. Robert Anthony Orsi, *The Madonna of 115th Street: Faith and Community in Italian Harlem, 1880–1950* (New Haven, Conn.: Yale University Press, 1985), 4–5.

18. Christa Ressmeyer Klein, "The Jesuits and Catholic Boyhood in Nineteenth-Century New York: A Study of St. John's College and the College of St. Francis Xavier 1846–1912" (Ph.D. diss., University of Pennsylvania, 1976), 249.

19. Colleen McDannell, *Material Christianity: Religion and Popular Culture in America* (New Haven, Conn.: Yale University Press, 1995), 155.

20. Colleen McDannell, *The Christian Home in Victorian America, 1840–1900* (Bloomington: Indiana University Press, 1986), 56, 60, 72.

21. Most Reverend John Ireland, *The Church and Modern Society* (Chicago: D.H. McBride, 1896), 138.

22. John Higham, *Strangers in the Land: Patterns of American Nativism 1860–1925* (New York: Atheneum, 1963), 75.

23. Von Rahden, "Beyond Ambivalance," 18.

24. Rev. A.H. Walburg, *The Question of Nationality in Its Relations to the Catholic Church in the United States* (Cincinnati: B. Herder, 1889), 57.

25. Quoted in *Amerika*, Sept. 14, 1887, 6.

26. Quoted in *Verhandlungen der zweite allgemeinen deutsch-amerikanischen Katholiken Versammlung in Cincinnati, Ohio*, Sept. 3–4, 1888 (St. Louis, Mo.: B. Herder, 1888) 115–16.

27. Quoted in Colman J. Barry, *The Catholic Church and German Americans* (Milwaukee: Bruce Publishing, 1953), 293.

28. Quoted in Barry, *The Catholic Church and German Americans*, 306.

29. Ireland, *The Church and Modern Society*, 174, 188, 189.

30. Quoted in Barry, *The Catholic Church and German Americans*, 120.

31. Ibid., 313–15.

32. Quoted in Dolan, *The American Catholic Experience*, 298–99.

33. Thomas S. Preston, "American Catholicity," *American Catholic Quarterly Review* 16, no. 62 (April 1891), 397.

34. See Ireland, *The Church and Modern Society*, for his talks on this theme uniting the church and the age.

35. Ireland, *The Church and Modern Society*, 89.

36. Ibid., 390, 95.

37. Dennis J. Dease, "The Theological Influence of Orestes Brownson and Isaac Hecker on John Ireland's Ecclesiology" (Ph.D. diss., Catholic University of America, 1978), 221.

38. Ibid., 244.

39. Gabriel Daly, *Transcendence and Immanence: A Study in Catholic Modernism and Integralism* (Oxford: Clarendon Press, 1980), 20.

40. Quoted in Dolan, *The American Catholic Experience*, 310.

41. Quoted in Barry, *The Catholic Church and German Americans*, 323–24.

42. See Ireland, *The Church and Modern Society*, 94, 101ff.

43. Quoted in Dolan, *The American Catholic Experience*, 303.

44. Quoted in Barry, *The Catholic Church and German Americans*, 323.

45. Quoted in John Louis Ciani, "Across a Wide Ocean: Salvatore Maria Bandi, S.J., and the *Civilta Cattolica*, From Americanism to Modernism 1891–1914" (Ph.D. diss., University of Virginia, 1992), 147–48.

46. Quoted in ibid., 209.

47. Quoted in ibid., 222.

48. Quoted in John Tracy Ellis, ed., *Documents of American Catholic History* (Chicago: Henry Regnery, 1967), 2: 502.

49. W. Elliott, *Le Pere Hecker* (Paris: V. Lecoffre, 1897), xxiv.

50. Charles Maignen, *Le Pere Hecker Est-Il Un Saint?* (Rome: Desclee, Lefebvre et Cie., 1899), 390.

51. See Ellis, *Documents of American Catholic History*, 2: 539, 546.

52. Quoted in Ciani, "Across a Wide Ocean," 238.

53. Albert Reynaud, Ph.D., "Collective and Individual Religion: A Synthesis," *The New York Review* (June–July, 1905), 302.

54. R. Scott Appleby, *Church and Age Unite: The Modernist Impulse in American Catholicism* (Notre Dame, Ind.: University of Notre Dame Press, 1992), 7–8.

55. Ibid., 3.

56. Roger Aubert, *The Church in a Secularised Society* (New York: Paulist Press, 1978), 191.

57. Appleby, *Church and Age Unite*, 36.

58. Quoted in Joseph M. White, *The Diocesan Seminary in the United States: A History from the 1780s to the Present* (Notre Dame, Ind.: University of Notre Dame Press, 1989), 230.

59. Appleby, *Church and Age Unite*, 109.

60. Ibid., 109, 163.

61. Quoted in White, *The Diocesan Seminary*, 263.

62. Michael V. Gannon, "Before and After Modernism: The Intellectual Isolation

of the American Priest," in *The Catholic Priest in the United States: Historical Investigations*, ed. John Tracy Ellis, (Collegeville, Minn.: St. John's University Press, 1971), 341.

63. Martin E. Marty, *Modern American Religion*, Vol. 1, *The Irony of It All 1893–1919* (Chicago: University of Chicago Press, 1986), 200.

64. Frank Sheed, *The Church and I* (Garden City, N.Y.: Doubleday, 1974), 95.

65. William Seton, "The Higher Education of Woman and Posterity," *Catholic World* 73 (May 1901), 147; Nancy Woloch, *Women and the American Experience* (New York: McGraw-Hill, 1984), 269.

66. Quoted in Karen Kennelly, C.S.J., "Ideals of American Catholic Womanhood," in *American Catholic Women: A Historical Exploration*, ed. Karen Kennelly (New York: Macmillan, 1989), 4.

67. Leslie Woodcock Tentler, *Seasons of Grace: A History of the Catholic Archdiocese of Detroit* (Detroit: Wayne State University Press, 1990), 213.

68. L.A. Toomy, "Some Noble Work of Catholic Women," *Catholic World* 57 (May 1893), 234. This section on gender is based on the work of Kathleen A. Sprows, "New Footsteps in Well-Trodden Ways: Gender, Religion and Ethnicity in Irish America, 1890–1910" (Ph.D. diss., University of Notre Dame, 1999).

69. A Married Working Woman, "Should Married Women Work?" *Donahue's Magazine* 29 (1893), 633.

70. "The Public Rights of Women," *Catholic World* 59 (June 1894), 302–3, 307, 320.

71. Quoted in Dolan, *The American Catholic Experience*, 329.

72. Marguerite Moore, "A New Woman's Work in the West of Ireland," *Catholic World* 64 (January 1897), 458; "Educators' Views On Education For Women," *Catholic World* 45 (1901), 180.

73. See Philip Gleason, *Contending with Modernity: Catholic Higher Education in the Twentieth Century* (New York: Oxford University Press, 1995) for a study of the development of higher education at the turn of the last century.

74. Quoted in Mary J. Oates, "Introduction," in *Higher Education for Catholic Women*, ed. Mary J. Oates (New York: Garland, 1987), n.p.; Austin O'Malley, "College Work for Catholic Girls," *Catholic World* 68 (November, 1898), 162.

75. Quoted in Oates, ed., *Higher Education for Catholic Women*, 38, 46.

76. Quoted in ibid., 63.

77. O'Malley, "College Work for Catholic Girls," 162.

78. Sister Margaret Marie Doyle, *The Curriculum of the Catholic Woman's College* (Ph.D. diss., University of Notre Dame, 1932), 79.

CHAPTER 4

1. *New World*, Sept. 3, Sept. 10, 1920.

2. Quoted in Eileen M. McMahon, *What Parish Are You From? A Chicago Irish Community and Race Relations, 1916–1970* (Lexington: University Press of Kentucky, 1995), 44.

3. Ibid., 31–33.

4. Ibid., 27, 71, 78.

5. Ibid., 74; see also Jeffrey M. Burns, "Que es esto? The Transformation of St. Peter's Parish, San Francisco, 1913–1990," in *American Congregations*, vol. 1, *Portraits of Twelve Religious Communities*, ed. James P. Wind and James W. Lewis (Chicago: University of Chicago Press, 1994), 398.

6. John T. McGreevy, *Parish Boundaries:The Catholic Encounter with Race in the Twentieth-Century Urban North* (Chicago: University of Chicago Press, 1996), 22.

7. Quoted in Thomas E. Blantz, *George N. Shuster: On the Side of Truth* (Notre Dame, Ind.: University of Notre Dame Press, 1993), 69.

8. Quoted in Jay P. Dolan, *The American Catholic Experience: A History From Colonial Times to the Present* (Garden City, N.Y.: Doubleday, 1985), 206.

9. Quoted in James Terence Fisher, *The Catholic Counterculture in America 1933–1962* (Chapel Hill: University of North Carolina Press, 1989), 17; quoted in McGreevy, *Parish Boundaries*, 79; quoted in McMahon, *What Parish Are You From?*, 53; Andre Siegfried, *America Comes of Age* (New York: Harcourt, Brace, 1927), 51.

10. Ibid., 33.

11. Lizabeth Cohen, *Making A New Deal: Industrial Workers in Chicago, 1919–1939* (Cambridge Mass.: Cambridge University Press, 1990), 29, 55.

12. Sam Bass Warner, Jr., *The Private City: Philadelphia in Three Periods of Growth* (Philadelphia: University of Pennsylvania Press, 1968), 169, 183; Robert H. Lord, John E. Sexton, and Edward T. Harrington, *History of the Archdiocese of Boston*, 3 vols. (New York: Sheed and Ward, 1944), 725ff.

13. John Higham, *Strangers in the Land: Patterns of American Nativism 1860–1925* (New York: Atheneum, 1963), 266, 287.

14. Leonard J. Moore, *Citizen Klansmen: The Ku Klux Klan in Indiana, 1921–1928* (Chapel Hill: University of North Carolina Press, 1991), 23.

15. Quoted in ibid., p.20; quoted in Kenneth T. Jackson, *The Ku Klux Klan in the City, 1915–1930* (New York: Oxford University Press, 1967), 21; Higham, *Strangers in the Land*, 291.

16. Quoted in Moore, *Citizen Klansmen*, 21.

17. Quoted in Lynn Dumenil, "The Tribal Twenties: 'Assimilated' Catholics' Response to Anti-Catholicism," *Journal of American Ethnic History* 11 (Fall 1991), 26.

18. Quoted in Martin E. Marty, *Modern American Religion*, Vol. 2, *The Noise of Conflict 1919–1941* (Chicago: University of Chicago Press, 1991), 81.

19. Edward R. Kantowicz, *Corporation Sole: Cardinal Mundelein and Chicago Catholicism* (Notre Dame Ind.: University of Notre Dame Press, 1983), 72.

20. Ibid., 119.

21. Cohen, *Making a New Deal*, 86.

22. Dolan, *The American Catholic Experience*, 300–301; Joseph John Parot, *Polish Catholics in Chicago, 1850–1920* (DeKalb, Ill.: Northern Illinois University Press, 1981), 211–12.

23. Kantowicz, *Corporation Sole*, 80.

24. George J. Sanchez, *Becoming Mexican American: Ethnicity, Culture and Identity in Chicano Los Angeles, 1900–1945* (New York: Oxford University Press, 1993), 95, 98, 103, 105.

25. Jeffrey M. Burns, "The Mexican Catholic Community in California," in *Mexican Americans and the Catholic Church 1900–1965*, ed. Jay P. Dolan and Gilberto M. Hinojosa (Notre Dame, Ind.: University of Notre Dame Press, 1994), 189.

26. Quoted in ibid., 191–92.

27. Sanchez, *Becoming Mexican American*, 13.

28. See Cohen, *Making a New Deal*, 8 and passim for this argument.

29. John J. Bukowczyk, *And My Children Did Not Know Me: A History of the Polish Americans* (Bloomington: Indiana University Press, 1987), 83.

30. *The Commonweal* 1, no. 1 (Nov. 12, 1924), 5.

31. "The Bishops' Program of Social Reconstruction," in *American Catholic Thought on Social Questions*, ed. Aaron I. Abell (New York: Bobbs-Merrill, 1968), 327.

32. Francis L. Broderick, *Right Reverend New Dealer John A. Ryan* (New York: Macmillan, 1964), 105.

33. Rodger Van Allen, *The Commonweal and American Catholicism* (Philadelphia: Fortress Press, 1974), 5; Carlton J.H. Hayes, "Obligations to America," *The Commonweal* 1, no. 10 (Jan. 14, 1925) 26.

34. William M. Halsey, *The Survival of American Innocence: Catholicism in an Era of Disillusionment, 1920–1940* (Notre Dame, Ind.: University of Notre Dame Press, 1980), 85.

35. Ibid., 87.

36. George N. Shuster, *The Catholic Spirit in America* (New York: Dial Press, 1927), x.

37. Quoted in Robert Brooke Clements, "*The Commonweal*, 1924–38: The Williams-Shuster Years" (Ph.D. diss., University of Notre Dame, 1972), 3.

38. Shuster, *The Catholic Spirit*, 118.

39. Gustave A. Weigel, "A Quarter Century Review," *Thought* 26, no. 100 (1951), 108.

40. Arnold Sparr, *To Promote, Defend, and Redeem: The Catholic Literary Revival and the Cultural Transformation of American Catholicism, 1920–1960* (New York: Greenwood Press, 1990), 15–16.

41. Frank Sheed, *The Church and I* (Garden City, N.Y.: Doubleday, 1974), 96, 88.

42. Dolan, *The American Catholic Experience*, 404.

43. Philip Gleason, *Contending with Modernity* (New York: Oxford University Press, 1995), 120.

44. Robert W. McElroy, "Catholicism and the American Polity: Murray As Interlocutor," in *John Courtney Murray and the Growth of Tradition*, ed. J. Leon Hooper, S.J., and Todd David Whitmore (Kansas City, Mo.: Sheed and Ward, 1996), 3.

45. J. Leon Hooper, "The Theological Sources of John Courtney Murray," in Hooper and Whitmore, *John Courtney Murray*, 110.

46. Joseph Komonchak, "John Courtney Murray and the Redemption of History: Natural Law and Theology," in Hooper and Whitmore, *John Courtney Murray*, 65–68.

47. Donald E. Pelotte, S.S.S., *John Courtney Murray: Theologian in Conflict* (New York: Paulist Press, 1975), 118.

48. Pelotte, *John Courtney Murray*, provides a thorough account of Murray's conflict with Roman authorities.

49. John Courtney Murray, S.J., *We Hold These Truths: Catholic Reflections on the American Proposition* (New York: Sheed and Ward, 1960), 185–90.

50. See Kathleen Tobin-Schlesinger, "Population and Power: The Religious Debate over Contraception, 1916–1936" (Ph.D. diss., University of Chicago, 1994) for a very informative discussion of the Catholic position in this debate.

51. Leslie Woodcock Tentler, *Seasons of Grace: A History of the Archdiocese of Detroit* (Detroit: Wayne State University Press, 1990), 478.

52. Ibid., 478–83.

53. This discussion is based on the essay by John T. McGreevy, "Thinking on One's Own: Catholicism in the American Intellectual Imagination, 1928–1960," *Journal of American History* 84, no. 1 (June 1997), 97–131. Quote is found on 106–7.

54. Paul Blanshard, *American Freedom and Catholic Power* (Boston: Beacon Press, 1950), 10, 303. The anti-Catholic bigot reference is from Martin E. Marty, *Modern American Religion*, Vol. 3, *Under God, Indivisible 1941–1960* (Chicago: University of Chicago Press, 1996), 158.

55. Pelotte, *John Courtney Murray*, 10.

56. Ibid., 76–77. The reference to the three great faiths is from Will Herberg, *Protestant–Catholic–Jew: An Essay in American Religious Sociology* (Garden City, N.Y.: Doubleday, 1955).

57. Tentler, *Seasons of Grace*, 404.

58. Alan Ehrenhalt, *The Lost City: The Forgotten Virtues of Community in America* (New York: Basic Books, 1995), 113.

59. Robert A. Orsi, "'He Keeps Me Going': Women's Devotion to Saint Jude and the Dialetics of Gender in American Catholicism, 1929–1965," in *Belief in History: Innovative Approaches to European and American Religion*, ed. Thomas Kselman (Notre Dame Ind.: University of Notre Dame Press, 1991), 144; Robert A. Orsi, *Thank You, St. Jude: Women's Devotion to the Patron Saint of Hopeless Causes* (New Haven, Conn.: Yale University Press, 1996), 41.

60. Ibid., 49, 66.

61. Joseph P. Chinnici, O.F.M., "The Catholic Community at Prayer, 1926–1976," unpublished paper, 56. Chinnici's paper examines the changing patterns of prayer among Catholics in the twentieth century.

62. Lynn Dumenil, *The Modern Temper: American Culture and Society in the 1920s*

(New York: Hill and Wang, 1995), 100; Woloch, *Women and the American Experience*, 388.

63. Ibid., 439–40.

64. Jeffrey M. Burns, *American Catholics and the Family Crisis 1930–1962, The Ideological and Organizational Response* (New York: Garland Press, 1988), 2–3, 158.

65. Ibid., 131.

66. Colleen McDannell, "Catholic Domesticity, 1860–1960," in *American Catholic Women: A Historical Exploration*, ed. Karen Kennelly, C.S.J. (New York: Macmillan, 1989), 74.

67. Anthony Burke Smith, "Prime-Time Catholicism in 1950s America: Fulton J. Sheen and 'Life is Worth Living,'" *U.S. Catholic Historian* 15, no. 3 (Summer 1997), 59, 71.

68. Quoted in Timothy Ignatius Kelly, "The Transformation of American Catholicism: The Pittsburgh Laity and the Second Vatican Council, 1950–1980" (Ph.D. diss., Carnegie Mellon University, 1990), 199 and 197ff for detailed discussion of this theme.

69. See Barbara Corrado Pope, "A Heroine Without Heroics: The Little Flower of Jesus and Her Times," *Church History* 57 (March 1986), 46–60; Monica Furlong, *Therese of Lisieux* (London: Virago Press, 1987).

70. Woloch, *Women and the American Experience*, 496.

71. William H. Chafe, *The American Woman: Her Changing Social, Economic, and Political Roles, 1920–1970* (New York: Oxford University Press, 1972), 135–36.

72. Woloch, *Women and the American Experience*, 446, 472, 502.

73. Quoted in Dolan, *The American Catholic Experience*, 414.

74. Jeffrey M. Burns, "Catholic Laywomen in the Culture of American Catholicism in the 1950s," *U.S. Catholic Historian* 5, no. 3–4 (Summer-Fall 1986), 392.

75. Cohen, *Making a New Deal*, 8.

76. Herberg, *Protestant–Catholic–Jew*, 1.

77. See Robert S. Ellwood, *The Fifties Spiritual Marketplace* (New Brunswick, N.J.: Rutgers University Press, 1997), 1–13.

78. Herberg, *Protestant–Catholic–Jew*, 161.

79. Doris Kearns Goodwin, *Wait Till Next Year: A Memoir* (New York: Simon and Schuster, 1997), 84–86.

80. Ehrenhalt, *The Lost City*, 91, 121.

81. Ibid., 120.

82. Ibid., 280.

83. Quoted in Steven M. Avella, *This Confident Church: Catholic Leadership and Life in Chicago, 1940–1965* (Notre Dame, Ind.: University of Notre Dame Press, 1992), 75.

84. Jay P. Dolan, R. Scott Appleby, Patricia Byrne, and Debra Campbell, *Transforming Parish Ministry* (New York: Crossroad, 1990), 309.

85. Andrew M. Greeley, *The Church and the Suburbs* (New York: Sheed and Ward, 1959), 56.

86. Ibid.

87. Leo R. Ward, *Catholic Life, U.S.A.* (St. Louis: B. Herder, 1959), 2, 10.

88. Dolan et al., *Transforming Parish Ministry*, 153.

89. Ibid., p.51.

90. John Tracy Ellis, *American Catholics and the Intellectual Life* (Chicago: The Heritage Foundation, 1956), 57.

91. Gleason, *Contending with Modernity*, 292.

92. Ehrenhalt, *The Lost City*, 120.

CHAPTER 5

1. Martin E. Marty, *Modern American Religion*, Vol. 3, *Under God, Indivisible 1941–1960* (Chicago: University of Chicago Press, 1996), 4; Jay P. Dolan, *The American Catholic Experience: A History From Colonial Times to the Present* (Garden City, N.Y.: Doubleday), 422.

2. Todd Gitlin, *The Sixties: Years of Hope, Days of Rage* (New York: Bantam Books, 1987), xiv.

3. Garry Wills, *Bare Ruined Choirs* (Garden City, N.Y.: Doubleday, 1971), 21.

4. James D. Davidson, Andrea S. Williams, Richard A. Lamanna, Jan Stenftenagel, Kathleen Maas Weigert, William J. Whalen, and Patricia Wittberg, S.C., *The Search for Common Ground* (Huntington, Ind.: Our Sunday Visitor Press, 1997), 195.

5. Robert Wuthnow, *The Restructuring of American Religion* (Princeton, N.J.: Princeton University Press, 1988), 5.

6. John T. McGreevy, *Parish Boundaries: The Catholic Encounter with Race in the Twentieth-Century Urban North* (Chicago: University of Chicago Press, 1996), 161.

7. Jim Castelli, *The Bishops and the Bomb: Waging Peace in a Nuclear Age* (Garden City, N.Y.: Doubleday, 1983), 180.

8. Ibid., 197.

9. Patrick W. Carey, *The Roman Catholics* (Westport, Conn.: Greenwood Press, 1993), 124.

10. Timothy A. Byrnes, *Catholic Bishops in American Politics* (Princeton, N.J.: Princeton University Press, 1991), 103.

11. *Economic Justice for All: A Pastoral Letter on Catholic Social Teaching and the U.S. Economy* (Washington, D.C.: U.S. Catholic Conference, 1987), 1.

12. Ibid., 2.

13. *Pastoral Constitution on the Church in the Modern World*, sec. 51, in *The Documents of Vatican II*, ed. Walter M. Abbott, S.J. (New York: America Press, 1966), 256.

14. Quoted in Byrne, *Catholic Bishops*, 55.

15. Jose Casanova, *Public Religions in the Modern World* (Chicago: University of Chicago Press, 1994), 206.

16. Hayes, "Obligations to America," 26. See chapter four for emergence of public Catholicism.

17. Jim Naughton, *Catholics in Crisis: An American Parish Fights for Its Soul* (Reading, Mass.: Addison-Wesley, 1996), 10, 37; Robert F. Keeler, *Parish* (New York: Crossroad, 1997), 13, 166.

18. Michael J. McNally, "A Peculiar Institution: A History of Catholic Parish Life in the Southeast (1850–1980)," in *The American Catholic Parish: A History from 1850 to the Present*, vol. 1, ed. Jay P. Dolan (New York: Paulist Press, 1987), 198.

19. David C. Leege, *Notre Dame Study of Catholic Parish Life, Parish Life Among the Leaders*, Report No. 9 (Notre Dame, Ind.: University of Notre Dame, 1986), 6.

20. Thomas W. Spalding and Kathryn M. Kuranda, *St. Vincent De Paul of Baltimore: The Story of a People and Their Home* (Baltimore: Maryland Historical Society, 1995), 149, 237.

21. Jeffrey M. Burns, "Building the Best: A History of Catholic Parish Life in the Pacific States," in *The American Catholic Parish: A History from 1850 to the Present*, vol. 2, ed. Jay P. Dolan (New York: Paulist Press, 1987), 99.

22. Carey, *People, Priests and Prelates*, 291–92.

23. William V. D'Antonio, James D. Davidson, Dean R. Hoge, and Ruth A. Wallace, *Laity: American and Catholic* (Kansas City, Mo.: Sheed and Ward, 1996), 160.

24. William Petersen, Michael Novak, and Philip Gleason, *Concepts of Ethnicity* (Cambridge, Mass.: Harvard University Press, 1982), 111.

25. Richard Polenberg, *One Nation Divisible* (New York: Penguin Books, 1980), 52.

26. James T. Patterson, *Grand Expectations: The United States 1945–1974* (New York: Oxford University Press, 1996), 326.

27. Will Herberg, *Protestant–Catholic–Jew* (Garden City, N.Y.: Doubleday, 1960), 31.

28. Ibid., 37.

29. Polenberg, *One Nation Divisible*, 244, 246.

30. Moises Sandoval, "The Organization of a Hispanic Church," in *Hispanic Catholic Culture in the U.S.*, ed. Jay P. Dolan and Allan Figueroa Deck, S.J. (Notre Dame, Ind.: University of Notre Dame Press, 1994), 132.

31. Ibid., 140.

32. Moises Sandoval, *On the Move: A History of the Hispanic Church in the United States* (Maryknoll, N.Y.: Orbis Books, 1990), 80.

33. Sandoval, "The Organization of a Hispanic Church," 144.

34. *The Hispanic Presence: Challenge and Commitment* (Washington, D.C.: U.S. Catholic Conference, 1984), 3, 5, 30.

35. *National Pastoral Plan for Hispanic Ministry* (Washington, D.C.: U.S. Catholic Conference, 1988), 7.

36. *The Hispanic Presence*, 24.

37. *Pastoral Constitution on the Church in the Modern World*, sec. 58, in *The Documents of Vatican II*, ed. Abbott, S.J., 264.

38. *Call to Action*, Recommendation on Ethnicity and Race, in *Origins* 6, no. 21 (Nov. 4, 1976), 334.

39. *Cultural Pluralism*, in *Origins* 10, no. 31 (Jan. 15, 1981), 487.

40. Pastoral in *Origins* 14, no. 18 (Oct. 18, 1984), 281.

41. Robert F. Keeler, *Parish* (New York: Crossroad, 1997), 23.

42. Burns, "Building the Best: A History of Catholic Parish Life in the Pacific States," 113; Peter Steinfels, "Ancient Rock in Crosscurrents of Today," *New York Times*, May 29, 1994, 1.

43. Charles Shanabruch, *Chicago's Catholics: The Evolution of an American Identity* (Notre Dame, Ind.: University of Notre Dame Press, 1981), 175.

44. Quoted in Dolan, Appleby, Byrne, and Campbell, *Transforming Parish Ministry*, 296.

Theology (*continued*)
tury, 59, 69; and Catholicism between 1880 and 1920s, 77, 78, 102, 104, 115; and Catholicism between 1920s and 1950s, 152–53, 156, 157–62, 173; and devotional Catholicism, 173; and historical conditioning of religious truths, 194; and immutability of Catholic dogma, 194; and public Catholicism, 152–53, 156, 157; and Romanization of American Catholicism, 59, 69; and science, 76; and Vatican II, 194
Thérèse of Lisieux, 176
Tibet, 135
Time (magazine), 168
Tobias, Sheila, 226
Tocqueville, Alexis de, 83–84
Tradition: and Americanization of doctrine, 110, 159–60, 162; and Catholicism between 1780 and 1820s, 30; and Catholicism between 1880 and 1920s, 110; and Catholicism between 1920s and 1950s, 159–60, 162, 175–76, 178–79; and Catholicism in 1950s, 184, 189; and democracy, 30; faith, 69; and gender issues, 175–76, 178–79; and identification of culture of Catholicism, 8; and immigrants, 32; influence of culture on Catholic, 5–6; as prevailing over change in Catholicism, 110; and Romanization of American Catholicism, 45
Transcendentalism, 67
Trappist monks, 181

Tridentine Catholicism, 37–38, 44, 45
Trinity College (Washington, D.C.), 122
Trustees: and bishops, 43; and Catholicism between 1780 and 1820s, 29–34, 38, 40, 42, 43; and Catholicism in mid nineteenth century, 47–49, 50; and Catholicism between 1880 and 1920s, 78, 80, 82; and democracy, 29–34, 38, 40, 42, 43, 78, 80, 82, 204; election of, 43; and Romanization of American Catholicism, 47–49, 50
Turner, James, 76

Ukrainian Americans, 82, 165
Ultramontanism, 44, 51, 52, 59
Unbelief: age of, 76
United Farm Workers, 217
United Nations, 251
United States: bicentennial of, 219; fears of Catholic takeover of, 166, 167–68; papal recognition by, 166
Universal Declaration of Human Rights (U.N., 1948), 251
Universities. *See* Colleges and universities; Seminaries; *specific college or university*
University of Georgia, 57
University of Notre Dame, 87, 113, 149, 186
University of Pennsylvania, 57
Urban issues, 61, 185, 199, 241

Vatican: and Americanization of doctrine, 99, 102, 105, 106, 107–8,

45. Nancy Woloch, *Women and the American Experience* (New York: McGraw-Hill, 1984), 496.

46. Quoted in Paul A. Carter, *Another Part of the Fifties* (New York: Columbia University Press, 1983), 88.

47. Woloch, *Women and the American Experience*, 509, 502.

48. Sheila Tobias, *Faces of Feminism: An Activist's Reflections on the Women's Movement* (Boulder, Colo.: Westview Press, 1997), 58, 62.

49. Woloch, *Women and the American Experience*, 491; Tobias, *Faces of Feminism*, 75.

50. Mark Chaves, *Ordaining Women: Culture and Conflict in Religious Organizations* (Cambridge, Mass.: Harvard University Press, 1997), 1, 5; Robert Wuthnow, *The Restructuring of American Religion* (Princeton, N.J.: Princeton University Press, 1988), 228.

51. Chaves, *Ordaining Women*, 49; Susan Hill Lindley, *You Have Stept Out of Your Place: A History of Women and Religion in America* (Louisville, Ky.: Westminster John Knox Press, 1996), 423.

52. Chaves, *Ordaining Women*, 78.

53. Quoted in Jay P. Dolan, *The American Catholic Experience: A History From Colonial Times to the Present* (Garden City, N.Y.: Doubleday, 1985), 232.

54. "Decree on the Apostolate of the Laity," in *The Documents of Vatican II*, ed. Abbott, S.J., 500.

55. Philip J. Murnion, *New Parish Ministries* (New York: National Pastoral Life Center, 1992), 9, 11; Philip J. Murnion and David DeLambo, *Parishes and Parish Ministers: A Study of Parish Lay Ministry* (New York: National Pastoral Life Center, 1999), iii.

56. *National Catholic Reporter*, July 16, 1999, 6.

57. D'Antonio et al., *Laity*, 121–22.

58. Charles R. Morris, *American Catholic* (New York: Random House, 1997), 389; *National Catholic Reporter*, June 30, 2000, 5, where it summarizes the U.S. Bishops' Study of the Impact of Fewer Priests in Pastoral Ministry; this report lists 2,334 parishes without a resident priest.

59. Morris, *American Catholic*, 389, 391.

60. Patricia Wittberg, S.C., *The Rise and Fall of Catholic Religious Orders* (Albany: State University of New York Press, 1994), 213–14.

61. Jay P. Dolan, R. Scott Appleby, Patricia Byrne, and Debra Campbell, *Transforming Parish Ministry* (New York: Crossroad, 1990), 166.

62. Ibid., 157.

63. Lora Ann Quinonez, C.D.P., and Mary Daniel Turner, S.N.D. deN., *The Transformation of American Catholic Sisters* (Philadelphia: Temple University Press, 1992), 92, 93, 87.

64. Ibid., 74.

65. D'Antonio et al., *Laity*, 11.

66. Lindley, *You Have Stept Out of Your Place*, 425.

67. Quoted in Mary Jo Weaver, *New Catholic Women* (Bloomington: Indiana University Press, 1995), 185; see also 182–83 for alternative spiritualities.

68. Sheila Durkin Dierks, *Women Eucharist* (Boulder, Colo.: Woven Word Press, 1997), 14.

69. Internet Data Base—Contemporary Women's Issues: Women's Ordination Conference-Organizational History.

70. Dierks, *Women Eucharist*, 27.

71. Center of Concern, Occasional Papers, "Comments on the First Draft NCCB Pastoral Letter Partners in the Mystery of Redemption," June 13, 1988, 17.

72. Thomas J. Reese, "Women's Pastoral Fails," *America* 167, no. 18 (Dec. 5, 1992), 443.

73. Comments of Bishop Raymond Lucker in *Origins* 22, no. 6 (June 18, 1992), 92; Reese, "Women's Pastoral Fails," 444.

74. Chaves, *Ordaining Women*, 192.

75. "The Church and Women: Exchange of Views: Archbishop Weakland and Cardinal O'Connor," in *Origins* 22, no. 31 (Jan. 14, 1993), 533.

76. Timothy Ignatius Kelly, "The Transformation of American Catholicism: The Pittsburgh Laity and the Second Vatican Council, 1950–1980" (Ph.D. diss., Carnegie Mellon University, 1990), 387; Davidson et al., *The Search for Common Ground*, 45, 124.

77. Patrick L. Malloy, "The Re-Emergence of Popular Religion Among Non-Hispanic American Catholics," *Worship* 72, no. 1 (Jan. 1998), 5–6.

78. Michael S. Driscoll, "Liturgy and Devotions: Back to the Future," in *The Renewal That Awaits Us*, ed. Eleanor Bernstein, C.S.J., and Martin F. Connell (Chicago: Liturgical Training Publications, 1997), 86.

79. Sister Thea Bowman, F.S.P.A., "The Gift of African American Sacred Song," in *Lead Me Guide Me: The African American Catholic Hymnal* (Chicago: G.I.A. Publications, 1987), n.p.

80. James P. Lyke, "Liturgical Expression in the Black Community," *Worship* 57, no. 1 (Jan. 1983), 18.

81. *What We Have Seen and Heard: A Pastoral Letter on Evangelization from the Black Bishops of the United States* (Cincinnati: St. Anthony Messenger Press, 1984), 4, 31.

82. D. Reginald Whitt, O.P., "Varietates Legitimae and an African-American Liturgical Tradition," in Diana L. Hayes and Cyprian Davis, O.S.B., *Taking Down Our Harps: Black Catholics in the United States* (Maryknoll, N.Y.: Orbis Books, 1998), 270.

83. Arturo J. Perez, "The History of Hispanic Liturgy since 1965," in *Hispanic Catholic Culture in the U.S.: Issues and Concerns*, ed. Dolan and Deck, S.J., 365.

84. Ibid., 364.

85. Ibid., 370.

86. Ibid., 378.

87. Ibid., 382.

88. Quoted in ibid., 397.

89. Andrew M. Greeley, *The American Catholic: A Social Portrait* (New York: Basic Books, 1977), 143.

90. Davidson et al., *The Search for Common Ground*, 131.

91. John Courtney Murray, "This Matter of Religious Freedom," *America* 112, no. 2 (Jan. 9, 1965), 41, 43.

92. Abbott, *Documents of Vatican II*, 673

93. John T. Noonan, Jr., *The Lustre of Our Country* (Berkeley: University of California Press, 1998), 2.

94. Ibid., 353.

INDEX